D1480512

Quality of Life in Asia

Volume 8

This series, the first of its kind, will examine both the objective and subjective dimensions of life quality in Asia, especially East Asia. It will unravel and compare the contours, dynamics and patterns of building nations, offering innovative works that discuss basic and applied research, emphasizing inter- and multi-disciplinary approaches to the various domains of life quality. Thus, the series will appeal to a variety of fields in humanities, social sciences and other professional disciplines. Asia is the largest, most populous continent on Earth, and it is home to the world's most dynamic region, East Asia. In the past three decades, East Asia has been the most successful region in the world in expanding its economies and integrating them into the global economy, offering lessons on how poor countries, even with limited natural resources, can achieve rapid economic development. Yet while scholars and policymakers have focused on why East Asia has prospered, little has been written on how its economic expansion has affected the quality of life of its citizens. The series will publish several volumes a year, either single or multiple-authored monographs or collections of essays.

More information about this series at http://www.springer.com/series/8416

Daniel T.L. Shek · Robert M. Hollister
Editors

University Social Responsibility and Quality of Life

A Global Survey of Concepts and Experiences

 Springer

Editors
Daniel T.L. Shek
Department of Applied Social Sciences
Hong Kong Polytechnic University
Kowloon
Hong Kong

Robert M. Hollister
Department of Urban and Environmental
 Policy and Planning
Tufts University
Medford, MA
USA

ISSN 2211-0550   ISSN 2211-0569   (electronic)
Quality of Life in Asia
ISBN 978-981-10-3876-1   ISBN 978-981-10-3877-8   (eBook)
DOI 10.1007/978-981-10-3877-8

Library of Congress Control Number: 2017930951

Printed on acid-free paper

This Springer imprint is published by Springer Nature
The registered company is Springer Nature Singapore Pte Ltd.
The registered company address is: 152 Beach Road, #21-01/04 Gateway East, Singapore 189721, Singapore

Preface

The contemporary world is facing many problems such as global warming, poverty, income disparities, refugees, aging populations, and new diseases. Obviously, how to solve these problems is a challenging task for leaders in the national, regional, and global contexts. As universities are commonly regarded as incubators for knowledge and solutions to promote quality of life, it is important to ask how universities can help to build a better world. In fact, it is the public expectation that universities should generate knowledge which can solve real-life problems which can eventually promote quality of life.

In the business sector, the notion of "corporate social responsibility" (CSR) has received growing attention in the past few decades. Fundamentally, the spirit of CSR maintains that besides maximizing profits, business enterprises should also look at how they can fulfill their social responsibilities such as promotion corporate governance, reduction of corruption and collusion, limiting negative and maximizing positive environmental and other impacts of their operations, and provision of voluntary service to the underprivileged and needy groups. Major corporations throughout the world regard CSR as a desired attribute of a company which would eventually promote corporate image and reputation.

As universities are corporations, the notion of CSR is applicable to universities to some extent. Nevertheless, as maximization of profit is not a common goal of universities and educational service is different from commercial activities, there is a need to explore the notion of "university social responsibility" (USR) as an emergent field of academic inquiry and practice. When we look at the experiences of different universities, different ways of promoting USR are evident. Some examples of USR missions include the following: establishment of communities within and outside the University which promotes social responsibilities in different stakeholders; promotion of activities which are ethical, inclusive, and beneficial to the public; emphasis on environmental conservation, sustainability, and balanced social development; promotion of welfare and quality of life of people, especially the needy and vulnerable populations; and commitment to building a better world. Typically, these missions are accomplished via teaching, research, and services within the university community and in collaboration with other bodies. There clearly is a growing movement among institutions of higher education to expand and strengthen these functions.

To promote USR in universities, several universities from different parts of the world have established the University Social Responsibility Network (USR Network). At this stage, in the USR movement it is especially timely to document and disseminate the work-in-progress of universities. Documenting and sharing institutional experiences of different types of universities and across borders can be particularly productive at this time of innovation, ferment, and growing activity. This book documents and reflects upon diverse USR experiences in different universities. We are publishing this volume to mark the beginning of the USR Network.

There are several unique features of this book. First, the role of universities in social responsibilities in different contexts is explored. Second, the background of the establishment of the pioneer USR Network and its possible future directions are described. Third, an innovative project on the possible assessment of USR is reported, which provides a first step in the exploration of the possible assessment of USR. Fourth, USR experiences in different parts of the world, including universities in North America, South America, Europe, Africa, Middle East, Australia, and Asia are presented and analyzed.

From the experiences revealed in these chapters, several observations can be highlighted. First, different universities have different goals and strategies with respect to their USR initiatives. Second, different USR programs with different levels of sophistication, resources, and commitment have been designed, which can provide excellent reference points for the development of the USR policies and programs of other institutions. Third, stakeholders including teachers, non-teaching staffs, and students can be (and are) involved in USR activities. Fourth, there is a need to step up work on the assessment of USR initiatives, a need to conduct more evaluation work of USR efforts, particularly with reference to the impact of USR on different stakeholders. Obviously, having good intentions to promote well-being is not enough. We need rigorous evaluation to demonstrate the impact. Fifth, as USR initiatives are mostly done within the context of a single university, there is a need to further promote inter-institutional USR initiatives. As such, the USR Network is an excellent vehicle to promote inter-institutional USR initiatives. Finally, as USR theory and research are still in their infancy, there is a need to strengthen the theoretical framework and basic research on USR. For example, it is important to know what basic qualities should be nurtured in students so that they can participate competently in USR activities such as service-learning, and in order to maximize what they learn in the process. In the recent decades, different ranking systems have been designed to rank universities and these regimes powerfully influence university strategic planning and decision-making. For example, in the *Times Higher Education World University Rankings*, performance indicators in five areas are used. These include teaching (reputation survey, staff to student ratio, doctorate to bachelor ratio, doctorate awards to academic staff ratio), research (volume, income and reputation), citations per paper, international outlook (ratio of international to domestic staff, ratio of international to domestic students, and international collaboration), and industry income. Unfortunately, no indicator of USR performance is included. Similarly, USR criteria are not included in the *QS World University Rankings* in which indicators related to academic peer review, faculty–student ratio, citations for faculty, employer reputation, international student ratio, and international staff ratio are employed. Again, USR activities are not included in the assessment. Of course, some criteria employed such as citations per faculty staff are an important indicator for assessing academic impact of a university. However, having strong academic impact does not necessarily mean that the university is excelling in improving the well-being of the society. Alternatively, we can argue that the percentage of students who have taken service-learning subjects may give a better indication of a university's service to the community. As such, we earnestly hope that the university rankings will start to incorporate USR activities in future. By doing this, universities would be reminded about the important responsibility that they have to promote quality of life of the society and the world, and their efforts to do so will be reinforced. At present, the complete lack of attention to USR in the rankings seriously undercuts their social responsibility obligations and opportunities, and skews their work toward other functions.

This book would not exist without the enthusiastic support of colleagues from different member institutions in the USR Network. Therefore, we must express our deep gratitude to them. In the Chinese culture, there is the saying of "throwing a brick to attract a jade" (pao zhuan yin yu). Hence, we treat this book as a "brick" which can attract "jades" in future and it is our modest wish that this book is a kickoff step in the book series on university social responsibility. We hope very much that colleagues in the field of USR will devote more effort in the future to documenting and assessing USR experiences.

Kowloon, Hong Kong   Daniel T.L. Shek
Medford, MA, USA   Robert M. Hollister

Contents

About the Editors

Daniel T.L. Shek Ph.D., FHKPS, BBS, SBS, JP is the chair professor of applied social sciences at the Department of Applied Social Sciences and associate vice president (undergraduate program) of Hong Kong Polytechnic University. He has taught social work students at the undergraduate and postgraduate levels for over thirty years. He was dean of students (1996–1998) and dean of general education (2006–2008) at New Asia College, the Chinese University of Hong Kong. He is editor in chief of the Journal of Youth Studies and Applied Research on Quality of Life and serves on the editorial board of many international refereed journals including Social Indicators Research and Journal of Adolescent Health. To date, he has published over 85 books, 154 chapters in various books, and more than 500 articles in international refereed journals.

Robert M. Hollister is founding executive director emeritus and co-founder of the Talloires Network, a global coalition of over 350 universities in 76 countries committed to strengthening civic engagement and social responsibility in higher education. He was founding dean of the Jonathan M. Tisch College of Citizenship and Public Service at Tufts University (2000–2011), where he is currently a professor at the Department of Urban and Environmental Policy and Planning. A pioneer in the engaged university movement, Prof. Hollister led the creation and development of the Tisch College Civic Life, a uniquely comprehensive university-wide program to prepare students in all fields for lifetimes of active citizenship—and to produce citizen engineers and citizen physicians, citizen humanists, and citizen business people. A specialist in citizen participation in public affairs and in the leadership and management of nonprofit organizations, Prof. Hollister is a co-author of *The Engaged University: International Perspectives on Civic Engagement* and *Development Politics*.

Part I
Introduction

Chapter 1
The Project: Theoretical Framework and Global Institutional Experience

Robert M. Hollister

Abstract Goals of this book are to: improve the theoretical framework about university social responsibility (USR); disseminate the USR experience of a geographically diverse group of twelve universities; demonstrate the value of global exchange on this topic; further develop the sponsoring organization, the University Social Responsibility Network; and encourage and guide further research. The introductory chapter highlights key themes with respect to conceptualization of USR and discusses six common themes that are explored in the institutional case accounts: opportunities and challenges about university-community partnerships, processes and strategies of institutional change, national policies that are influencing USR, student programming and the impacts of these initiatives on students' development, application of research to addressing societal problems, and the corporate social responsibility of universities—social responsibility impacts of university institutional policies and practices.

Keywords University social responsibility · University Social Responsibility Network · Theory

This book is a multi-university, global project with several goals. First, to conceptualize (and reconceptualize) the field of endeavor called "university social responsibility" (USR), to help strengthen theoretical frameworks with respect to this dimension of higher education. Second, to document and share the experience of twelve institutions of higher education that are committed to elevating their social responsibility, and to illustrate the work-in-progress of a geographically diverse

Robert M. Hollister, Professor Emeritus, Tufts University; Founding Dean Emeritus, Tisch College of Civic Life, Tufts University; Founding Executive Director Emeritus, Talloires Network.

R.M. Hollister (✉)
Department of Urban and Environmental Policy and Planning,
Tufts University, Talloires Network, Medford, USA
e-mail: robert.hollister@tufts.edu

© Springer Nature Singapore Pte Ltd. 2017
D.T.L. Shek and R.M. Hollister (eds.), *University Social Responsibility and Quality of Life*, Quality of Life in Asia 8,
DOI 10.1007/978-981-10-3877-8_1

group of universities. We aim in this volume to present fresh knowledge about USR, and contribute to overcoming the predominance in the literature of experience and perspectives from the Global North. We hope that these accounts will inform others' efforts to strengthen USR—initiatives by individual universities and also by public policy-makers. A third function is to demonstrate the value of global exchange on this important topic. As the global USR movement is rapidly gaining momentum, it is especially timely to disseminate information about what constitutes effective USR in diverse settings, so that the next wave of institutional initiatives can benefit from what peer universities have learned. The featured institutions are located in nine countries and represent all continents. They include universities that are advanced and widely recognized for their social responsibility (SR) work, and others that are deeply committed to strengthening this dimension of their operations, but are at earlier stages in its development.

Fourth, through this project of the University Social Responsibility Network (USRN), we strive to strengthen and further develop the Network itself. With its commitment to building sustained collaboration on a few selected challenges, the University Social Responsibility Network is playing a unique international leadership role in advancing USR. And finally, the book seeks to encourage and guide future research about university social responsibility. To date, the USR movement has been long on rhetoric, but short on evidence about its impacts and about what constitutes effective strategies. There is an urgent need, and also a great collective opportunity, to build a broader and deeper factual foundation about USR. The knowledge base should represent the full range of experience around the world.

The opening chapter "University Social Responsibility Network: A Platform to Promote University Social Responsibility" describes the origins, goals and distinctive features of this global alliance. The next section explores conceptual and theoretical underpinnings. Then a set of case studies describe and analyze selected aspects of the SR work of twelve universities that represent a diverse cross-section of higher education. A concluding chapter highlights key themes and advocates directions for future action and research.

In the section on "Concepts and Theoretical Considerations," two chapters review alternative concepts of USR, trace its evolution over time, and examine factors that have shaped changing approaches to USR. These chapters provide theoretical framework for reading the institutional cases presented in the next section. These theoretical directions may also be useful to practitioners and researchers more broadly.

Carlos Wing-Hung Lo, Rose Xue Pang, Carolyn P. Egri, and Pansy Hon-Ying Li in "University Social Responsibility: Conceptualization and an Assessment Framework" note that while USR has grown rapidly, its conceptual foundation has been slow to develop. Their chapter helps to address this gap. Defining USR as "a progressive management system for pursuing sustainability", the authors review the evolution of USR, then propose a specific conceptual model, and offer a framework for assessing institutional performance. Causal factors examined include the corporate social responsibility movement, global growth in the number of students, the unique role that universities play in their respective regions, and technological innovation. Primary dimensions of the proposed model are values, process and impact. These dimensions are defined in relation to five major functions: university governance, teaching and learning, research, community service, and environmental sustainability. The model is organized around the roles and perspectives of a comprehensive set of stakeholders (students, employees, the environment, government and funding bodies, communities, peer universities, and suppliers).

In "From Historical to the Contemporary Challenges", Daniel T.L. Shek, Angelina W.K. Yuen-Tsang, and Eddie C.W. Ng analyze the changing nature and the context of higher education in a time of advancing globalization, and how these trends shape USR. The chapter focuses on component trends of globalization, including increasing student mobility and curriculum development in a global marketplace that emphasizes preparing students for employment and the overall economic development impacts of higher education. The authors call for clarifying what is meant by university social responsibility and for strengthening collective understanding of how best to improve USR. The institutional accounts presented in the section on "Global Experience" address the challenges articulated by Shek et al. —to elevate conceptual clarity and also to sharpen awareness of effective strategic approaches.

In a global context, "university social responsibility" is the phrase that is used most widely to describe the public and community service activities and impacts of institutions of higher education. It is often used to refer to what Global Northern representatives call "civic engagement" and "community engagement." In many discussions, the terms "social responsibility" and "civic engagement" are used interchangeably. However, it is important to note that "university social responsibility" also can be, and in practice often is, a more encompassing concept, one that includes the social impacts of the full range of university functions, and includes corporate social responsibility issues such as the energy efficiency of building design, employment policies, purchasing and financial management. There is considerable division of opinion among university leaders and stakeholders as to whether their social responsibility efforts should take this more inclusive approach. As the opening chapter indicates, this more inclusive meaning of "university social responsibility" is indeed embraced by the University Social Responsibility Network. Therefore, a number of the institutional profiles pay attention to institutional policies and practices that reach beyond student volunteering and service learning, and applied research.

Some of the case studies that follow in the section on "Global Experience" present an overview of the institution's SR activities; others focus on selected programs or dimensions. As a group, the cases explore a number of common themes—university-community partnerships, processes and strategies of institutional change, the influence of national policies on USR, student programming, impacts on students and their development, research applied to community and societal problems, and the social responsibility of institutional policies and practices beyond teaching, research and service activities. The cases provide a broad range of examples of different kinds of societal issues that USR work addresses, including, for example, the needs of older people (The University of Manchester), poverty alleviation (Peking University), health (Sichuan University and University of Pretoria), disaster response and management (Sichuan University), sustainability (The Hong Kong Polytechnic University), social conflicts (University of Haifa), the needs of children and adolescents (University of São Paulo), and economic development (University of Pretoria).

A rich dimension of a number of the cases, including University of Haifa, The University of Manchester, Kyoto University, and Washington University in St. Louis, is their focus on *opportunities and challenges with respect to university-community partnerships*. The University of Haifa account reviews the literature on university-community partnerships, noting the breadth and vagueness of this concept, and summarizing research about common barriers to effective university-community collaboration. The authors then challenge the conventional perspective, "the binary concept of cooperation and conflict as opposing concepts." They offer an alternative framework organized around four paradoxes and use these to explain the University of Haifa experience—top-down work versus bottom-up work, organizational relationships versus organizational effectiveness, egalitarian approach vs. hierarchical structures, and forging a common vision versus celebrating multiple identities. They use these paradoxes to explain the work to date of the University of Haifa's Flagship program, an interdisciplinary initiative to combat social exclusion and to promote solidarity among conflicting population groups. The Haifa co-authors state, "This perspective gives room for the many contradictions, tensions and dichotomies that characterize the complex relationship between academy and community." In other words, these opposites co-exist in the Haifa experience. The authors suggest that this framework can help to guide project planning and implementation of university-community partnerships in other settings.

The University of Manchester chapter presents an extensive university-community research partnership that aims to develop "age-friendly" communities in the city. The Manchester project involves older people as co-investigators, training and supporting them to participate directly in the conduct of research. This case describes the process of organizing the research collaboration, shares results, and discusses challenges encountered. The impacts of the study are impressive in terms of the creation of fresh knowledge, the direct use of the findings by political actors and policy stakeholders, and also the positive contributions to the capabilities of the older Manchester residents as they "co-produce" fresh knowledge.

Processes and strategies of institutional change receive considerable attention in the institutional accounts. A number of the cases relate how the university's SR efforts have changed over time and why, and describe strategies for strengthening the institution's SR, including new organizational arrangements. The University of Pretoria chapter describes how that university moved from a needs-based, community service approach to a community development orientation. As the latter paradigm took hold, charity-like projects and services that bred dependency were replaced and the university involved and empowered "people in communities in determining their own priority needs as well as in planning, implementing and evaluating development programs." The University of Pretoria established a Unit for Development Support to support its expanding community engagement programs, and community engagement is a significant priority in its Strategic Plan 2025. The Hong Kong Polytechnic University has taken the dramatic step of requiring all undergraduates to complete an academic credit-bearing community service learning course. In order to successfully implement this new graduate requirement, the university has established an Office of Service Learning to expand and sustain partnerships with community organizations and to enhance the ability of faculty members to teach service learning courses. Tufts University established a university-wide college that functions and that is a resource to all schools and academic units to promote education for active citizenship across the curriculum. The University of New South Wales has made the promotion of social responsibility as a major strategy priority, and has put in place a new organizational structure and a senior Deputy Vice-Chancellor position to deliver on this commitment. At the University of São Paulo, the Pro Rectory of Culture and Extension mobilizes and coordinates an impressive set of arts and cultural resources of the University to address societal needs and to reduce inequalities of all sorts. In order to elevate its social responsibility efforts with its host city and region, Kyoto University has established a new Education and Research Unit for Regional Alliances and also initiated a Unit for Promotion of Education and Research in Cooperation with Local Communities.

A few of the cases show how in some countries *national policy is playing an influential role in advancing USR*. A strategic theme in the Chinese National Plan for Medium and Long-term Education Reform and Development (2010–2020) calls on universities to enhance "students' sense of social responsibility to serve the country and the people." This national policy directive has guided and accelerated the development of SR programs at Beijing Normal University, Peking University, Sichuan University, and The Hong Kong Polytechnic University. Haifa University's SR efforts have been directly encouraged by policies of the Israeli Council for Higher Education that explicitly encourages institutions of higher education to organize academic-community partnerships and to develop civic engagement courses. Post-apartheid South African national education policy has motivated and shaped significantly the expanding SR efforts at University of Pretoria. In 1997, the new national policy stated an expectation that institutions of higher education "demonstrate social responsibility" and that they "promote and develop social responsibility and awareness amongst students of the role of higher education in social and economic development through community service programs."

Student programming and the impacts of these initiatives on students' development is discussed in all of the cases and is the focus of the accounts from Washington University in St. Louis and the University of New South Wales. The Washington University in St. Louis chapter presents that institution's commitment to developing "reciprocal, mutually-beneficial partnerships with local community groups" and emphasizes the civic values and skills that students learn by participating in these university-community partnerships. The authors note that the literature about civic learning strategies and outcomes pays scant attention to the role and effects on the students of university-community partnerships. "A community partnership approach is absent from civic learning frameworks, outcomes, and assessment tools." They review existing major frameworks for assessing changes in civic learning and then describe how they have used at Washington University the Civic-Minded Graduate model developed by the Center for Service and Learning at Indiana University-Purdue University Indianapolis.

The University of New South Wales (UNSW) utilizes two different co-curricular approaches to develop socially responsible students through volunteering—an intensive program that involves students seeking an opportunity for deep engagement, and a less intensive option in which a larger number of students participate. The intensive option involves students in a broad range of community service activities, supported by preparatory workshops and reflection sessions. The second program places a larger number of UNSW students in schools in disadvantaged communities to support K-12 students' academic progress and to elevate their educational aspirations. The university assesses the impacts of both programs on students' sense of social responsibility and also involves community partners in the evaluation process.

The Beijing Normal University chapter describes "Three Approaches to Cultivating College Students' Sense of Social Responsibility"—academic, professional, and public services. The academic approach involves integrating social responsibility education into a wide range of courses and students' participation in research projects. Through the professional strategy, students have multiple opportunities to apply their classroom learning in practice. Receiving greatest emphasis at present is the third, public services approach, an extensive array of student volunteer projects.

Peking University has a rich history of student volunteering including, for the past 35 years, the One Hundred Villages' Social Investigation through which many PKU students collect information about the health and living conditions of retirees in towns and villages across the country. More recently, the Loving Heart Society has grown into an extensive set of student voluntary programs in local communities.

Several of the institutional cases describe how a major dimension of the university's social responsibility is the *direct application of research to addressing societal and community problems*. Sichuan University, in addition to promoting social responsibility through many courses and student volunteer associations, has mobilized its research capabilities in a major effort on natural disaster prevention and response. The Sichuan institutional account also describes several applied research initiatives to address pressing regional challenges, including building the capacity of women in rural areas, developing new health service models for the elderly, and establishing a birth defects pedigree database and DNA bank. The Hong Kong Polytechnic University case describes substantial research programs to promote sustainability. At Peking University, eight academic departments have undertaken a long-term poverty alleviation initiative in Yunnan Province that combines research, training and direct provision of health and human services.

As was noted earlier, the corporate social responsibility movement has significantly influenced the growth of university social responsibility. USR includes *the SR impacts of university institutional policies and practices*. It is about not only that social responsibility goals and impacts of academic institutions' defining missions of teaching, research and service, but also extends to the social responsibility aspirations and achievements of their policies and practices as *corporate* entities. The University of Pretoria case includes a section on its corporate social responsibility, discussing the example of its procurement and employment policies. An expression of corporate social responsibility at Sichuan University is its creation of smoke-free campuses and hospitals. The Hong Kong Polytechnic University chapter describes the university's efforts "to promote sustainability in planning, development and operation of the campus environment and facilities as well as to develop sustainability initiatives in education, research and community service activities."

A concluding chapter "Global Experience to Date and Future Directions" summarizes major points that emerged from the institutional case studies and suggests future opportunities for action and research, organized around the same six common themes discussed above—university-community partnerships, processes of institutional change, national policy, student programming, applied research, and universities' corporate SR.

Chapter 2
USR Network: A Platform to Promote University Social Responsibility

Daniel T.L. Shek, Angelina W.K. Yuen-Tsang and Eddie C.W. Ng

Abstract Higher Education is facing rapid and enormous change, one of which is the corporatization of higher education. Given the market-driven nature of university education, a natural and reasonable concern is its social responsibility towards the community it serves, particularly when corporate social responsibility is the normative expectation of contemporary organizations by the general public. This is also an intrinsic mission of the university. This chapter aims to outline the importance of University Social Responsibility (USR) and the emergence of such an initiative entitled University Social Responsibility Network (USRN) initiated by The Hong Kong Polytechnic University. In particular, we pay close attention to the network development of the collective effort, in contrast to the endeavor of a single institution. The rationale, mission, organizational structure and strategy of USRN, as well as the strengths and challenges of this partnership approach, will also be discussed particularly drawing on the lessons learned from other similar and related initiatives. Ideas for the future development of the USRN are also discussed.

Keywords University social responsibility · The Hong Kong Polytechnic University · USR network · Civic engagement · Partnership approach

2.1 Background

The call for increased community engagement of the higher education sector has received attention for some time. A recent attempt, under the notion of University Social Responsibility (USR), has received much attention given the enormous

---

This work is financially supported by the Global Youth Leadership Institute at The Hong Kong Polytechnic University.

D.T.L. Shek (✉) · A.W.K. Yuen-Tsang · E.C.W. Ng
The Hong Kong Polytechnic University, Kowloon, Hong Kong
e-mail: daniel.shek@polyu.edu.hk

changing environment in the higher education setting. Especially the commercialization of higher education with the increasing trend of for-profit higher education has gained much notice (Morey 2004; Vasilescu et al. 2010). While universities are steering towards the market mechanism but still enjoying much autonomy and academic freedom, social responsibility becomes the normative expectation of nowadays organization (including university) by the general public (Vasilescu et al. 2010). On one hand, some traditional top tier universities still focus on the narrow perspective on knowledge (e.g., technical rationality) and enjoy the prestige gained from academic "ivory tower" (Hoyt and Hollister 2014). On the other hand, other newly established universities benefit from the "massification" and rapid expansion of higher education system, primarily emphasizing student enrolment and providing traditional curricula. No wonder some scholars will doubt if universities "miss what matters most" (Basken 2016, p. 3).

Apart from the reactive response to the accountability issue towards the society and relevant stakeholders, proactively speaking, USR could also play a significant role in the societal development. Herrera (2009) notes that educators have to be creative and use multidisciplinary strategies to ensure the sustainable development of people, while USR is one such approach because USR includes wide ranges of actions and processes, which help facilitate the greater alignment between the university and the societal need in an appropriate manner and with a strong sense of ethics. Herrera even argues that USR is seriously needed in the present, as the globalization and the over-reliance on the economic development have created many social ills, which the university could solve by utilizing their knowledge. "This approach is of great importance because globalization and the application of neo-liberal models of economic development have led to social crises to which universities must respond by providing innovative solutions to the complexity of the current problems at the national and regional levels (Herrera 2009, p. 40)." Therefore, while the traditional and more civic oriented mission of higher education is slowly giving way to the profit motive in the practice of some higher education providers, raising the profile of USR could not only restate the often ignored, if not lost, mission of the higher education, but also raise the spirit and aspiration of educators for the greater good of the society.

This chapter outlines the importance of USR and the emergence of an initiative, University Social Responsibility Network (USRN) initiated by The Hong Kong Polytechnic University. In particular, we pay close attention to the network development of the collective effort, in contrast to the endeavor of each institution (which will be presented throughout this volume). Besides the rationale, mission, organizational structure and strategy of USRN, the strengths and challenges of this partnership approach will also be discussed particularly drawing on the lesson learned from the other similar and related endeavor. Ideas for the future development of the USRN are also discussed.

2.2   Definition of USR

The social relevance of higher education has been discussed in the literature. De Ketele (2009) highlights that the importance of higher education is best expressed through the variety of "academic services" it offers for the society, while taking into consideration the needs of people and society. Herrera (2009) notices that the new notion of USR steps further to request educational policies, which could "encourage greater correspondence between the fundamental objectives of universities and the environment in which they operate" (p. 40). In practice, it is to promote the social usefulness of knowledge, as a result contributing to improving the quality of life. As Herrera notes, USR requires "a two-way perspective between universities and society, which involves directly multiplying the critical uses of knowledge in society and the economy" (p. 40).

Acknowledging that USR is a wide-ranging and evolving concept, which is open to interpretations, we propose, in its broad meaning, that university social responsibility could be understood as the responsibility shared by universities in contributing to social betterment through the integration of social responsibility policies into institutional management, teaching, research, services and public activities. Consistent with the view of Vasilescu et al. (2010), our underlying rationale for USR is that, as corporations, universities should have corporate social responsibility, which we call university social responsibility. Furthermore, USR can renew the traditional mission of universities to improve human quality of life and address societal needs (Glass and Fitzgerald 2010; Herrera 2009; Watson et al. 2011).

2.3   The Need to Set Up a USR Network

The idea of USR does not only deserve further examination but also have to be implemented to create changes in real life. As such, there is an increasing interest in creating platform or infrastructure to help promote USR in an individual institution or as a coalition. For example, Spiru Haret Univeristy (Vasilescu et al. 2010) and the chapters presented in the present volume are examples of individual efforts at the institutional level. Nevertheless, to bring the impact of the individual efforts to a higher level, network or alliance should also be formed to promote USR. For example, there are a few strong regional networks focusing on specific countries, such as (e.g., Ma'an Arab University Alliance for Civic Engagement and the South African Higher Education Community Engagement Forum, Engagement Australia) (Hoyt and Hollister 2014).

Internationally, University Social Responsibility Alliance (now renamed Global University Social Responsibility Network) was set up in San Francisco in 2008 to advocate for the idea that social responsibility has to be incorporated into the fundamental basis of all university education. As such, the global citizen with sense of responsibility can be developed. The members of the network, mainly from the Asian Pacific, North America, and Western Europe, includes business-related parties, international organizations, and governmental sectors, all of which share the same objective to promote social responsibility in higher education (Global University Social Responsibility Network 2016).

A closely related initiative, mainly derived from universities, was the formation of Talloires Network in 2005, which targeted international coordination and exchange at the senior management level of higher education (Hollister et al. 2012). As the largest international network focused on the community engagement of higher education, Talloires Network composed of 367 higher education institutions in 77 countries combined with an enrollment of over 6 million students. Their primary goal is "for the exchange of ideas and understandings (of community engagement in higher education) and for fostering collective action" (Hollister et al. 2012, p. 83). Watson et al. (2011) also have a nice summary of the information about other active higher education networks that focus on civic engagement.

Another important organization, The Global University Network for Innovation (GUNi), is an international network created in 1999 and supported by UNESCO, the United Nations University (UNU) and the Catalan Association of Public Universities (ACUP), which hosts the organization's secretariat and presidency. GUNi's mission is to strengthen the role of higher education in society contributing to the renewal of the visions and policies of higher education across the world under a vision of public service, relevance, and social responsibility. The network is currently composed of 209 members from 78 countries, and includes the UNESCO Chairs in Higher Education, higher education institutions, research centers and networks related to innovation and the social commitment of higher education (Global University Network for Innovation 2016). The GUNi book series on the social commitment of universities "Higher Education in the World" is also an invaluable resource of USR, providing both global and regional analysis of higher education in the world and delicate discussion on the key issues and challenges facing higher education in the 21st century. These collective efforts are important as they could facilitate the deeper exchange of knowledge and practice, and also raise greater awareness of the issue.

While these networks or organizations are conducive to the USR movement, they vary in number, size of membership and capability. In addition, the experiences from the Northern part of the globe and the western societies are still dominating the discourse and practice. Furthermore, the idea of USR is ambiguous and interchangeable with community engagement/action or social innovation, which requires further clarification and refined understanding.

2.4   USRN: A Global Initiative

In view of the world facing huge economic, social, cultural and environmental challenges, USR has not only become a central topic of discussion in the higher education sector but also appears to be a potential pathway towards the solution (Herrera 2009; Vasilescu et al. 2010). Furthermore, the expansion of higher education system and the rapid expansion of online educational offering provide a rare but timely opportunity for the university to influence the public life (Hoyt and Hollister 2014). Thus, USR, focusing on the alignment between educational practice in the universities and the societal needs are enormously and timely needed.

It is in such a context the University Social Responsibility Network (USRN) was established in 2015 based on the belief that universities have an obligation to work together to address these challenges and find solutions so as to make the world more just, inclusive, peaceful and sustainable. As compared to the large network, the size of USRN was kept small in the beginning stage to create uniqueness and strength of the network. The USRN places emphasis on collaboration, coalition, and networking among members and with other networks and alliances. It recognizes the importance of advancing USR in networks of co-responsibility that link each other and link with key stakeholders and the wider society. It is hoped that the network endeavors, together with other initiatives, can push forward the emerging trend of higher education sector, taking seriously the community needs as their core business.

There are several missions of the USRN. First, it provides a platform for the exchange of ideas, resources, policies, practices, problems and solutions to foster USR among the Network members. Second, it develops collaborative USR projects with varied scope and scale among the Network members. Finally, it steers and contributes to the global discussions and development of USR through networking and partnership within the Network, and with other networks and alliances.

In the establishment stage, fourteen universities joined the network as the founding members. They are (in alphabetical order), Beijing Normal University (China), Clare Hall, University of Cambridge (U.K.), Kyoto University (Japan), Peking University (China), Sichuan University (China), The Hong Kong Polytechnic University (Hong Kong, China), The University of Manchester (U.K.), Tufts University (U.S.), University of Haifa (Israel), University of New South Wales (Australia), University of Pretoria (South Africa), University of Sao Paulo (Brazil), Washington University in St. Louis (U.S.), Yonsei University (Korea). Selection criteria for membership cover track record in USR, geographical location, commitment to USRN and institutional reputation in a country/region.

The Network's decision-making body is the Executive Committee, with representation from each of the founding members of the Network. The Committee is tasked with setting strategic direction and providing development plans for the Network. The Secretariat is set up at The Hong Kong Polytechnic University. The Secretariat provides support to the work of the Committee and the Network, including creating and maintaining a website as the platform for collaboration and for members to exchange and disseminate information and views, and share best practices. The Hong Kong Polytechnic University is initially responsible for soliciting the fund needed for the operation of the Secretariat.

To generate impact and become hallmarks of the network, USRN is strategic and focuses on a selected few collaborative initiatives. In the initial phase, it was agreed that collaborations surround four major areas. The first area is joint research and publications. Collaboration on USR-related research in disaster management, and culture and design is proposed while the sharing of research results concerning student learning outcomes in community engagement with in USRN are being facilitated. This joint research is valuable as it could facilitate cross-country comparison and mutual learning, hopefully with the beneficial results in student learning. Furthermore, research on USR index is under discussion, which can help to promote the adoption of USR as a core mission of all universities in future. In addition to the joint research, a joint publication is also under preparation, while this edited book is an example of collaboration which will document the USR practices and case studies. This joint publication has potential to develop into a book series.

Besides research and publications, student programs and scholarships are being established. To facilitate stronger student programs, student exchange are being actively pursued among USRN member institutions. Students of USRN are encouraged to join hands in initiating projects to promote inter-cultural understanding, youth leadership, and community service. Furthermore, student community engagement programs (such as summer volunteer opportunities) are being made available to students of other member universities, while scholarships are provided to enable students of member institutions to participate in USR related activities among the network universities. What is more, we will set up Faculty Exchange & Visiting Fellowship program through which staff can learn from the host country's USR experiences. Currently, annual staff development program has been firmly established with visit and workshop organized by a member institution. Finally, to further promote USR globally, a USRN website was developed to provide an open platform for member institutions to share their experiences, research results, resources, and programs/projects/events related to USR. Also, USR Summit is being held every two years to facilitate further discussion and mutual learning.

2.5   Uniqueness and Challenges of USRN

Compared to the other alliances or networks with similar nature, USR has both common and unique features. Similar to the Talloires Network, USRN also targets the senior management of the university and solicit for their support. The representatives of the USRN founding members are mainly the key persons who are not only in charge of the associated USR practice in the school but also may play a strategic role or are in a position to mobilize the university practice (such as vice-presidents or chair person in the university council). As Hollister et al. (2012) note, in their experience, getting the support from the university leaders is critical in institutionalizing engagement.

Furthermore, USRN is global in nature. While many existing networks are targeting a specific country or are primarily US based (Hollister et al. 2012; Watson et al. 2011), USRN include members from the U.S., the U.K., Australia, Brazil, South Africa, Israel, Korea, Japan, China and Hong Kong. It is also expecting that several more universities will join the Network soon. Global presence and representation are important because it not only raises public awareness and displays the unifying force, but also demonstrates the collective effort and shows the collaboration to be real and viable.

USRN is unique in several aspects. First, the founding members of USRN have quite a strong commitment and track record in USR practice when they joined the network (please refer to the detailed examples provided throughout this volume). Instead of just paying the lips service or taking advantage of the benefits offered by joining those networks (e.g., recognition or eligibility for associated Prize), as observed by Hollister et al. (2012) in their Talloires Network experience, the rich and various experiences shared among the USRN members work as a source of inspiration for more consolidated work. Second, despite the fact that at the current stage USRN has relatively few members, the dynamic and interaction between the USRN members are favorable, if not optimal. As the network members have agreed, the key at this stage is not to increase the number of members, but to generate impact, which could underpin further collaboration in the future. Thus, small is beautiful at this stage.

Third, USRN is strategic and realistic. Instead of doing some common global project, which failed finally in Talloires experience (Hollister et al. 2012), USRN is wise to focus on a few collaborations. As Roussos and Fawcett (2000) highlight in their study, that the outcome of a project matters a lot in the coalition process as it could further boost human and financial support. Nevertheless, as the essence of USR is closely related the community itself, which varies in its cultural, economic and political situation, the USR practice across the globe will not be uniform. Therefore, instead of standardizing the USR practice or working on some highly ambitious and grand projects, the diversity of USR practice create many opportunities for research and learning. USRN, surrounding their works on research and student and faculty learning (i.e., the four area mentioned above), is making sense. Last but not least, the presence of China in the Network is worth noting. While the abovementioned network or other related higher education networks with a primary focus on civic engagement may involve South East Asia countries, the involvement of China is almost non-existent. As China is a country with rapidly expanding higher education, the lessons learned in this context will be valuable to the global community.

The use of network approach is with strengths and challenges, which we discuss below. Watson et al. (2011) highlight that global network could be an ideal platform for synergy and collective power. Hoyt and Hollister (2014) also argue that the power of network related to university civic engagement lies in the coalitions, which are "effective vehicles for the exchange of experience as well as capacity-building and collective voice in policy advocacy" (p. 132). For example, USR network could provide a "gateway to diverse experiences and knowledge that cut across cultural, political and economic boundaries." (p. 228). This could nurture and facilitate innovation through sharing good practice and exchange of ideas. Hoyt and Hollister (2014) also highlight many innovative examples regarding the university engagement in the Global South from which the universities in western societies could learn (e.g., how to move forward the civic engagement initiatives with fewer resources or under the constraint by authoritarian regimes).

In terms of capacity building, the network could help build up local resources, such as broadening and encouraging partnerships with the local and regional funders. Furthermore, working collectively and as a unifying force, the network is more likely to influence the policy development, and thus enabling changes that would be difficult for a single institution to do alone. Therefore, we can say that the nowadays, network approach could be better-suited to handle and address complex issues facing society. This approach has already been commonly used in addressing community problems or health issues (Butterfoss et al. 1993; Roussos and Fawcett 2000; Wolff 2001a). We are also witnessing an increasing number of regional or global networks formed to promote the social responsibility and civic engagement of higher education (Hoyt and Hollister 2014).

Nevertheless, the network approach comes with challenges as well. First and foremost, financial sustainability is essential (Hoyt and Hollister 2014; Watson et al. 2011). While Watson et al. observe that the networks could receive funding from a variety of sources, including private foundations, government, investments by the initial host university, and international organizations, sustaining ongoing resources will be difficult. Second, Watson also raises the important role of the leadership and the associated challenge of inevitable change in the leadership in the network development process. Third, maintaining a shared vision is not easy. Watson noted that it is difficult to change the perceptions of faculty and community partners about the social role of the university. It is particularly apparent in the academic circle as the incentive structure for USR practice is minimum, if there are any. This may pose a great challenge to keep the momentum for the socially responsible way of engaging the higher education in the society and as an engine for institutional change. Last but not least, relationship building among the network members, maintaining an effective platform for co-operation (in term of organizational structure and membership), technical assistance (e.g., administrative support and communication among members), and the broader environment (the societal readiness for USR) are all challenges facing various kinds of partnership and critical factors leading to the success of coalition (Butterfoss et al. 1993; Wolff 2001b).

2.6 The Way Forward

USRN is still in its spawning stage. As such, its mission and vision are to be realized and much more work needs to be done. There are several tasks ahead of us. First, the students' work could be further cultivated. Hollister et al. (2012) noticed that while they have done a good work to solicit support from the university leaders, not enough work had been done to build up a sustainable community of students. Thus, how to cultivate the next generation and translate the USR spirit from the senior level to students' level is critical. Good practices and experiences accumulated among the USRN members could be shared and would be a good start to develop further action. Besides, financial resources for USR initiatives are required, both in the institutional or network level had the ideal of USR be realized. Thus, helping line up or develop relationships with appropriate funders may be a potential pathway to success. Talloires Network had tried to raise the interest of several key funders, as a result providing critical financial support to some innovative local initiatives. Thus, documenting and publicizing the emerging impact of effective USR practices can help encourage the funders to understand how USR can be a promising investment opportunity (Hoyt and Hollister 2014) and may invite and expand new sources of funding.

Furthermore, systematic and rigorous evaluation of USR is enormously needed to demonstrate the impact of a higher level coordination at the policy level of higher education, despite the difficulty. The impact could be measured at multiple levels, including the student (e.g., students' civic awareness and engagement), faculty (e.g., staffs' engaged scholarship), institution (e.g., USR could become a key performance indicator in the University ranking game), and society (e.g., whether the USR practice of the university is related to the subjective well-being of people in the specific area). Last but not least, attention should also be paid to building an effective partnership. Though the success of USRN also depends on the broader environment (such as the community readiness for USR or government policy), facilitating an effective partnership and managing well all the nuts and bolts (e.g., having a clear vision and mission, supporting leadership, documentation and ongoing feedback on progress, technical assistance and support, expansion of coalitions, as reflected in Butterfoss et al. 1993; Roussos and Fawcett 2000; Wolff 2001b) are certainly critical if we envision a larger and bigger change in the policy level. All in all, USR could be a timely response to the global society facing rapid change and challenge, but more collective work has to be done, collective voice has to be advocated and collective wisdom needs to be shared and learned through active partnership and exchange. This is what USRN aims to achieve.

References

Basken, P. (2016, January 24). Is University Research missing what matters most? *The Chronicle of Higher Education* (pp. 3–7). Retrieved from http://www.chronicle.com/article/Is-University-Research-Missing/235028?cid=cp27

Butterfoss, F. D., Goodman, R. M., & Wandersman, A. (1993). Community coalitions for prevention and health promotion. *Health Education Research, 8*(3), 315–330. doi:10.1093/her/8.3.315.

De Ketele, J. M. (2009). The social relevance of higher education. In Global University Network for Innovation. (Ed.), *Higher education at a time of transformation: New dynamics for social responsibility*. Basingstoke: GUNI/Palgrave Macmillan.

Glass, C. R., & Fitzgerald, H. E. (2010). Engaged scholarship: Historical roots, contemporary challenges. In H. E. Fitzgerald, C. Burack, & S. D. Seifer (Eds.), *Handbook of engaged scholarship: Contemporary landscapes, future directions*. East Lansing: Michigan State University Press.

Global University Network for Innovation. (2016). Retrieved from http://www.guninetwork.org

Global University Social Responsibility Network. (2016). *History*. Retrieved from http://globalusrnetwork.org/history.html

Herrera, A. (2009). Social responsibility of universities. In Global University Network for Innovation. (Ed.), *Higher education at a time of transformation: New dynamics for social responsibility*. Basingstoke: GUNI/Palgrave Macmillan.

Hollister, R. M., Pollock, J. P., Gearan, M., Reid, J., Stroud, S., & Babcock, E. (2012). The Talloires Network: A global coalition of engaged universities. *Journal of Higher Education Outreach and Engagement, 16*(4), 81–102.

Hoyt, L. M., & Hollister, R. M. (2014). Moving beyond the ivory tower: The expanding global movement of engaged universities. In Global University Network for Innovation. (Ed.), *Higher education in the world 5: Knowledge, engagement and higher education: Contributing to social change*. Basingstoke, Hampshire: Palgrave Macmillan.

Morey, A. I. (2004). Globalization and the emergence of for-profit higher education. *Higher Education, 48*(1), 131–150.

Roussos, S. T., & Fawcett, S. B. (2000). A review of collaborative partnerships as a strategy for improving community health. *Annual Review of Public Health, 21*(1), 369–402. doi:10.1146/annurev.publhealth.21.1.369.

Vasilescu, R., Barna, C., Epure, M., & Baicu, C. (2010). Developing university social responsibility: A model for the challenges of the new civil society. *Procedia-Social and Behavioral Sciences, 2*(2), 4177–4182. doi:10.1016/j.sbspro.2010.03.660.

Watson, D., Hollister, R. M., Stroud, S. E., & Babcock, E. (2011). *The engaged university: International perspectives on civic engagement*. New York: Routledge.

Wolff, T. (2001a). Community coalition building—Contemporary practice and research: Introduction. *American Journal of Community Psychology, 29*(2), 165–172. doi:10.1023/a: 1010314326787.

Wolff, T. (2001b). A practitioner's guide to successful coalitions. *American Journal of Community Psychology, 29*(2), 173–191. doi:10.1023/a:1010366310857.

Part II
Concepts and Theoretical Considerations

Chapter 3
University Social Responsibility (USR): Insight from the Historical Roots to the Contemporary Challenges

Daniel T.L. Shek, Angelina W.K. Yuen-Tsang and Eddie C.W. Ng

Abstract The relationship between higher education (HE) and the wider society is dynamic but poorly understood. This chapter aims to provide a brief historical account of the development of higher education. In particular, multiple roles and functions are identified to highlight the dynamic interplay between higher education and the societal need and development. Then we examine the changing nature of higher education and the globalization challenges facing contemporary higher education. Drawing on the historical roots of higher education, we summarize key insights based on the current review and propose how the university can maintain its intellectual endeavors while fulfilling its social mission.

Keywords University social responsibility · Historical account · Higher education · Globalization · Civic engagement

3.1 Introduction

The relationship between higher education (HE) and the wider society is dynamic but poorly understood. Sometimes, universities are seen as institutions of the state providing the society with the manpower needs of the bureaucracy. In other times, they are regarded as autonomous to the state control (Brock 2009, p. 24). Despite its fluid nature and the inherent complexity of the relationship between higher education and the society, articulation of social missions and the role of universities in the society is enormously important, particularly when universities are not only the most enduring institutions of civilization but also now becoming a global knowledge industry.

The preparation for this chapter is financially supported by the Global Youth Leadership Institute at The Hong Kong Polytechnic University.

D.T.L. Shek (✉) · A.W.K. Yuen-Tsang · E.C.W. Ng
The Hong Kong Polytechnic University, Kowloon, Hong Kong
e-mail: daniel.shek@polyu.edu.hk

© Springer Nature Singapore Pte Ltd. 2017
D.T.L. Shek and R.M. Hollister (eds.), *University Social Responsibility and Quality of Life*, Quality of Life in Asia 8,
DOI 10.1007/978-981-10-3877-8_3

This chapter aims to provide a brief historical account of the development of universities, with particular reference to its social mission. Then we examine the changing nature and context of higher education with reference to globalization. In particular, puzzles and challenges facing the globalized educational environment will be highlighted. Next, we would summarize key insights that can be drawn from the historical roots of higher education and examine how the university can maintain its intellectual core business while fulfilling its social mission.

3.2 Historical Development of Universities

The idea of the university can be traced back to the Classical Greece or other ancient civilization (Brock 2009; Lay 2004) with their primary focus dedicated to education and inquiry. The normal practice was for students to follow a famous master, while the "first such institution was established in 392 BC by an upper-class Athenian, Isocrates", who offered "to train students in practical arts of rhetoric" (Lay 2004). The advanced education was valued as an aristocratic accomplishment. The Roman Empire later modified the educational curriculum to better serve their practical needs. While Rhetoric and Philosophy remained the core components of traditional schooling, specialized legal training was also developed (see Clark 1963, in Lay 2004). While suspicion happened at the very beginning, advanced learning was gradually accepted by orthodox citizens (e.g. seen as providing civic pride or even financial benefit) and embraced by society. Nevertheless, classical HE system never developed the concept of institutional autonomy, which was basically an achievement of the medieval world. Instead, the HE was closely aligned to the needs of the government. The graduates were normally promised a better career path in some administrative role. Nevertheless, by the 6th century, institutional higher education collapsed after the slow disintegration of the Roman Empire, and only re-emerged until the medieval renewal of interest in the 11th century.

The renewal of interest in higher education in Renaissance was both a "rebirth" of classical Greco-Roman and Christian scholarship, and also a greater exposure to other culture or civilization. Acknowledging that there were relatively open opportunities to become a master and that advanced education could enhance upward social mobility, opposition to expansion was expressed by some scholars or elites, resulting in various forms of regulation and control measures. The degree and boundary of inclusion/exclusion and expansion also became the political arena of various parties with a vested interest, and this was also an enduring theme over the following centuries (Brock 2009). It is in such a context that institutional autonomy was gradually developed as the key characteristic that distinguished the medieval university from the forerunner in the previous generation.

According to Lay (2004), the students of Bologna in 1195 organized themselves into two groups (known as "universities"), one for Italian and the other for non-Italian students. Each group elected their own representative to protect their rights in the face of civic impositions. They even appointed their own lecturer and directed the curriculum to be taught. By 1245, foreign students were granted protection under the city law and less than a decade later the statutes of the universities were recognized by the Bolognese authorities. Thus, the University of Bologna was considered to be the first true university (Patterson 1997, in Lay, 2004). In parallel, the masters also tried to defend their interests through collective efforts, particularly in French. They not only maintained their economic and intellectual importance but also succeeded in the complex power struggles going on in the society and between various kinds of stakeholders, be they religious or secular. Through a series of happenings and fights for the right, Pope Gregory IX issued the papal decree Parens Scientiarium (mother of Knowledge) in 1231, granted the university papal protection and freedom from local church or civil author, and allowed the university to establish its own laws for self-governance (Patterson 1997, in Lay 2004). In fact, the advancement of the cause of the universities by the political or religious leaders was "not simply because of their intellectual or economic value, but rather due to the implications of this support on wider patterns of political power" (Lay 2004, p. 37). Also, the *Licentia docendi*, the license to teach, was also set up to maintain the exclusivity and the access to a store of knowledge, resulting in both examination and the degree structure. Thus, both the freedom from legal or religious constraint and the division and appropriation of knowledge are a complementary process leading to institutional autonomy (a fundamental characteristic of modern universities) and formalization of the relationship between society and the university.

During the medieval period, the primary focus of higher education was oriented toward teaching and the learned professions, while the universities' roles were to fulfill the social demand and to provide the required educated priests, administrators, lawyers, physicians or personnel for business (Scott 2006). Thus, serving the emerging state is a natural progression and by-product. While the philosophical goal of the medieval university was "the pursuit of divine truth and learning", the chancellors (of the university) often served the church and their kingdom at the highest level, and the monarchs also relied on the university doctors to serve as judges in the secular court system. Scott (2006) even noticed that "during the early 1500s Henry VIII consulted the Universities of Oxford, Paris, and Salamanca regarding his controversial divorce case" (p. 11).

In the 17th century, the higher education underwent a period of stagnation in which the university "withdrew from society but only concentrated on maintaining the privileges gained during the earlier phases of expansion" (Lay 2004, p. 20). Instead of engaging with new intellectual development, universities retreated to primarily preserve society's store of knowledge; universities also changed from providing training for a particular profession into an instrument of social control and a means for social demarcation and exclusion. Brock (2009) even depicted a dim picture of HE that, "corruption was rife and standards low ... in the 17th and 18th centuries" (p. 159). Critics of traditional university system even wondered about the justification for the university in the modern world, resulting in the university reform in the following century to counter the threat (Cowley and Williams 1991, in Lay 2004).

In the 19th century, to better serve the post-industrial society, there was an increasing emphasis on practical knowledge and the importance of professional accreditation (Watson et al. 2011). For example, since the twelfth century, Oxford and Cambridge were almost duopoly of higher education and considered themselves colleagues in an autonomous collective (Lay 2004). Thus, in response to the resistance to change of the Oxbridge system, University of London was developed to provide a more practical curriculum and greater accessibility to people. They also allowed the setting of examination and the awarding of degrees to students of institutions that might be affiliated later. As a result, the University of London "quickly grew in size… and a series of linked institutions were founded across the country." (Lay 2004, p. 46).

Another major reform in the 19th century was initiated in Germany. Wilhelm von Humboldt was charged to propose a new model for the old universities, resulting in the establishment of the University of Berlin in 1810. Fundamental to this new vision of the university "was an emphasis on scholarship, and the assertion that the true university accord equal significance to research and training" (Lay 2004, p. 48). According to this new vision, "the ideal university aimed to increase the sum total of human knowledge through research" (Lay 2004, p. 48). The Humboldt reform was well recognized and conceived to reinvigorate the university and revitalize the intellectual dimensions of the nations (Brock 2009; Lay 2004). It also has a massive influence on the future of higher education not only in Germany, but also Britain and US throughout the 19th century and into the 20th century. This reform also established the research mission of higher education which many universities still embrace today.

The development of the university in the 20th century has a multiplicity of forms, resulting in varied institutional forms and functions. In addition to the teaching and research roles as well as the purpose of serving the government and nation-state mentioned before, higher education was also with the aim to support the public service and democratization in the society (Scott 2006). Particularly noted is the Americans' experience. According to Scott (2006), since the founding of the nation, democratization was the inherent mission of American higher education throughout the 19th century and "through education, the Republican value of liberty and self-government were to be reinforced in young people" (p. 14). He further noted that this democratization mission was later "embodied in the formal public service mission of the 20th and 21st centuries" (Scott 2006, p. 15). Lay (2004) observed that while the early American institutions (following the Oxbridge model) underwent a conservative period by primarily offering education for elites population, their ongoing resistance to change finally led the federal government to create a new form of institution, the Land Grant College and the passing of the Morrill Act in 1862. The act not only provided the state with land and financial support to establish the state-administered educational facilities but also recognized the importance of more utilitarian studies (such as agricultural science which was valuable to the local needs in that period), which deserved equal standing with the traditional liberal studies within the same facility. Furthermore, women and the African Americans were also benefited with more equalitarian admission. Thus,

Cantor (2012) even argued that "The Morrill Act launched a revolution in higher education by providing for what would become known as 'democracy's colleges' (p. 2)."

Later, the University of Wisconsin "joined the ranks of the land-grant institution in 1866, and by 1885 was reaching 50,000 farmers with its first offering of a wintertime farmer's institute" (Cantor 2012, p. 2). The sessions gave the professors and the farmers a chance and platform to talk and give feedback to each other. In this spirit, the President of the University of Wisconsin committed to serving the entire population of that rural state in 1904, by vowing that he would "never be content until the benefits influence of the University reaches every family in the state" (Cantor 2012, p. 3). The landmark "Wisconsin Idea" not only realized the public service ideal among state universities, but also "influenced many other state universities to elevate public services as a core mission equal to teaching and research" (Scott 2006, p. 26). As a result, this became the foundation of social engagement of higher education while the emphasis of service became one of the key pillars of universities.

Nevertheless, in the meantime, many scholars in the US were also enthusiastic about the German model and advocated the ideal of scholarship as the defining characteristic of the University. As compared to its German counterpart, the American graduate school had a strong ethos of public service by making available to society academic research. Also, in the 20th century, the American universities were called upon by the federal government to perform research and contribute knowledge to the military invention or other societal issues/concern, such as the nation's defense, health, space program and economic growth (Chambers 2005; Scott 2006). Thus, Lay (2004) argued that the US developed its unique higher education model which was a "product of European traditions being selectively transported in response to local societal needs" (p. 60). We can also see how they were "flexible and capable of meeting both cultural and technical needs of the growing nation" (Lay 2004, p. 60).

The above review provides a rough sketch of the historical root of higher education across the centuries, particularly about the societal need and development. The roles and functions of universities are multiple and varied, depending on the broader social context and internal dynamic of universities. While the traditional role of higher education emphasizes more on general education and research and prepares administrators for the regime, the recent development also highlights the diverse role of higher education, such as the importance of professional school and the service to the society and economic world. In addition, promoting the civic society and a sustainable human development is also expected of higher education whether they fulfill their contemporary role in society (Brennan and Naidoo 2008; Cortese 2003; Parsons 2014; Scott 2006). Fairly speaking, the teaching role is consistently the primary focus of HE while the other non-teaching functions of universities are the relatively recent product of higher education addressing the societal needs and tailored to the local context. Nevertheless, due to the globalized nature of HE, the successful experience in one area will quickly spread to the other region in the world. Therefore, to understand the role and function adequately played by the universities and the promise of university social responsibility in the contemporary world, we have to examine in detail the changing nature of society and the globalization challenge facing the universities nowadays, which we now turn to.

3.3 Changing Nature of Universities: Puzzles and Challenges

While the changing nature of the higher education is discussed, the globalization challenge facing the higher education is most critical and with enormous impact (Altbach et al. 2009). The opportunities for study and research are no longer limited by the national boundaries. Instead, many universities may take the advantage of the globalization and become internationalized, such as recruiting students overseas or "sending students to study abroad, setting up a branch campus, or engaging in some inter-institutional partnership" (Altbach et al. 2009, p. 24). In addition to internationalization, a related trend of globalization influence on higher education is the corporation and privatization of universities. As such, universities are not only public service to the society but also can generate income from research funds, the sale of university-related products, consulting, research service and university-industry linkage in the global market (Altbach et al. 2009; Parsons 2014). The impact of globalization on higher education can be understood in different aspects outlined in the following paragraphs.

Firstly, student mobility will increase. To meet the demand brought by the massification of higher education, universities nowadays have developed many strategies to attract non-resident students and to reap the benefit from the new global environment. As Altbach et al. (2009) observed, "globally, the percentage of the age cohort enrolled in tertiary education has grown from 19% in 2000 to 26% in 2007" (p. iv). Nevertheless, Altbach et al. also noticed that the improved tertiary education mainly focuses on upper middle countries, while the tertiary level participation in low-income countries has improved only marginally. Thus, this implies that the internationalization and massification of HE benefit the relatively well-off countries and those who can afford, rather than at the service of others in less advantaged part of the world (Stromquist 2007). Thus, we can fairly argue that the higher education nowadays is not only in popular demand, but also becomes an industry with the promising return.

Secondly, the curriculum will also be influenced as the globalization trend may give pressure on, if not force, the universities to produce graduates that can contribute to the labor market. As a result, the focus of curricula will tend to be more professional or skill based program with lesser attention to the general or comprehensive education (Altbach et al. 2009; Stromquist 2007). Parsons (2014) also noted that the corporatization of the university or the privatization of higher education "has led to an increased emphasis on vocational programs and economic pursuits and a decreased emphasis on programs that focus on social and environmental issues" (p. 29). Thirdly, in addition to influence on students and curriculum, the globalization may also impact the internal governance of higher education institutions. In particular, the influence of faculty on decision making will give way to the administrators or executive person, resulting in the primary focus on corporate or managerial concern (e.g. cost recovery, industry links) rather than intellectual interest or social responsibility (Altbach et al. 2009; Parsons 2014; Stromquist 2007). Related to this are the imbalance in stakeholder relationship and imbalance in the evaluation process (Parsons 2014). Parsons explained that to be able to succeed, if not survive, in the globalized market, there will be increased dependence of higher education sectors on the industry stakeholders for financial support, while humanities or social science stakeholders may be seen as a lower priority, resulting in lesser influence. Furthermore, evaluation of the performance of universities will be more likely to be based on economic factors or indicators. Parsons (2014) also expressed her serious concern that universities have been merely defined in terms of their role in the economic development or "measured based on their ability to contribute to economic growth and development as opposed to their capacity to provide social value" (p. 29).

The implication of globalization influence is huge. In the age of globalization, the neo-liberal market orientation has led to increased competition among universities, resulting in marketization and commodification of higher education. Given the primary focus of higher education to serve the labor market and economic development, higher education is no longer viewed as a public good (Altbach et al. 2009; Glass and Fitzgerald 2010; Parsons 2014). Instead, higher education has been readily considered to be a private good, largely benefiting individuals. Thus, financing higher education is no longer the governments' sole responsibility. The public good-private good debate also results in the heavier role in academic institutions and their students' contribution to the cost of postsecondary education and the growth of private higher education sector (Altbach et al. 2009).

In response to the reduced public spending for higher education, universities become a competitive enterprise searching for and securing resources from students' intake, research funding, industry partnership or private foundation. As a result, competition among universities for faculty, students and ranking become the normative practice (Altbach et al. 2009; Stromquist 2007). There is also competition between both the public and private sectors, with the state administrators playing the regulating role. Altbach et al. (2009) also noticed private higher education institutions, whether for-profit or quasi for profit, are now the fastest growing sector worldwide while they are mostly run on a business model. Singh (2012) observed that, to retain its accountability after losing its noble social goal, the discourse on higher education is being "thinned down and reduced to the terms of market responsiveness" and the discourse of accountability "is narrowly but overwhelmingly framed by the drive for economic growth and competitiveness or even economic survival with a global area" (p. 9). Under this context, many may worry that the "university is no longer a social institution but an industry, subservient to blind market forces like any other business" (Scott 2006, p. 28). As such, the discussion of university social responsibility is timely and highly relevant. While universities are steering towards the market mechanism but still enjoying much autonomy and academic freedom, social responsibility becomes the normative expectation of organization nowadays (including university) by the general public (Vasilescu et al. 2010).

3.4 Lessons Learned

In no doubt, higher education sectors have changed a lot in the past few decades and the age of globalization. Particularly, higher education has changed from primarily offering for the elites to open system of mass education (Altbach et al. 2009; Morey 2004). In response to the rapid growth of knowledge, the expansion of demand for higher education, the competing demand of higher education for the service of economy and society, higher education sectors are at the crossroad what function and appropriate role they have to play so as to fulfill its unique role in the society. In the age of profane marketization and commodification of higher education, how and for what value could higher education maintain its social mission and purpose? Scott (2006) argued that to face the rapid social change, universities have to set clear missions so as to facilitate decision making, align associated academic policy and practice, enhance communication internally and externally, and to promote organizational improvement. Otherwise, they will easily get lost in the rampant competition (such as a ranking game). In other words, without a clear mission, the university could not define to itself and society as a whole exactly what it is and, more importantly, what it can offer to others. Thus, tracing the historical roots and mission of higher education is timely as it could provide insight and inspiration to what higher education should aspire to do.

Looking back to the higher education history since the medieval period, Scott (2006) identified six key missions higher education sectors had played, namely teaching, research, nationalization, democratization, public service and internationalization. As he noted, the university teaching mission since the medieval age included both the liberal education and the professional education for undergraduate and graduate students. The research mission emerged in the German universities embracing Humboldtian model, where research (both basic and applied research) was incorporated into classroom teaching and started to stand out as true scholarship. Also, Scott observed the monarchies of England and Spain had fully utilized and nationalized the universities for the service of the government, while in the US, the goal of democratization was promoted and endorsed in some higher education institutions. Related to the democratization mission is the public service mission in the US briefly mentioned above. Through the Morrill Act of 1862 and 1890, the public service was developed as a regular mission of higher education in America, and since then many universities started to consider public service as one of the major missions similar to teaching and research. Last but not least, Scott also became aware of the internationalization mission facing the postmodern universities. The internationalization mission of higher education not only served the nation-states but also cut across the existing multiple missions of the university. In other words, under this goal, the university will internationalize its mission of teaching, research and public service in the global information society.

Despite the difference and diverse function of universities, Scott concluded that the major theme running through all six missions is the service. He argued that whatever the form (e.g. teaching, research or services to the government, public or individual) is, universities are designed and established to provide higher education service. Lay's (2004) summary of the rise and fall of the higher education (e.g. the period of stagnation in the 17th century or American's successful transplantation experience) also reminded us that universities flourished while they met and responded to the societal need, and waned while they became complacent and alienated from the societal concern. Following this logic, we contend that it is the time to reiterate the social mission of higher education and the idea of higher education as a public good, especially when the commercialization of higher education with the increasing trend of for-profit higher education has gained much notice (Morey 2004; Vasilescu et al. 2010). It is not only because the value of higher education, from its historical origin, is building on its service to the society and its ability to serve the society. More importantly, higher education will most likely get lost in the age of globalization, if its core mission is not emphasized enough. As Altbach et al. (2009) recognized, the idea of higher education as a public good is "fundamentally important and must be supported … because this aspect of higher education is easily neglected in the rush for income and prestige" (p. xxi). In addition, as far as the accountability issue is concerned, reinstating the HE as a public good (rather than merely a business product) could fulfill the social responsibility expected for the university by the general public. Furthermore, proactively speaking, realizing the social mission of universities, by the use of the teaching, research and service (such as service learning initiative) could address the social ills and contribute significantly to the societal development and the global world in which we are now locating.

3.5 Way Forward and Questions to Be Considered

Nevertheless, even if the social mission or the notion of higher education as a public good could be established among the universities, there are still two main issues to be considered. While the first is conceptual, the second is practical.

Firstly, and most importantly, the idea of public good has to be clarified. What are actually the social mission of higher education and required accomplishment for higher education to be viewed as a public good? Indeed, there are different understandings related to the idea of "public good". While some may worry about the shifting of the curriculum away from a broad discipline towards a narrow vocational focus, others may argue that program focusing on the market orientation truly contributes to the local industry and economy. Related to this, while many pursuing higher education may wish to acquire the applied knowledge so as to reap the tangible benefit of education (such as better career prospect), others will worry the overemphasis on the applied knowledge may threaten or marginalize some equally important disciplines (such as arts and humanities), and the more intangible aspects of public good which is often associated with higher education (such as academic autonomy, deeper human understanding or civic sense) (Singh 2012).

Furthermore, while the growth of for-profit higher education may be due to the greater accessibility to higher education and opportunities for those who could not be provided elsewhere (Morey 2004), others may concern that the massification of higher education may lead to the overall lowering of academic standard (Altbach et al. 2009). In relation to research, Basken (2016) observed that while many scientists are good at turning research into products, disproportionally fewer scientists make the same effort to turn their work into solutions for society's thorny problems. Thus, the notion of public good and further discussion of what is expected of higher education to play in the contemporary society is much needed and imperative. That involves the discussion of the degree and boundary of inclusion/exclusion for higher education, the curriculum and associated competence (general vs. specialized) we are expecting from our graduates, and the criteria for the true scholarship. The fruitful discussion of these important topics will advise the higher education how to realize its noble mission- service to the public, and in what way higher education can become a public good.

In particular, to fulfill the broader social (instead of merely economic) purpose of higher education, we propose the higher education to respond to the expectation of society in the area of teaching, research and service with responsibility and integrity. For example, greater access to higher education for the disadvantaged population is certainly needed for more attention, especially when the education equity is at serious stake (Brennan and Naidoo 2008; Singh 2012). With respect to the knowledge and curriculum, it is certainly inadequate if only the very narrowly focused and specialized knowledge is delivered at the expense of the more general competences which is equally important in the world full of global challenge nowadays (Singh 2012; Stromquist 2007). Some argued that promoting social responsibility and educating students to be citizens of a global society are an urgent need nowadays and a good way to develop students' global perspective (Chickering and Braskamap 2009). In term of research, Glass and Fitzgerald (2010) has a nice discussion of engaged scholarship through which the university and society can develop a more reciprocal engagement and mutually beneficial exchange.

Secondly, in addition to the clarification of the conceptual issue, another equally important question pertaining to the social mission of higher education is the practical question of how. To go beyond the reminiscence of the good old days, we also need to understand the strategy and associated support as we wish to bring the ideal of social mission to its full fruition.

Checkoway (2001) proposed three key strategies on renewing the civic mission of the American research university, namely strengthening student learning, involving the faculty and increasing institutional capacity. On students, Checkoway suggested that we can involve students in research projects that address societal issues. Furthermore, we can also involve students in for-credit service learning courses so that they can both serve the community and learn from the experience. In addition, Checkoway reckoned that involving the student in cocurricular activities with a strong civic purpose (e.g. intergroup dialogues or programs promoting global citizens) could also be a powerful way to develop the civic sense of students. With respect to the faculty, Checkoway recognized the important role the faculty can play in renewing the social mission of the university. They could not only "manage the curricula and teach the course that can help prepare students for their own civic roles", but also can "conduct research that involves and improves communities, employing methodologies that treat communities as partners and participants rather than as human subjects and passive recipients of information." (Checkoway 2001, p. 133). Certainly, faculty can also share and disseminate their knowledge by providing consultation and assistance to local communities and organization. Concerning the institutional capacity, Checkoway also noted that some institutional restructuring will be required (e.g. centralized office or new institutional units that increase interdisciplinary interaction) so as to facilitate the relevant community engagement process (e.g. referral procedure, bridging mechanism). Certainly, Checkoway realized obstacles pervade (such as the conservative academic culture, reward structure, lacking structure for university community partnership or leadership in the university).

Thus, a closer examination of successful and innovative examples of higher education institutions will be invaluable for us to learn from others who can hold on the broader social notion of accountability (Singh 2012). Pertaining to this may be related to how the university can "balance the different requirements of good scholarship, entrepreneurial efficiency and social justice commitment" (Singh 2012, p. 16), the exploration of the systemic and institutional forms which could support such a (i.e. broader social) notion, the understanding of the leadership, management and governance practice at different levels of higher education, and mobilization of different stakeholders (e.g. faculty or donor).

Without a better understanding of all the nuts and bolts of the implementation process, the higher education as a public good could be just an ideal and utopia. More theoretical and practical efforts have to be paid. Nevertheless, in order not to narrow down the role of higher education to merely an economic benefit, and to account for the public expectation of the social responsibility for the university, we cannot elude the social mission anymore. Instead, we align with Singh's (2012) broader notion of higher education as a public good because it is not only a noble mission rooted in our historical heritage but also allows the university to become the witness of the time and the changing agent for the improvement of the society nowadays.

References

Altbach, P. G., Rieisberg, L., & Rumbley, L. E. (2009). *Trends in global higher education: Tracking an academic revolution: A report prepared for the UNESCO 2009 World Conference on Higher Education*. France: UNESCO.

Basken, P. (2016). Is university research missing what matters most? *The Chronicle of Higher Education*, January 24, 2016. http://www.chronicle.com/article/Is-University-Research-Missing/235028. Accessed 1 Jan 2016.

Brennan, J., & Naidoo, R. (2008). Higher education and the achievement (and/or prevention) of equity and social justice. *Higher Education, 56*(3), 287–302. doi:10.1007/s10734-008-9127-3

Brock, C. (2009). Historical and societal roots of regulation and accreditation of higher education for quality assurance. In Global University Network for Innovation (Ed.), *Higher education at a time of transformation: New dynamics for social responsibility*. Basingstoke: GUNI/Palgrave Macmillan.

Cantor, N. (2012). The public mission of higher education: Barn_Raisings a century later. http://docplayer.net/20984770-The-public-mission-of-higher-education-barn-raisings-a-century-later.html. Accessed 1 Jan 2016.

Chambers, T. C. (2005). The special role of higher education in society: As a public good for the public good. In A. J. Kezar, A. C. Chambers, & J. Burkhardt (Eds.), *Higher education for the public good: Emerging voices from a national movement* (1st ed.). San Francisco, CA: Jossey-Bass.

Checkoway, B. (2001). Renewing the civic mission of the American research university. *The Journal of Higher Education, 72*(2), 125–147. doi:10.2307/2649319

Chickering, A., & Braskamap, L. A. (2009). Developing a global perspective for personal and social responsibility. *Peer Review, 11*(4), 27–30.

Clark, D. L. (1963). *Rhetoric in Gaeco-Roman education*. New York: Columbia University Press.

Cortese, A. D. (2003). The critical role of higher edcuation in creating a sustainable future. *Planning for Higher Education, 31*(3), 15–22. http://www.scup.org/sustainability/telecast-resources/cortese.pdf

Cowley, W. H., & Williams, D. (1991). *International and historical roots of American higher education*. New York: Garland.

Glass, C. R., & Fitzgerald, H. E. (2010). Engaged scholarship: Historical roots, contemporary challenges. In H. E. Fitzgerald, C. Burack, & S. D. Seifer (Eds.), *Handbook of engaged scholarship: Contemporary landscapes, future directions*. East Lansing: Michigan State University Press.

Lay, S. (2004). *The interpretation of the Magna Charta Universitatum and its principles*. Bologna: Bononia University Press.

Morey, A. I. (2004). Globalization and the emergence of for-profit higher education. *Higher Education, 48*(1), 131–150.

Parsons, A. (2014). *Literature review on social responsibility in higher education*. http://dspace.library.uvic.ca:8080/bitstream/handle/1828/5221/Parsons_Amy_MA_2014.pdf?sequence=1&isAllowed=y

Patterson, G. (1997). *The university from Ancient Greece to the 20th century*. Palmerston North: The Dunmore Press.

Scott, J. C. (2006). The mission of the university: Medieval to postmodern transformations. *The Journal of Higher Education, 77*, 1–39.

Singh, M. (2012). Re-inserting the "public good" into higher education transformation. In B. Leibowitz (Ed.), *Higher education for the public good: Views from the South*. Stellenbosch: Trentham Books.

Stromquist, N. (2007). Internationalization as a response to globalization: Radical shifts in university environments. *Higher Education, 53*(1), 81–105. doi:10.1007/s10734-005-1975-5

Vasilescu, R., Barna, C., Epure, M., & Baicu, C. (2010). Developing university social responsibility: A model for the challenges of the new civil society. *Procedia—Social and Behavioral Sciences, 2*(2), 4177–4182. doi:10.1016/j.sbspro.2010.03.660

Watson, D., Hollister, R. M., Stroud, S. E., & Babcock, E. (2011). *The engaged university: International perspectives on civic engagement*. New York: Routledge.

Chapter 4
University Social Responsibility: Conceptualization and an Assessment Framework

Carlos Wing-Hung Lo, Rose Xue Pang, Carolyn P. Egri
and Pansy Hon-Ying Li

Abstract This chapter presents a systematic review of the evolution and current status of the University Social Responsibility (USR) concept. USR advances that universities should go beyond the core functions of teaching, research, and service and voluntarily act beyond legal requirements to promote the public good and environmental sustainability. There is a growing recognition that USR should be integrated with university strategy and operation practices. Thus, we propose a Values, Process and Impact (VPI) conceptual model and formulate a USR performance assessment framework based on a stakeholder perspective. This assessment framework provides a methodology for constructing a USR index that would rate and benchmark universities, as well as promote USR as a management model. Further, the USR performance assessment framework can be utilized as a management tool to further universities' USR efforts to achieve triple-bottom-line sustainability.

Keywords University social responsibility (USR) · USR index · Conceptual framework · Assessment · Social engagement

C.W.-H. Lo (✉) · R.X. Pang · P.H.-Y. Li
The Hong Kong Polytechnic University, Kowloon, Hong Kong
e-mail: carlos.lo@polyu.edu.hk

R.X. Pang
e-mail: xue.pang@connect.polyu.hk

P.H.-Y. Li
e-mail: pansyhy.li@polyu.edu.hk

C.P. Egri
Simon Fraser University, Vancouver, Canada
e-mail: egri@sfu.ca

© Springer Nature Singapore Pte Ltd. 2017
D.T.L. Shek and R.M. Hollister (eds.), *University Social Responsibility and Quality of Life*, Quality of Life in Asia 8,
DOI 10.1007/978-981-10-3877-8_4

4.1 Introduction

There have been emerging efforts among universities around the world to undertake social responsibility initiatives and practices. This is the result of growing recognition that universities should go beyond research and education to actively contribute to the sustainable development of human society. Universities at the forefront have established social responsibility organizational structures, either a committee or an office, to strategically plan, coordinate, adopt, and implement social responsibility and sustainability projects (US Fed News Service 2010). More progressive institutions have already published their own university social responsibility (USR) or sustainability reports (e.g., Harvard University, University of Bologna, University of Manchester, University of California-Berkeley, Michigan State University, etc.). What appeared to be individual and discrete actions have gradually evolved into joint and network endeavors as exemplified by the Talloires Network and the USR Alliance. In this process, the scope of social responsibility commitment and activities has evolved from being solely community-focused to include environmental sustainability, and more recently towards a holistic view of triple-bottom-line sustainability.

In contrast to the growing popularity of USR, its conceptual development has been slow and is still in the formative stage as demonstrated by the broad range of definitions, scope, and management approaches. In order to effectively promote USR in the global community as well as enhance university social performance, there is an urgent need for a coherent USR conceptual framework, an appropriate management model, and an assessment framework. This chapter provides a systematic review of the evolution of the concept of USR and its current status. In particular, we propose a conceptual model and formulate a performance assessment framework based on a stakeholder perspective of university responsibility management.

4.2 The Concept of Social Responsibility

The idea of social responsibility owes its origin to the business community, where the progressive but unorthodox view of "more than profit making" was raised in the 1930s to temper the excessive profit-orientation in business pursuits. During subsequent decades, a heated debate on the proper role of business in society stimulated scholarly and professional efforts to explore the business relevance of social responsibility. In turn, the concept of corporate social responsibility has developed and been entrenched as an important dimension of business management. The conceptual evolution of the definition of social responsibility has undergone a process of "a hundred competing schools of thought". One stream of research considered social responsibility as voluntary acts motivated by advancement of the social good (Manne and Wallich 1972). Classical economists represented by

Friedman (1970) insisted that profit maximization and obeying the law were the essence of corporate social responsibility. Scholars including McGuire (1963) and Backman (1975) considered social responsibility as additional acts going beyond economic and legal confines to promote societal well-being. Steiner (1972) conceptualized social responsibility as a continuum, ranging from "traditional economic" at one end to "expectation beyond reality" at the other end. These divergent approaches have made it difficult to reach consensus on a definition of social responsibility. Carroll (1979) attempted to resolve this debate by proposing a three-dimensional model of corporate social performance—the philosophy of social responsiveness, social responsibility categories, and social issues involved—to inform the strategic direction, content and action of corporate social responsibilities. Accordingly, the totality of social responsibilities embodies a CSR pyramid of economic, legal, ethical and discretionary categories of business performance. These four categories of social responsibility are not mutually exclusive, and in many cases co-exist simultaneously. Economic responsibility, namely the provision of goods and services, is the fundamental basis for an organization's activities. The other corporate requirement is the legal responsibility to comply with laws and regulations to fulfill social contracts. The next category is the ethical responsibility to meet the social norms and expectations of conduct in different social contexts. At the top of the pyramid is discretionary responsibility, which is voluntary and subject to firm-specific judgment and commitment.

Carroll's pyramid model has been influential in advancing the acceptance of CSR as corporate acts for social well-being that go beyond legal compliance. At the same time, CSR has been increasingly conceptualized from a stakeholder perspective which posits that corporations should actively take care of stakeholders in the process of profit making (Freeman 1984). Following increasing societal expectations of business participation in sustainability development in the wake of the 1987 Earth Summit in Rio, environmental protection has become an integral part of CSR, either expressed in a modified notion of CSER (corporate social and environmental responsibility) or with the biophysical environment being treated as a core stakeholder along with customer, investor, supplier, employee, and community stakeholders. Eventually, Elkington's (2001) triple-bottom-line view of business paved the way for a holistic view of CSR by linking corporate, individual stakeholder responsibilities with economic, social and environmental sustainability.

4.3 Universities and Social Responsibility

CSR informs the conceptualization of USR by considering universities as one form of organizations in human society. Like business organizations, universities should go beyond the core functions of teaching, research, and service (Clugston and Calder 1999) and voluntarily act beyond legal requirements to promote the public good and environmental sustainability. Individual researchers have advanced various definitions of USR. For example, in their study of university sustainability practices, Velazquez et al. (2006) defined a sustainable university as "a higher educational institution, as a whole or as a part, that addresses, involves and promotes, on a regional or a global level, the minimization of negative environmental, economic, societal, and health effects generated in the use of their resources in order to fulfill its functions of teaching, research, outreach and partnership, and stewardship in ways to help society make the transition to sustainable life-styles" (Velazquez et al. 2006, p. 812). Reiser (2008, p. 2) focused on the management of university impacts in defining USR as "a policy of ethical quality of the performance of the university community (students, faculty, and administrative employees) via the responsible management of the educational, cognitive, labor and environmental impacts produced by the University, in an interactive dialogue with society to promote a sustainable human development". Vasilescu et al. (2010, p. 4178) conceptualized the university from a citizenship perspective to define USR as "the need to strengthen civic commitment and active citizenship; it is about volunteering, about an ethical approach, developing a sense of civil citizenship by encouraging the students, the academic staff to provide social services to their local community or to promote ecological, environmental commitment for local and global sustainable development". As demonstrated by this variety of definitions, USR is a living concept still in an exploratory stage.

As identified by Vasilescu et al. (2010, p. 4179), "[g]lobalization, the knowledge society, innovation, the development of technologies, a growing emphasis on the market forces" and environmental degradation, have had significant impacts on "the universities' mission, organization and profile, the mode of operation and delivery of higher education". All these trends in development have expanded universities' footprint in society, and rising social expectations have contributed to increased recognition of the importance of universities' responsibility to various stakeholder groups.

In terms of management and operations practices, universities are increasingly resembling business organizations as higher education becomes a business activity (Jónasson 2008) under growing pressure to generate income to ameliorate the impact of severe cuts in government funding during the last few decades (e.g. Sawasdikosol 2009). This marketization trend in education (Bok 2003) has required universities to be responsive to demands made by individual stakeholder groups. As such, there are common dimensions between CSR and USR. For instance, government as a regulator in the business sector is equally important in the education sector, where it is also the largest sponsor of public university education and research. A similar reasoning holds for important stakeholders in university operations, including employees, suppliers, local communities, and the environment.

Another factor contributing to the importance of USR is the fast growing number of students globally. Across nations, the total number of students enrolled in higher education is forecast to more than double to 262 million by 2025. Nearly all of this growth will be in the developing world, with more than half being in China and India alone (Maslen 2012). This fast growing trend indicates that universities are becoming larger communities and that their related activities will have a greater impact on society as a whole.

A third issue is the unique role that universities play in their respective regions. Universities support and promote local industries through technology innovation and application (Lindqvist 2012). They cooperate with local governments to improve the quality of labor markets. Universities play a unique role in social responsibility fulfillment, not only as critical educational organizations that impact human society, but also by fostering awareness of social responsibility for the younger generations (Muijen 2004).

Another urgent reason to initiate university transformation is technological innovation. Universities are now facing disruptive threats from the emergence of digital education systems such as Massive Open Online Courses (MOOC) (The Economist 2014). MOOC provides online degree courses at much lower costs than traditional university courses. Despite issues under debate, such as degree recognition, this flexible form of digital education has developed rapidly and now poses a real threat to traditional education systems. One implication of this trend in education is that choices for receiving education have become more diverse. As a source of inspiration, as well as a signal to embrace change, universities now face real pressure to optimize their organizational routines. Under the rubric of USR, universities can adopt digital technology as an effective strategy to responsibly innovate in education delivery and management.

In sum, there is growing recognition of the relevance and importance of USR.

4.4 The Development of USR

While the transcendent view of universities as "ivory towers" has withered in the last century, there has been a rapid secularization of universities' strategic vision and positioning, with more salient social orientation and a stronger sense of social responsibility to promote societal welfare around the world (Bok 1982). Major systematic undertakings in university responsibility began with environmental sustainability. Sustainability in higher education first emerged in 1990 with the Talloires Declaration, when 22 university leaders voiced their concerns regarding the prospect of building a sustainable future, and stressed the critical role universities should play in this campaign. As of May 2012, 440 university leaders in over 50 countries have signed the Talloires Declaration, which is a 10-point action plan for incorporating sustainability and environmental knowledge in teaching, research, operations and outreach at universities (Shi and Lai 2013). The declaration marked the official start of university sustainability campaigns and has gained wide influence. As universities responded to the call, a number of other declarations appeared, such as the Halifax Declaration in 1991, the Swansea Declaration in 1993, and the Declaration of Barcelona in 2004. (Alshuwaikhat and Abubakar 2008). The primary impetus has been to establish a sustainable campus by providing guidelines and assessment templates. As a result, significant progress has been made in terms of both environmental education and practices on university campuses (Shi and Lai 2013).

In 2005, the Higher Education Associations Sustainability Consortium (HEASC) was founded in the United States. The purpose of the HEASC is to learn and to work jointly to advance sustainability education, as well as to develop sustainable products and tools. The HEASC recognized the need to create a university sustainability rating system that could address all dimensions of campus sustainability. The Association for the Advancement of Sustainability in Higher Education was the first to respond to this call, developing the Sustainability Tracking, Assessment and Rating System™ (STARS) in 2006 (https://stars.aashe.org/pages/participate/reporting-process.html; Shi and Lai 2013). Several other rating systems have subsequently emerged.

Recognition of the social dimension of universities' responsibility owes much to the social mission of higher education institutions as being to "educate highly qualified graduates and responsible citizens, giving students opportunities to develop their own full ability with a sense of social responsibility" (UNESCO World Conference of Higher Education 1998, p. 24). Concurrently, acceptance of the triple-bottom-line concept has extended the social linkages between universities and societies. The idea that universities should serve broader communities has led to an increased focus on community and civic engagement among universities around the world. Among the early endeavors was the Community Knowledge Initiative established in 2001 by NUI Galway in Ireland (with funding support from Atlantic Philanthropies) to create deeper pathways between the university and the wider society. This initiative later developed into a national network in 2007 and has been international since 2010. More recently, the adverse impact of universities' growing concern over their global rankings on civic engagement has been widely perceived, in fear of their diversion of their resources and effort away from social responsibility.

Initiatives supporting and promoting USR ideas and practices have proliferated in the last decade in Europe, North America, Latin America, Asia, Oceania, and even Africa (see Dima et al. 2013; Mohamed 2015; Vasquez et al. 2014). The milestone event of this global movement was the first International Conference on University Social Responsibility, organized by the University Social Responsibility Alliance in 2009 for the purpose of "establish[ing] a dialogue between attending universities, which addresses their responsibility to society, and … a culture of social responsibility" (Dima et al. 2013). International and regional academic events and networking on USR have followed. In 2014, The Hong Kong Polytechnic University convened the Second Summit on University Social Responsibility, which culminated in the establishment of the USR Network in 2015. As a result of this process, the view that social responsibility should have a central role in universities has become more prevalent.

Scholarly attention on the social responsibility of universities started in the late 1990s, with the initial focus being on universities' responsibility for environmental protection in response to the global call for sustainable development. Apart from the conceptual clarification and definition, academic research has focused on formulating a framework to operationalize and assess university (environmental) sustainability performance. For instance, Viebahn (2002) designed an environmental management model to enable universities to commence a purposive effort to reduce resource consumption. Alshuwaikhat and Abubakar (2008, p. 1777) proposed a framework for achieving campus sustainability "through the integration of three strategies, namely, university environmental management system, public participation and social responsibility, and promoting sustainability in teaching and researching". The first systematic effort to develop a tool for assessing sustainability in higher education was undertaken by Shriberg (2002) in the close examination of 11 cross-institutional assessment tools. Cole and Wright (2003) used a participatory action research approach to design a framework for assessing campus sustainability among Canadian universities. Velazquez et al. (2006) proposed a managerial model consisting of education, research, outreach and partnership, and sustainability initiatives on campus as a comprehensive framework to achieve a sustainable university. More recently, Shi and Lai (2013) proposed an improved university sustainability rating framework that was based on a critical review of three existing university rating frameworks (SARS, ACUPCC, the Green Report Card). The search for an effective management framework to achieve university environmental sustainability and assess green university performance continues.

Another stream of scholarly research regards the social responsibility of universities as a multi-dimensional construct with CSR as the benchmark. Accordingly, USR should go beyond the narrow confines of environmental protection to integrate economic, social and ethical issues into a holistic framework. The conceptual link between USR and sustainability has been gradually established: USR is a means for achieving university sustainability in economic, social and environmental domains (Sawasdikosol 2009). At the same time, different approaches for practising USR have been advanced, with case illustrations of best practices from universities in both developed (Vasilescu et al. 2010) and developing countries (Alzyoud and Bani-Hani 2015; Chen et al. 2015). For example, in their review of the social achievements of the Romanian higher education system, Dima et al. (2013) proposed a model of social responsibility focusing on the academic domain that had six dimensions: alumni-oriented projects, inter-university cooperation, university-high school cooperation, university-business cooperation, international cooperation, and socio-cultural and ecological projects. Vallaeys et al. (2009) suggested four steps for the implementation of USR practices, namely, commitment, self-diagnosis, fulfillment, and reporting and communication. Mohamed (2015) took USR one step further by integrating it with strategic management from a stakeholder perspective. Increasingly, USR is seen as a progressive concept and practice that will help universities to "achieve development, sustainability and competitiveness" (Alzyoud and Bani-Hani 2015, p. 1857).

In contrast, scholarly research on the assessment of USR is less developed, although many universities have undertaken their own assessment of sustainability efforts (e.g. University of Minnesota, Miami University, Bates University). One rare major effort was undertaken by Lozano (2006), who, by modifying the Global Reporting Initiative (GRI) Sustainability Guidelines, formulated a Graphical Assessment of Sustainability in Universities (GASU). Accordingly, the sustainability efforts of individual universities are assessed based on published sustainability or USR-related reports. Sets of indicators in each of four dimensions—economic, environmental, social and educational—are graded to obtain dimension performance scores, which are then added to obtain an overall sustainability score. In this way, GASU serves as an assessment tool "for the analysis, longitudinal comparison and benchmarking of universities' sustainability efforts and achievement" (Lozano 2006, p. 963).

Cross-university USR assessment has given rise to the idea of USR international rankings. With the focus on curriculum design and teaching, the USR Alliance is a major advocate in that "[u]niversity social responsibility ranking and awards are essential tools to motivate the university to inculcate the teachings of social responsibility as the essential means of man's survival and advancement" (Sawasdikosol 2009). However, given that USR is still an evolving and somewhat elusive concept, a robust and comprehensive USR assessment framework is not yet available. This is the major obstacle that impedes the promotion of USR worldwide and the establishment of comparable ratings and rankings as a motivator for adoption. Therefore, we aim to fill this gap by proposing a generic USR assessment framework designed for cross-institutional comparison.

4.5 A Holistic and Progressive USR Assessment Framework: The VPI Model

The development of a generally applicable USR assessment framework has lagged behind the development of USR itself. Existing assessment frameworks have mainly focused on university environmental sustainability. One example is STARS (the Sustainability Tracking, Assessment and Rating System), which is a transparent, self-reporting framework allowing colleges and universities to measure their sustainability performance (https://stars.aashe.org/pages/participate/reporting-process. html). Another example is ACUPCC, the American College and University Presidents' Climate Commitment, which specifically addresses global warming and climate change issues (http://ecoamerica.org/programs/american-college-university-presidents-climate-commitment/). There are certain limitations in existing formulations. First, university social responsibility should go beyond environmental sustainability to include the social and economic dimensions of sustainability. In addition, previous models suffer from either criteria redundancy or over simplification with some key factors missing. For example, the campus sustainability assessment framework proposed by Alshuwaikhat and Abubakar (2008) has 'environmental management and improvement' criteria that overlap with its green campus criteria. However, in their social justice category, only 'equity issues' and 'care for handicapped' are mentioned, omitting other important social issues for universities. A second issue concerns variability in the framework coverage of USR practices. The STARS assessment has 247 and the Green Report Card 120 criteria, while the ACUPCC has only 70 criteria (Shi and Lai 2013). A more comprehensive assessment framework is needed to address these shortcomings in order to establish a valid and reliable USR index and rating system.

In developing a generic and credible USR index, five key issues need to be addressed (Shriberg 2002). First, the framework needs sequential logic linking a university's USR strategy with its operations. This internal logic will enable universities to improve their strategic management and seek continuous improvement in undertaking their social responsibilities. Second, a systematically constructed framework should be able to capture USR practices in a relatively comprehensive way. All key issues should be organized in a logical manner in order to minimize missing items or redundancy. Third, for the purpose of overall performance comparison, a composite indicator is desirable. Based on systematic criteria, a single aggregated USR score can be constructed based on sub-dimension assessments for individual types of USR engagement. As such, one requirement for the assessment framework is that it can be meaningfully integrated and also segregated for multi-level comparisons. Fourth, the criteria selection needs to be non-redundant, so that the same item/factor is not counted in more than one USR indicator. Fifth, indicators or criteria to evaluate USR performance need to be representative and quantifiable. Information for criteria assessment should be from widely available sources, and multiple sources of information need to be consulted. In this process, it is imperative to avoid interdependency among criteria or indicators.

There has been a growing recognition that USR should be integrated with university strategy and operation practices. In the process of conducting research and teaching, consideration should be accorded not only to knowledge creation and talent cultivation, but also to the wider concerns of economic efficacy, social development and environmental protection. Our conceptual model of university sustainability, integrating a multiple stakeholder perspective is presented in Fig. 4.1.

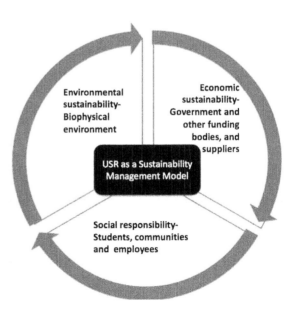

Fig. 4.1 Conceptual model of university sustainability

Fig. 4.2 Conceptualization
of VPI model

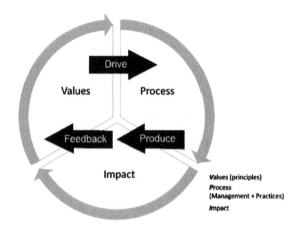

How should universities pursue USR? Based on Wood's (1991) Corporate Social Performance (CSP) model, we developed the Values-Process-Impact (VPI) model for a holistic conceptualization. As shown in Fig. 4.2, the VPI model consists of three aspects. The sustainability values (V) of a university require the formulation of a vision and mission of USR and university sustainability that are conceptually sufficient to inform its strategic positioning. The process (P) of practicing USR asks a university to institutionalize the management of USR and deliver USR projects that translate its vision and mission into action. The impact (I) of USR practices obliges a university to evaluate the contribution of its USR endeavors to economic, social and environmental sustainability in terms of the well-being of various stakeholder groups. The virtuous cycle of VPI takes the form of the values driving the process, the process generating an impact, and the impact providing feedback for improvement. As such, the VPI approach makes the USR model interactive and progressive, and accordingly to guide universities in achieving sustainability through continuous improvement.

Based on these two conceptual models, we propose a USR assessment logics framework that combines university stakeholder management and the strategic management of operational functions. As shown in Fig. 4.3, the first step in the framework concerns the university's values: whether the university has written policies to direct its social responsibility engagement and which stakeholders are involved in its USR. From the perspective of institutional change, leadership is the definitive element for advocating USR (Allen 1999). Leaders who have the power to make decisions regarding policy making and resource allocation with clear awareness of social responsibility can initiate top-down change. The second step in the framework concerns the university's USR management system: USR goals and plans; USR programs in progress; the university's USR budget; release of annual USR report for stakeholder communication; and organizational structure of USR management. Without well-structured managerial procedures, the work of USR is difficult to initiate, implement and monitor. The third step involves creating a university stakeholder-strategy matrix that links USR practices with key

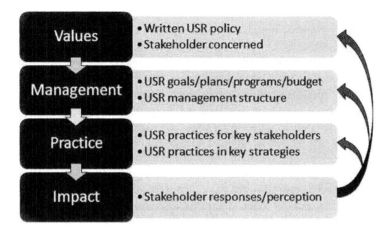

Fig. 4.3 USR assessment logics framework

stakeholders and university strategies. For this matrix, clearly defined and quantifiable USR criteria are derived for each stakeholder group and the corresponding major university functions. The framework's fourth step considers the impact and benefits of USR engagement on stakeholder groups. These assessments then serve as feedback for validation or revision of the previous framework steps.

4.6 A Stakeholder Perspective of University Social Responsibility

Business sustainability has been increasingly conceptualized in terms of CSR from a stakeholder perspective (e.g., Dyllick and Hockerts 2002). The fundamental idea is that enterprises that are responsible to their stakeholder groups in the process of doing business are more likely than non-responsible enterprises to sustain the life span of their business operation. There is growing evidence to show that enterprises that adopt CSR are prone to building a positive corporate image, nurturing high employee commitment, cultivating customer loyalty, acquiring community popularity, becoming environmentally friendly, and ultimately, to reducing business risks (Godfrey et al. 2009). In addition, research on corporate social performance has generally found that being responsible to stakeholders helps to strengthen enterprises' competitive advantage and financial performance in the long run (Cheng et al. 2014). All these are necessary conditions for business sustainability. In this way, CSR provides an avenue to enable enterprises to achieve economic, social and environmental sustainability—the so-called triple bottom line.

The CSR stakeholder perspective informs the USR assessment framework, which is stakeholder focused in order to achieve an aggregated value by being concerned with all major stakeholders' interests and caring for their well-being. In this way, the first step of the assessment design is to identify the key stakeholders for universities.

The operation of a university involves a wide range of stakeholders. University staff and academic faculty teach and nurture students to serve society. Besides teaching, academics also conduct research in different fields and disciplines for knowledge creation. In order to maintain daily operations and to develop teaching and research capabilities, universities need to secure funding support from government or relevant bodies in order to deliver education and engage in research. From the management perspective, universities cater to the welfare and well-being of their students and staff members through the careful selection of service and resource suppliers. They also have to take care of the adverse environmental consequences of their operations, and to promote societal well-being through service to social and business communities. Universities also cooperate as well as compete with their peers. They cooperate with each other for education delivery and research exchange, share and leverage resources, and collectively contribute to social development. They also compete with each other for the admission of students, recruitment of academic staff, and to secure funding support. Therefore, key stakeholder groups are identified as: students, employees, government, community, peer universities, environment, and suppliers. We next elaborate on the nature of each stakeholder group in greater detail.

Students The sub-groups of students include undergraduates, postgraduates, continuing education, and prospective students. Undergraduate students are often the main body of the university population. They spend most of their time on campus participating in a wide range of curricular and extracurricular activities. Therefore, they generally require more care from their university than other student groups. Introducing the concept of social responsibility in curriculum design and arranging related extracurricular activities serve the purpose of cultivating young and socially responsible generations. Student responsibility practices demonstrate a university's commitment to its students by providing high-quality education delivery including complete information, responding to student complaints and suggestions, and adopting curriculum design and teaching practices that meet student needs and expectations.

Employees A university needs a variety of staff to meet its teaching and research missions, as well as to maintain its daily operation, including administrative staff and front-line functional staff. In general, employee responsibility practices emphasize organizational fairness and support in employee relations, including equitable treatment of employees irrespective of gender and ethnicity, and supporting employee educational development, and work-family life balance. In particular, the policy of employee management should encourage social responsibility practices on campus as well as in the local community. USR brings additional requirements for university employees who are teaching staff and academic researchers. Social responsibility has become an important field of teaching and research in various disciplines, such as the science, engineering, business, the arts and humanities, social work, etc. Publications focusing on this topic also contribute to promoting social and environmental responsibility.

Environment The biophysical environment as another key stakeholder has multiple implications. Internally, campus sustainability is a long-term goal. In this regard, universities develop green policies and establish environment management systems to guide daily operations, such as in resource and energy saving, pollution prevention, greening projects, etc. Externally, the university's research on environmental sustainability is an important form of contribution to knowledge and practice in society. Further, it has a responsibility to disseminate an environment-friendly message to the public, such as by attending and holding environment-friendly activities, and encouraging university volunteers to support environmental initiatives. In sum, university environmental responsibilities integrate environmental sustainability goals and objectives in organizational operations such as voluntarily exceeding government environmental regulations and implementing environmental management systems.

Government and funding bodies Government and other funding bodies are major sponsors for public and private universities respectively. They provide financial and other forms of resources to support university development, support education as part of their social responsibility fulfillment, and develop cooperative programs. It is important to acknowledge that modern universities, however independent in their teaching and research, need to be responsive to government policies and initiatives. Although governments should not directly instruct universities on what to research and what to teach in a political sense, the relationship between government or funding bodies and universities within the broad framework of policy, especially education policy, needs careful exploration. Government and funding body responsibility practices incorporate their interests in education and research decisions by seeking their input on strategic decisions, responding to their needs and requests, and providing a positive return on their education investment.

Communities Universities and local communities frequently interact with each other. Communities are the closest channels that are impacted by universities. University community responsibility practices demonstrate a university's voluntary commitment to improving the quality of life in its local communities through charitable activities such as philanthropic donations, and organization and sponsorship of cultural, sports, and education programs. Universities can impact communities via organizing voluntary work or activities that are provided by university staff and students. Such university-organized and -supported activities can have a significant impact on local citizens' lives. Alternatively, communities provide universities with a venue for employment, student recruitment, industrial support, and field research. The reciprocal interaction between university and community is the key link where knowledge can be discovered and transformed into productivity and innovation.

Peer Universities Peer universities are considered both competitors and collaborators. Fair competition must be ensured through fair resource acquisition, fair recruitment policy, and transparent information disclosure. Cooperation among institutions, including student exchange programs, academic visits, and organizing conferences, may effectively enhance teaching and research outcomes through shared communication platforms. Peer university responsibility practices indicate mutual respect, resource sharing, and networking in order to better serve other stakeholders' interests.

Suppliers Suppliers provide services and products for supporting universities' daily operations. Universities have an obligation to select qualified and responsible suppliers who share the idea of sustainability. They need to establish an effective purchasing system to select, evaluate and maintain relationships with qualified and responsible suppliers. Supplier responsibility practices involve the development of long-term collaborative relationships based on communication and information sharing, as well as cooperative goals and decision making.

In the proposed USR assessment framework, the stakeholder perspective is aligned with universities' key strategic areas to capture individual USR practices. We conceptualize a university's strategic areas in terms of its major functions, namely, university governance, teaching and learning, academic research, community service and environmental sustainability. These five functions reflect the major strategic areas for improving USR engagement. University governance is the institutional arrangement that guides university operation, and prescribes policies and regulations for defining relations and interactions with various stakeholders. A well-structured USR management system can enhance the decision-making process, enable stakeholders' participation, and facilitate policy implementation. In accordance with the stakeholder groups previously identified, teaching and learning, and academic research are primarily the responsibilities of academic staff. Environmental sustainability involves the upstream of green suppliers to the downstream of the environmental footprints of individuals and communities. Community service refers to the outreach of university activities, especially university support of social development and promoting a sense of social responsibility society.

The ticks in each box in Table 4.1 are examples of how the framework integrates stakeholders and strategic areas in a relational logic. Assessment criteria under each stakeholder group's responsibility practice and impact will be linked with their relational strategic areas.

Table 4.1 Assessment matrix linking USR strategic areas with stakeholders

Stakeholder/strategy	Teaching and learning	Academic research	University governance	Community service	Environmental sustainability
Student	✓	✓		✓	
Employee	✓	✓			
Environment			✓		✓
Government/funding bodies			✓		
Peer universities	✓	✓	✓		
Communities				✓	✓
Suppliers			✓		✓

4.7 The University Social Responsibility Assessment Framework

As described in previous sections, the proposed USR assessment framework consists of three domains to evaluate universities' engagement in USR: values, process (management and practice), and impact.

USR engagement needs to be initiated, managed and delivered by the university management system. It is guided by appropriate USR values embedded in the university's public policies and strategies, which provide an institutional foundation for all USR endeavors. The assessment framework evaluates the university's values as identified by the USR vision statement, policy and strategy, the stakeholders to be cared for, and the overall USR conceptualization and its level of sophistication. With respect to management, the assessment framework examines the university's specific USR goals and plans, programs and budgets, and its USR management structure (e.g., an independent USR management committee, top executive involvement in USR management, and specific unit responsibility for USR implementation). In addition, the assessment includes the annual/periodical USR reports, and regular communication of USR activities and sustainability information to university stakeholders.

The evaluation of USR practices is the core of the assessment framework, with wider coverage than the values and management domains. The university stakeholder-strategy matrix covers a variety of key dimensions and sub-dimensions for eight individual stakeholder groups (namely, students, employees, government/funding bodies, peer universities, communities, the environment, and suppliers) (Table 4.2). The assessment criteria fulfill the major considerations of our USR definition as follows:

USR is about universities going beyond their legal obligations to manage the impact they have on the environmental and society. In particular, this includes how universities interact with their students, employees, government/funding bodies, peer universities, communities, the environment, and suppliers in a caring and responsible way to achieve university sustainability.

To complete the assessment framework, we include USR impact, as it is important to assess the outcomes of the USR practices implemented in terms of their effects on individual stakeholder groups. In particular, the assessment findings will provide feedback that will enable USR management to review the policy effectiveness and resource efficiency of its USR undertakings for continuous improvement. The list of USR impact criteria is provided in Table 4.3.

We have conducted pilot tests of this USR framework scheme to assess the USR efforts of a few universities. Although based on information provided on the universities' websites, preliminary results indicate that the USR assessment framework differentiates the VPI of USR across universities, with notable variance for all major assessment dimensions. Subject to further testing and refinement, the next stage will involve compiling a USR index for rating and benchmarking.

Table 4.2 Key dimensions for evaluating USR practices for individual stakeholder groups

Stakeholder		USR Practice
Students	1.	Program/course quality
	2.	Equality and diversity
	3.	Student welfares
	4.	Building social and environmental responsibility
	5.	Appeal/complaints channels
	6.	Communication and engagement
	7.	USR code of conduct
Employees	1.	Health and safety
	2.	Equality and diversity
	3.	Development and education
	4.	Employee welfare
	5.	Information transparency
	6.	Communication and engagement
	7.	USR code of conduct
Government/funding bodies	1.	Communication
	2.	Financial audit
	3.	Participate in USR programs (sponsored by this stakeholder)
	4.	Service for USR programs (sponsored by this stakeholder)
	5.	Advocacy of USR initiatives
Peer universities	1.	Fair competition
	2.	Information sharing
	3.	Joint USR initiatives
	4.	Communication and engagement
Communities	1.	Philanthropy
	2.	Employee support
	3.	Provision for voluntary service
	4.	Sponsorship
	5.	Communication and engagement
	6.	Sharing information/practice of USR
	7.	Community support
	8.	Joint social responsibility initiatives
	9.	Engagement in USR
Environment	1.	University environmental policy
	2.	Environmental management system
	3.	Environmental management budget
	4.	Green purchasing polices
	5.	Green HRM
	6.	Green communication
	7.	Green Publicity
	8.	Green awareness building
	9.	Environmental protection projects
	10.	Sponsor environmental activities
	11.	Collaboration with ENGOs
	12.	Recycling programs
	13.	Hazardous waste treatment and disposal program
	14.	Paperless office, library and education environment
	15.	Use of energy efficiency-certified IT hardware and devices

(continued)

Table 4.2 (continued)

Stakeholder	USR Practice	
	16.	Software installed to reduce energy consumption
	17.	Green non-compliance record
Suppliers	1.	Supplier responsibility policy
	2.	Support local procurement
	3.	Monitor suppliers' CSR performance
	4.	Communication
	5.	CSR engagement

4.8   Strategic Implications of USR

USR is a progressive management system for pursuing university sustainability. Since its implementation requires considerable investment of resources and effort, it is essential to approach USR from a strategic point of view. Like corporate social responsibility, USR can bring strategic advantages in several respects. The most immediate benefit to be achieved is cost saving by optimizing resource utilization. Upgrading traditional operational routines and raising the sustainability awareness of students and employees engender the adoption of environmentally friendly practices that reduce the consumption of energy or other materials. Waste recycling is supported when the university installs equipment with proper instructions. In these ways, changes in the daily consumption habits of these individual stakeholders can result in significant saving of resources. Eventually, this fosters a change in the university culture, which facilitates the translation of the USR strategy into action (Muijen 2004).

Apart from optimizing campus operations in environmental terms, USR is a strategic tool for enhancing legitimacy and competition. According to Carroll and Shabana (2010), if the organization is to maintain a sufficiently healthy climate to function in the future, it must take actions that will ensure its long-term viability and competitiveness. Conforming to institutionalized rules bestows legitimacy on the organization, which is critical for the organization's survival (DiMaggio and Powell 1983). Suchman (1995, p. 574) defines legitimacy as "a generalized perception or assumption that the actions of an entity are desirable, proper, or appropriate within some socially constructed system of norms, values, beliefs, and definitions". Undertaking social responsibility has increasingly been expected from the general public. Thus engaging in USR will help the university secure public recognition and build social identification. In addition, it is well documented that engaging in social responsibility will differentiate the organization from its competitors (Brammer and Millington 2008). Described as 'doing good to be different', USR promises to give universities a differential advantage in increasingly competitive local and international arenas. A socially responsible image will benefit the university in terms of recruiting students, faculty and staff; securing funding; and maintaining its reputation.

Table 4.3 USR impact criteria

Stakeholder		USR impact criteria
Students	1.	Student feedback
	2.	Employment rate in USR-related jobs
	3.	Percentage of students enrolled in USR-related courses
	4.	Percentage of students taking part in USR-related activities
	5.	Student USR awards earned
	6.	Admission diversity statistics (% race/ethnic minority groups)
	7.	Unsettled student complaints-student complaint statistics and trends
	8.	Number/percentage of students involved in USR-related exchange programs/field trips
	9.	Number/percentage of education projects with USR focus
	10.	Drop-out rate/graduation rate (normalized)
Employees	1.	Employee satisfaction level (% high/moderate levels)
	2.	Employee-related awards (number)
	3.	Percentage of employees participating in USR-related voluntary activities
	4.	Turnover rate (normalized)
	5.	Percentage of women holding management/senior positions
	6.	Percentage of race/ethnic minority groups (relative to local context) holding management/senior positions
	7.	Training/education—average hours per year per employee
	8.	Conference attendance related to USR—average number per teaching/academic/administrative staff member
	9.	Number/percentage of employees with disabilities
	10.	Number of meetings with employee associations on USR issues
	11.	Workplace injury rate
	12.	Number/percentage of employees engaged in training and development with USR focus
	13.	Number/percentage of research projects/papers on USR
Government/funding bodies	1.	Number of meetings on USR with government/funding bodies in attendance
	2.	Number of university management reports on USR to government/funding bodies
	3.	Number of USR initiatives supported by government/funding bodies
	4.	Number of meetings with government/funding bodies on USR issues
	5.	Number of USR policy initiatives proposed to government/funding bodies
	6.	Number of USR awards

(continued)

Table 4.3 (continued)

Stakeholder		USR impact criteria
Peer universities	1.	Experience sharing on USR issues/topics
	2.	Attendance at joint conferences/seminars on USR
	3.	Enrolment in joint classes on USR topics
	4.	Enrolment rate in exchange programs with USR focus
	5.	Enrolment in joint education programs on USR
	6.	Number of joint initiatives related to USR
	7.	Enrolment of joint education projects related to USR
	8.	Enrolment in joint social projects
	9.	Number of co-authored publications on social and environmental topics
	10.	Number of joint project awards (education, research)
Communities	1.	Number of donation (e.g. in kind, etc.) made
	2.	Number of ongoing community projects supported (3 years or more)
	3.	Number of community projects jointly organized with NGOs
	4.	Number of community projects supported
	5.	Number of community projects jointly organized with businesses
	6.	Percentage of staff members participating in community services
	7.	Number of hours accumulated by staff members participating in community services
	8.	Number of community USR awards received
	9.	Number of media reports of university community USR activities
	10.	Number of complaints from the community on USR
	11.	Number of business information sessions/talks on sharing and promoting USR
	12.	Number of projects involving knowledge transfer of USR to the business community
	13.	Number of endowments from the business community related to USR (e.g. research/education programs, faculty chairs, scholarships, etc.)
	14.	Number of USR awards received
Environment	1.	Energy consumption reduction
	2.	Water consumption reduction
	3.	Indoor air quality level/improvement
	4.	Recycling rate
	5.	Reduction of solid waste to landfills
	6.	Reduction of hazardous waste disposal
	7.	Frequency of ENGO collaboration
	8.	Number of complaints related to environment and pollution
	9.	Number of environmental programs organized/sponsored
	10.	GHG emissions reduction
	11.	Increase in green land areas
	12.	Green awards received

(continued)

Table 4.3 (continued)

Stakeholder	USR impact criteria	
Suppliers	1.	Number and percentage of local suppliers
	2.	Number and percentage of long-term suppliers (more than 3 years)
	3.	Number of meetings/inspections/monitoring with suppliers in the last year
	4.	Percentage of suppliers with USR collaboration
	5.	Number of complaints about suppliers (lodged by students or employees)
	6.	Number of complaints from suppliers
	7.	Number of cases of suppliers' violation of regulations/contracts

In sum, the strategic focus of USR identifies several potential benefits and outcomes for a socially responsible university. Possible positive effects range from a more respectable reputation to greater employee commitment, better student quality, sound financial performance due to more funding support and higher cost savings, and stronger competitiveness. In the final analysis, USR can serve as an effective risk management tool in university governance in that beyond-legal-requirement operation in all major stakeholder-related aspects will buffer policy and operational risks.

4.9 Limitations of Proposed USR Assessment Model

Although this study has adopted appropriate methodological approaches to conceptualize a generic and holistic USR assessment framework for evaluating individual universities' USR efforts and provided it with relevant theoretical underpinnings, it is still possible to detect limitations. Like CSR, USR is highly context dependent. Its operationalization is more an interpretation of the cultural and social context and subjective judgment than objective description. There is a potential limitation of the assessment framework in that certain activities that are perceived to be USR practices in one socio-cultural context might not be applicable in others. Although the assessment framework is intended to be generic, it is still necessary to address the variation in the effects of culture, social norms and stage of economic development across different geographical regions.

With similar logic, USR is evolving along with social and economic development. What used to be considered as USR practices that go beyond legal requirements today may later be written into local laws and regulations as the economic advances and society progresses. This will in turn raise the USR assessment standards. As a result, the criteria used in the assessment framework are required to be periodically reviewed and regularly revised accordingly. Otherwise, its reliability and credibility as an effective assessment tool will be gradually eroded.

Finally, the assessment is basically qualitative in nature. This qualitative approach has its own unique merits of being informative and rich in content. However, it is still desirable to quantify the measurements as far as practically possible in order to reduce the subjectivity of content analysis and strengthen its objective accuracy. The short history of USR has made the assessment difficult to be fully quantified at this stage.

4.10 Conclusion: The Sustainability Pathway for USR

USR is in an early stage of development and thus warrants continuous exploration, with attention paid to cultural differences and geographical diversities. Indeed, undertaking USR is an on-going process requiring long-term effort and commitment. USR is a complex and evolving concept contingent on social expectations, economic progress, and environmental needs, featuring by expanding scopes and moving targets. This informs the USR assessment framework, which should be reviewed regularly. Future empirical research will be conducted to validate the proposed assessment framework, as well as the means-ends relation between USR and university sustainability. We hope the USR conceptual model proposed in this chapter will serve to promote USR as a management model that can enable individual universities to achieve triple-bottom-line sustainability, and the assessment framework as a management tool to further their USR efforts on the path to sustainability.

References

ACUPCC (American College & University Presidents' Climate Commitment). http://ecoamerica. org/programs/american-college-university-presidents-climate-commitment/. Accessed June 16, 2016.

Allen, A. (1999). Institutional change and leadership in greening the campus. In W. L. Filho (Ed.), *Sustainability and university life: Environmental education, communication and sustainability* (pp. 105–128). Berlin: Peter Lang Scientific Publishers.

Alshuwaikhat, H. M., & Abubakar, I. (2008). An integrated approach to achieving campus sustainability: Assessment of the current campus environmental management practices. *Journal of Cleaner Production, 16*(16), 1777–1785.

Alzyoud, S. A., & Bani-Hani, K. (2015). Social responsibility in higher education institutions: Application case from the Middle East. *European Scientific Journal, 11*(8), 122–129.

Backman, J. (1975). *Social responsibility and accountability*. New York: New York University Press.

Bok, D. C. (2003). *Universities in the marketplace: The commercialization of higher education*. Princeton, NJ: Princeton University Press.

Bok, D. C. (1982). *Beyond the ivory tower: Social responsibilities of the modern university*. Cambridge, MA: Harvard University Press.

Brammer, S., & Millington, A. (2008). Does it pay to be different? An analysis of the relationship between corporate social and financial performance. *Strategic Management Journal, 29*(12), 1325–1343.

Carroll, A. B. (1979). A three-dimensional conceptual model of corporate performance. *Academy of Management Review, 4*(4), 497–505.

Carroll, A. B., & Shabana, K. M. (2010). The business case for corporate social responsibility: A review of concepts, research and practice. *International Journal of Management Reviews, 12* (1), 85–105.

Chen, S.-H., Nasongkhla, J., & Donaldson, J. A. (2015). University social responsibility (USR): Identifying an ethical foundation within higher education institutions. *TOJET: The Turkish Online Journal of Educational Technology, 14*(4), 165–172.

Cheng, B., Ioannou, I., & Serafeim, G. (2014). Corporate social responsibility and access to finance. *Strategic Management Journal, 35*(1), 1–23.

Clugston, R. M., & Calder, W. (1999). Critical dimensions of sustainability in higher education. *Sustainability and University Life, 5,* 31–46.

Cole, L., & Wright, T. (2003). Assessing sustainability on Canadian university campuses: Development of a campus sustainability assessment framework. Unpublished master's thesis, Royal Roads University, Victoria, BC.

Dima, A. M., Vasilache, S., Ghinea, V., & Agoston, S. (2013). A model of academic social responsibility. *Transylvanian Review of Administrative Sciences, 9*(38), 23–43.

DiMaggio, P., & Powell, W. W. (1983). The iron cage revisited: Collective rationality and institutional isomorphism in organizational fields. *American Sociological Review, 48*(2), 147–160.

Dyllick, T., & Hockerts, K. (2002). Beyond the business case for corporate sustainability. *Business Strategy and the Environment, 11*(2), 130–141.

Elkington, J. (2001). The triple bottom line for 21st century business. In R. Welford & R. Starkey (Eds.), *The Earthscan reader in business and sustainable development* (pp. 20–43). London: Earthscan Publications.

Freeman, R. E. (1984). *Strategic management: A stakeholder perspective.* Boston: Pitman.

Friedman, M. (1970). The social responsibility of business is to increase its profits. *New York Times Magazine, 13*(32–33), 122–126.

Godfrey, P. C., Merrill, C. B., & Hansen, J. M. (2009). The relationship between corporate social responsibility and shareholder value: An empirical test of the risk management hypothesis. *Strategic Management Journal, 30*(4), 425–445.

Jónasson, J. T. (2008). *Inventing tomorrow's university: Who is to take the lead?.* Bologna, IT: Bononia University Press.

Lindqvist, M. (2012). The roles of universities in regional development. http://www.nordregio.se/en/Metameny/Nordregio-News/2012/Issue-22012/The-Roles-of-Universities-in-Regional-Development/. Accessed May 15, 2016.

Lozano, R. (2006). A tool for a graphical assessment of sustainability in universities (GASU). *Journal of Cleaner Production, 14*(9), 963–972.

Maslen, G. (2012). Worldwide student numbers forecast to double by 2025. University World News, 209. http://www.universityworldnews.com/article.php?story=20120216105739999. Accessed September 19, 2016.

Manne, H. G., & Wallich, H. C. (1972). *The modern corporation and social responsibility.* Washington DC: American Enterprise Institute for Public Policy Research.

McGuire, J. W. (1963). *Business and society.* New York: McGraw-Hill.

Mohamed, A. T. E. (2015). A framework for university social responsibility and sustainability: the case of south valley university, Egypt. *World Academy of Science, Engineering and Technology, International Journal of Social, Behavioral, Educational, Economic, Business and Industrial Engineering, 9*(7), 2370–2379.

Muijen, H. S. (2004). Corporate social responsibility starts at university. *Journal of Business Ethics, 53*(1–2), 235–246.

Reiser, J. (2008). University Social Responsibility definition. http://www.usralliance.org/resources/Aurilla_Presentation_Session6.pdf. Accessed March 25, 2016.

Sawasdikosol, S. (2009). Driving universities' collaboration toward the new era of sustainable social responsibility. Paper presented at the University-Community Engagement Conference Penang, Malaysia.

Shi, H., & Lai, E. (2013). An alternative university sustainability rating framework with a structured criteria tree. *Journal of Cleaner Production, 61,* 59–69.

Shriberg, M. (2002). Institutional assessment tools for sustainability in higher education: Strengths, weaknesses, and implications for practice and theory. *International Journal of Sustainability in Higher Education, 3*(3), 254–270.

STARS. Reporting process. https://stars.aashe.org/pages/participate/reporting-process.html. Accessed July 25, 2016.

Steiner, G. A. (1972). Social policies for business. *California Management Review, 15*(2), 17–24.

Suchman, M. C. (1995). Managing legitimacy: Strategic and institutional approaches. *Academy of Management Review, 20*(3), 571–610.

The Economist. (2014). Massive open online forces. http://www.economist.com/news/finance-and-economics/21595901-rise-online-instruction-will-upend-economics-higher-education-massive. Accessed May 15, 2016.

UNESCO World Conference on Higher Education. (1998). Higher education in the twenty-first century: Vision and action. http://unesdoc.unesco.org/images/0011/001163/116345e.pdf Accessed July 25, 2016.

US Fed News Service (2010). Social responsibility should be part of a country's overall development strategy. https://www.highbeam.com/publications/us-fed-news-service-including-us-state-news-p138798. Accessed on July 16, 2016.

Vallaeys, F., De La Cruz, C., & Sasia, P. M. (2009). *Responsabilidad Social Universitaria, Manual de Primeros Pasos.* McGrawHill: Mexico D.F.

Vasilescu, R., Barna, C., Epure, M., & Baicu, C. (2010). Developing university social responsibility: A model for the challenges of the new civil society. *Procedia-Social and Behavioral Sciences, 2*(2), 4177–4182.

Vasquez, J. M. G., Alequin, B. M., & Vadi, J. C. (2014). University social responsibility: A social transformation of learning, teaching, research, and innovation. http://quest.uprrp.edu/Quest_files/ProceedingsQ9/Concurrent_session_VIII/university_social_responsibility.pdf. Accessed September 19, 2016.

Velazquez, L., Munguia, N., Platt, A., & Taddei, J. (2006). Sustainable university: What can be the matter? *Journal of Cleaner Production, 14*(9), 810–819.

Viebahn, P. (2002). An environmental management model for universities: From environmental guidelines to staff involvement. *Journal of Cleaner Production, 10*(1), 3–12.

Wood, D. J. (1991). Corporate social performance revisited. *Academy of Management Review, 16* (4), 691–718.

Part III
Global Experience

Chapter 5
A Comprehensive University-Wide Strategy to Educate Students in All Fields for Lifetimes of Active Citizenship

Robert M. Hollister

Abstract This chapter describes the vision of Tufts University to educate students in all disciplines to be "active citizens," people with the values and skills to be leaders for positive change in society, and the comprehensive approach it is using to achieve that end. The account describes the process of developing this ambitious, university-wide initiative. Then it describes core programs in the areas of student leadership development, faculty support and capacity-building, research, community partnerships, and institutional social responsibility. It discusses facilitating factors and challenges encountered, and how they have been managed. A concluding section reflects on future issues and opportunities. The chapter emphasizes distinctive features of Tufts' vision and strategy: its determination to reach all students and professors in all disciplines, collective leadership by all stakeholders, and a horizontal organizational structure.

Keywords University social responsibility · Active citizenship · Civic engagement · Tufts University

5.1 The Tufts University Vision: Prepare Students in All Fields for Lifetimes of Active Citizenship

Tufts University has a long history of encouraging and supporting student volunteering and has for many years administered several well-established academic programs with a core focus on preparing students for careers in public service. In

Robert M. Hollister, Professor Emeritus, Tufts University; Founding Dean Emeritus, Tisch College of Civic Life, Tufts University; Founding Executive Director Emeritus, Talloires Network.

R.M. Hollister (✉)
Department of Urban and Environmental Policy and Planning,
Tufts University, Medford, MA, USA
e-mail: Robert.hollister@tufts.edu

© Springer Nature Singapore Pte Ltd. 2017
D.T.L. Shek and R.M. Hollister (eds.), *University Social Responsibility and Quality of Life*, Quality of Life in Asia 8,
DOI 10.1007/978-981-10-3877-8_5

the late 1990s, building upon this tradition and these existing programs, Tufts decided to mount an ambitious university-wide initiative to prepare students in all field of study for lifetimes of active citizenship. This effort was led by the author of the present chapter. Our vision is to educate students in the entire range of disciplines to be not only competent in their chosen fields and professional paths, but also to equip them to be effective leaders for change—people who integrate in their diverse professional roles and personal lives the values and skills of civic leadership. Individuals who use their professional standing and skills to address pressing societal challenges and build healthy, prosperous communities. Our bold aspiration is to educate our students to be citizen engineers, citizen businesswomen and men, citizen mathematicians, and citizen artists. We aim to move beyond the traditional ivory tower model of higher education and to demonstrate that the "engaged university" can be a path to higher quality and higher impact teaching and research.

5.2   Process and Stages of Development

This account of Tufts University's recent social responsibility experience uses the terminology that stakeholders of the University consistently utilize—"active citizenship," "civic engagement," and "civic life," rather than "social responsibility." But this is indeed a case study of university social responsibility (USR). The terms are interchangeable in terms of the functions, values and competencies to which they refer. As other chapters in this book indicate, the conceptual vocabulary with respect to USR varies considerably around the world. In the U.S. and at Tufts University as well, the operative phrases are those noted above. However, if one looks closely at the goals and activities involved, these programs and activities fit comfortably under the rubric of USR. In the very first hour of the founding conference of the Talloires Network, the global coalition of engaged universities, hosted by Tufts University in 2005, university heads from beyond the U.S. commented that the conference preparatory materials were presented under the heading "civic engagement," while in their settings the common phraseology was "social responsibility." So the group immediately added social responsibility to the banner, talking henceforth about "civic engagement and social responsibility"—an overly long phrase, but one that sought to represent and respect the full range of perspectives and practices of the participating institutions.

In the late 1990s, Tufts University embarked on a major civic education initiative for three reasons. First, to address the urgent societal need for leaders who would more effectively address pressing societal challenges. Second, to respond to growing student demand for the skills required in order to make a difference with their lives. And third, to take greater advantage of what was already a distinctive strategic strength of the institution. Over a two-year period, the designated leaders of this effort and a widening circle of allies assessed the current assets of the institution and examined options for how to proceed. They decided to embrace an across-the-curriculum, across-the-institution approach that would infuse active citizenship throughout the university. Planners of the effort appreciated that essential ingredients of success would be maximum institutional commitment and an organizational structure to drive and support the project across the entire university. Therefore, they developed a proposal to establish a university-wide college, called the University College of Citizenship and Public Service. In 1999 the University Trustees voted to establish the new college. By taking this formal action, they made a forceful declaration of institutional commitment to achieving the College's educational mission—to prepare students in all disciplines to be active and effective citizens, agents for positive change throughout their lives. The College was set up not to be a separate degree-granting unit, but rather to be a catalyst and a resource to all schools and departments of the University—to encourage, assist and support them to infuse active citizenship in the curricula of all degree programs (Hollister 2002; Hollister et al. 2006, 2008).

Tufts' comprehensive infusion strategy has achieved significant results in its first fifteen years. Our progress to date can be attributed to several factors that include a rich history of institutional commitment to active citizenship, exceptionally strong leadership from three presidents and from other top administrators and the university's trustees, collective leadership by professors and other stakeholders, and support and guidance from sister institutions of higher education. We have, of course, encountered serious obstacles including traditional academic culture that regards public service activities and community-engaged teaching and research as somehow less rigorous or valuable than traditional, and competition for resources.

In its first years, the College placed a primary emphasis on undergraduate student programming and organized several programs to strengthen education for active citizenship in the curriculum and the co-curriculum. We invested heavily in supporting and building the capabilities of faculty members to elevate community-engaged teaching. The College later elevated its commitment to research and expanded its support for active citizenship in the University's graduate and professional schools. Then in 2016 a new strategic plan placed still greater emphasis on research and added a new focus on civic practice—activities to strengthen civic life and behavior in society at large.

In the U.S. an ironic challenge has been that at the same time that student volunteering was expanding dramatically, students level of participation in electoral politics was limited or declining. Students in droves were volunteering to clean up the environment, to combat poverty, and to improve public health, but they were holding back on political participation, not voting, and not working in political campaigns. A key challenge for institutions of higher education has been to bridge this gap—to encourage and support young people who are enthusiastic in their volunteer service to also participate fully and effectively in public decision-making about the same issues that have been the focus of their volunteering (Ehrlich 2000; Musil 2009; Youniss and Levine 2009).

From the very start, faculty leaders urged that the College increase its support for the research dimensions of active citizenship. They argued that the process of gaining full participation by professors would be accelerated by attending to the research side of their professorial responsibilities. They observed further that there were robust research opportunities with respect to citizenship and public service, and that Tufts had an opportunity to exert leadership on this topic. Therefore, a key direction of evolution has been to steadily increase the research work of the College. Faculty Fellows were supported to do research projects as well as curriculum development. A major step forward occurred in 2008 when a leading national research center, the Center for Information and Research on Civic Learning and Engagement, previously located at the University of Maryland, merged with Tisch College.

In 2016 fresh leadership of Tisch College completed a new strategic plan and decided to organize its work around three pillars: education—sharing knowledge, research—creating knowledge, and practice—applying knowledge. Going forward, the College would expand its research about civic life and the institutions that shape it, and to influence practice, not just at Tufts but broadly beyond the academy. "We will utilize that knowledge to promote practices that support the efforts of individuals and communities who seek the greater good (Tisch College of Civic Life 2016)." Priorities include to expand current research efforts through the Center for Information and Research on Civic Learning and Engagement, the Institute for Democracy and Higher Education, and the Tisch Community Research Center. In the area of practice, the College will apply "knowledge to improve democracy and civic life, and to engage citizens in addressing shared problems. We strive for impact in communities and in higher education." This new stage of development aims for substantial impact beyond the ivory tower—not only through the university's educational and research programs, but also through direct efforts to improve democratic and civic practice nationally and internationally. Goals include to "strengthen local and national partnerships with community-based organizations, schools, and government agencies," and to "expand our global reach through a stronger relationship with the Talloires Network, an international association committed to the civic role of higher education around the world (Tisch College of Civic Life 2016)."

The new strategic vision of Tisch College embraces Civic Studies as "an emerging interdisciplinary field that studies civic life and helps citizens improve it. It includes scholarship that combines ethics, knowledge, and strategies to guide citizens in shaping their communities." The College is building the Institute for Democracy and Higher Education "to be a leading venue for research, resources, and advocacy that will shape how colleges and universities foster political learning and engagement (Tisch College of Civic Life 2016)." A core program of the Institute is the National Study of Learning, Voting, and Engagement that provides data to 800 participating institutions of higher education about their students' voting registration and rates.

Environmental sustainability has played a major role in the University's civic engagement efforts in a number of ways. Our environmental and public service efforts have overlapped significantly and in a very positive and influential fashion. Over a decade prior to Tufts' major civic engagement initiative, the University undertook to promote environmental science and policy across the curriculum. This major interdisciplinary effort pioneered basically the same approach that Tisch College employed years later. As a result, when Tisch College was being organized, University faculty and staff already had had significant positive experience with a similarly ambitious university-wide effort organized around another substantive theme. Furthermore, active citizenship is fundamentally about trying to improve the world, and issues of environmental quality and sustainability are high on the list of pressing societal challenges. Therefore, it is natural and inevitable that an important portion of the public service-oriented teaching and research programs at Tufts focus on environmental issues. For several years a Tufts Environmental Literacy Initiative offered faculty members from diverse disciplines intensive training in how to integrate environmental values and competencies in their teaching and research. During that period, the University created the new position of Dean for Environmental Programs, a horizontal leadership role to elevate environmental programming throughout the institution. In 1990, the President of Tufts convened heads 22 universities from around the world to confer about how their institutions would address environmental challenges. The group co-signed the Talloires Declaration on Environmental Sustainability. Fifteen years later, Tufts President Lawrence Bacow hosted another gathering of 29 higher education leaders from 23 countries. The group issued the Talloires Declaration on the Civic Roles and Social Responsibilities of Higher Education. The 2005 Talloires conference organized an ongoing alliance, the Talloires Network, to gather additional signatories and to foster action on the Declaration.

5.3 Strategies

Tufts' primary strategies for strengthening its civic engagement and social responsibility have been to infuse active citizenship throughout the curriculum and the co-curriculum; support collective leadership by all stakeholders; put in place a horizontal organizational structure—a university-wide college; and participate in, and contribute to, the global higher education movement beyond the ivory tower.

5.3.1 Infuse Active Citizenship Throughout the Curriculum and the Co-curriculum

A central feature of our approach has been to integrate values and skills of active citizenship in the full range of academic disciplines and co-curricular activities, to create a web of opportunities and experience that reinforce one another. Today more than half of all undergraduate students participate in community service or other civic engagement activities. Ultimately, our aim is that virtually all students are exposed to, and have direct experience in, doing community service. As the scale of civic engagement activities continues to expand, it becomes almost evitable that every student will have multiple exposures and experiences with community service work, and that these experiences add up, creating greater impact on the development of individual students and also achieving real culture change—making active citizenship a shared ethos of all participants and stakeholders in the institution. The infusion strategy can achieve far greater impact than the alternative of concentrating active citizenship teaching and research in one or a few units. This across-the-curriculum, across-the-institution approach will mobilize the talents and person power of several times as many people as would a separate program or school.

5.3.2   Collective Leadership

Another key element of Tufts' approach has been a high level of collective leadership in designing and implementing its civic engagement activities. Our civic work has been, and continues to be, a story of both top-down and bottom-up leadership, of collective endeavor in all features of the enterprise. This is a story of initiative and creative action by presidents, professors, students, alumni, community partners and other partners. We have achieved significant progress and lasting cultural change largely through the combined strong leadership of this mix of constituencies.

Presidential leadership. The university-wide college that leads Tufts' civic work was initiated by President John DiBiaggio, and then benefitted enormously by forceful support and guidance from two successor presidents, Lawrence Bacow and now Anthony Monaco. In addition to starting the effort, DiBiaggio began a program of annual presidential awards that recognize the outstanding civic work of selected undergraduate and graduate students from all schools of the university. The Presidential Awards for Citizenship and Public Service, presented at a moving public ceremony, send a powerful message that this is an important value and commitment of the institution. While the college was in its planning phase, DiBiaggio personally co-taught an undergraduate course on Leadership for Active Citizenship which brought to campus leading exemplars of civic leadership. The next President, Lawrence Bacow vigorously raised funds and encouraged program development. Early in his tenure, he led a strategic planning process that designated active citizenship as one of three strategic priorities of the university. It would be difficult imagine a more forceful and consequential form of institutional support. He initiated an annual Presidential Symposium on Community Partnerships, a regular occasion that convenes professors, students and community partners to assess how well university-community partnerships are doing and how to improve them. Bacow also chaired the international conference of university heads that launched the Talloires Network global coalition of engaged universities. More recently President Monaco has taken the College to a wholly new level of accomplishment, elevating participation by the university's graduate and professional schools, and strengthening its research programs. President Monaco also has started to challenge the university on how to better incentivize and reward faculty members' civically-engaged teaching and research, including possible reform of tenure and promotion policies.

Professors have been major co-architects as well. They participated in a faculty-student task force that drew up plans for the new college. They designed new courses in a broad range of disciplines that integrate values and skills of active citizenship. Two professors organized a Civic Engagement Research Group that for several years convened over 25 professors to promote civic research, and to foster exchange and joint projects. The group co-authored a book *Acting Civically: From Urban Neighborhoods to Higher Education* that advanced research as a defining component of Tufts' civic endeavor (Ostrander and Portney 2007). Today 50 professors from all schools constitute the invisible faculty of this "college without walls," and a Faculty Executive Committee helps to guide the College.

Student leadership has been highly important, as many of the most effective civic experiences for students have taken place through their participation in community projects that their peers designed, organized and run. An increasing number of students report that Tufts' strong commitment to active citizenship is part of why they chose to enroll in our institution.

A distinctive feature of Tufts' experience has been active and influential participation by alumni in shaping Tisch College. When the university announced its plans for a bold university-wide civic education effort, graduates who were leaders in public service and civic life stepped forward to help their alma mater develop the initiative. They not only provided encouragement, advice and money, but they also started and ran programs that were significant building blocks. Alumni have organized and funded many summer public service internships, and personally mentor the Tufts students in these placements. Over 20 alumni chapters in different parts of the country created annual book awards to recognize local secondary school students who excelled in citizenship and public service. Many alumni serve on the Tisch College Board of Advisors. Primary financial support was provided first by alumni Pierre and Pamela Omidyar who gave over $25 million to launch and build the college. Later alumnus Jonathan M. Tisch contributed $40 million to endow the college and a subsequent gift of $15 to support new directions in the 2016 college strategic plan. Tisch also exemplifies the mission of the college that bears his name. A businessman who incorporates values and skills of active citizenship in his professional and personal life, Tisch states, "At Tisch College, we believe that each of us has a skill set that can, should, and must be used to forge collaborative and innovative solutions. … Higher education is among the most effective means to instill our shared responsibility to make a difference" (Tisch College of Civic Life 2016).

Community partners also have played a vital role in both planning and operating our civic initiative. They not only supervise student interns and service projects, they also contribute influentially to our strategic planning. Many of our community partners—leaders of local nonprofit organizations and government agencies—are co-educators and co-researchers. They participate directly in teaching our students and are inspiring role models to them. Through the Tisch Community Research Center, they help to conceive, plan and co-operate major research projects.

5.3.3 Horizontal Organizational Structure—A University-Wide College

When the planners of Tisch College scanned the landscape of U.S. higher education, they confirmed that the dominant approach being taken by colleges and universities seeking to elevate their public service work was to build up a separate center or school with special responsibility for that area of activity. There existed many well-established and impressive examples of this typical strategy. But we realized that this orientation would inevitably limit the proportion of faculty members involved and of students reached. Regardless of how extensive was its outreach, the "separate center" model would communicate the message, "If you are interested in doing community service, go over to the place with that name over the door. It's their responsibility and expertise." The planning group was determined to reach far greater impact. They asked themselves, "Why not involve all students?" Surely the complicated societal problems require the concerted attention of people with the insights and capabilities embedded in the full range of disciplines. In addition, as they inventoried the current academic assets of the institution, it was abundantly clear that Tufts already had in place some quite substantial programs that already were doing impressive work in educating active citizens. What would it take to grow, to expand, to build upon these efforts, which were thriving in a wide range of parts of the organizational structure? The university-wide college model communicates, "Education for active citizenship is everyone's opportunity and responsibility." The fundamental work involved is located in academic departments ranging from chemistry to economics, from literature to mechanical engineering (Hollister et al. 2006, 2008).

The University College of Citizenship and Public Service (now Tisch College of Civic Life) was initially located within the School of Arts and Sciences—to avoid creating a new piece of organizational infrastructure and to tie the new College directly to the unit responsible for educating the majority of undergraduate students. It soon became apparent that this position in the organizational framework would not provide sufficient stature and participation in higher-level decision-making with and among other schools. Therefore, Tisch College was given the same place in the organizational structure as the seven degree-granting schools. Like the deans of these schools, the Dean of Tisch College reports directly to the Provost and sits on the Provost's Council of school deans and other upper administrators. This arrangement has been very effective in facilitating strong representation of the active citizenship mandate in inter-school planning.

5.3.4 Participate in, and Contribute to, the Global Higher Education Movement Beyond the Ivory Tower

Tufts has charted a direction for its civic work that is shaped by its own history, context and special strengths. In addition, we have benefitted greatly from the experience of sister institutions. Given the reality that institutions of higher education often resist change, it has been very helpful to be able to cite the positive experience of other universities as we developed programs and policies. For example, the impressive community partnerships of the University of Pennsylvania with public schools in West Philadelphia was an important source of inspiration and guidance. Similarly, we were instructed by the dynamic leadership of Princeton University alumni in elevating the community service opportunities for undergraduates in that institutions. In addition, we learned from several public universities, including Michigan State University and the University of North Carolina, that were pioneering ways to recognize and reward faculty members for outstanding engaged teaching and research.

In addition, we have endeavored to share our uniquely comprehensive infusion approach with other institutions, and to collaborate with other universities on common challenges. Therefore, in 2005 Tufts initiated a pair of coalitions of universities to work together to advance their individual civic engagement and to grow the movement of universities beyond the ivory tower. These alliances are vital vehicles for exchange and fostering collaboration, and also for joint policy advocacy—with funders, governmental agencies and other sectors. Efforts to change individual institutions, Tufts included, are strengthened by being part of a broader movement. As was mentioned above, President Bacow convened the first international gathering of the heads of universities, planned in conjunction with Innovations in Civic Participation, to envision their future civic engagement and social responsibility. The group drafted and co-signed the Talloires Declaration on the Civic Roles and Social Responsibilities of Higher Education and launched the Talloires Network to foster action on this vision. Today the Talloires Network has grown to 363 institutions in 77 countries with a combined student enrollment of 6 million, and is the primary global alliance on university engagement (Hollister et al. 2012; Hoyt and Hollister 2014; Watson et al. 2011). Also in 2005, Tisch College and Campus Compact hosted a gathering of 13 U.S. research universities to explore the challenges and opportunities of that segment of higher education to advance their civic work. The group has grown to 40 institutions, including most of the top U.S. research universities; it continues to meet annually and is a regular forum and vehicle for exchange and collaboration.

5.4   Programs and Policies

Core programs and policies of Tisch College and Tufts University are student leadership development, faculty support and capacity-building, research, community partnerships, and institutional social responsibility.

5.4.1   Student Leadership Development

Tisch College offers a host of initiatives to reach students. These programs are so extensive that it now is rare for an undergraduate student to graduate without some significant participation in active citizenship curricular and/or co-curricular activities. One set of the opportunities for student engagement are intensive; they require substantial commitments of time and effort over a semester or longer. Other opportunities are less intensive; because they entail more modest investments of time, they are accessible to, and reach, larger numbers of students.

Intensive options include Tisch Scholars, an undergraduate leadership development program; Tisch Summer Fellows, public service internships; regular, year-long volunteering; and a new bridge-year service-learning program, Tufts 1 + 4.

Students can apply to participate in an intensive, multiple-year civic leadership development program, Tisch Scholars. The Scholars program combines academic courses, fieldwork in local communities, skills development and critical reflection. Scholars develop their own values and skills as transformative leaders and they work together to infuse active citizenship in the lives of their fellow students and to advance culture change at Tufts, to further embed active citizenship in the university's DNA.

Undergraduates also have access to the Tisch Summer Fellows program that offers 70 public service-oriented internships—35 hours per week for 10 weeks—in Washington, D.C., Massachusetts, and New York City, and internationally as well. Tisch College works to maximize prior preparation, guidance during these field experiences, and also critical reflection to elevate what students learn-by-doing. Alumni in Washington, D.C., created an ongoing program called Connecting Alumni and Student Experiences which also places students in paid internships, matches them with an alumni mentor, and offers weekly educational, career and networking events.

Throughout the academic year, over 60 undergraduates participate in Jumpstart, a national early education program that motivates and supports young children from disadvantaged backgrounds to learn and their families to support their education. In another intensive student experience program, the Student Teacher Outreach Mentorship Program, over 30 engineering students work regularly in local public elementary schools to enhance education in science and technology. The largest co-curricular group at Tufts is a volunteer service organization, the Leonard

Carmichael Society, which operates dozens of year-long, student-run local volunteer service programs to combat poverty, take care of homeless people, teach literacy, and address many other community needs.

A major new initiative is the Tufts 1 + 4 Program that supports incoming undergraduate students to do a year of full-time community service prior to matriculating. In the initial pilot year 2015–16, students worked in Brazil, Nicaragua and Spain, and in the U.S.—teaching and mentoring children, working on renewable energy projects and other community development programs. Tufts 1 + 4 key components include preparation, service, a blended learning for-credit course, immersion in communities, reflection, and then carrying with them and sharing their learnings with fellow students once they matriculate. The gap year or bridge year phenomenon is growing slowly but steadily in the U.S. To date, young people who do a year of service prior to starting university are almost entirely from economically privileged backgrounds. A unique feature of Tufts 1 + 4 is that it provides financial support to enable all students accepted into the program to participate regardless of their families' economic circumstances.

Less intensive opportunities for students include a common books project that reaches all new undergraduates, service-learning courses in all disciplines, short-term volunteer service projects, and a Fund for Civic Engagement that supports student initiatives. In addition, Resident Assistants integrate active citizenship programming into activities that take place in residential halls. During each national election, JumboVote encourages and supports students to participate in electoral politics, bringing to campus a wide range of speakers and providing assistance in the voter registration and voting process.

Through the common book project, each year a new text is chosen that illustrates and motivates inquiry into social problems and social action. The book is distributed to all incoming students and during orientation week students participate in discussion groups to reflect on this shared reading experience and the author comes to campus to speak about her/his book.

Each semester, a growing number of courses integrate service projects in academic-credit offerings. Because the vast majority of students' time is devoted to their academic studies, service learning course are an especially influential way to advance their development of civic values and skills. Furthermore, service learning is an ideal way to reach those students who may be less inclined to seek out community service opportunities on their own. To cite just a few examples, undergraduate service learning courses are offered in religion, foreign languages, biochemistry, urban sociology, soil remediation, and nutrition and community health.

Short-term volunteering projects are an important way to reach large numbers of students and to motivate them later to participate in more intensive civic learning and serving opportunities. Each year a myriad of faith-based groups, athletic teams and social organizations organize students to do service projects that range from environmental clean-ups to housing rehabilitation and to expanding recreational opportunities for disadvantaged youth.

The Tisch Fund for Civic Engagement invites students to compete for small grants to support their projects, events and programs that advance active citizenship. In 2015–2016 funded projects included a project of interviews with ordinary citizens and city leaders about how the city of New Orleans rebuilt following a devastating hurricane, a conference on African challenges and initiatives, a symposium on water contamination issues, a poetry workshop series and slam team for Asian and Asian American young people in Greater Boston to support their voices and civic leadership, and a microfinance project in rural Ecuador.

An important challenge with respect to our across-the curriculum strategy has been, how to recognize students' civic education achievements? Our integrative approach has engaged and influenced students who are majoring in all disciplines, but their acquisition of civic values, knowledge and skills was largely invisible. Students sought public validation and certification for the civic leadership competencies that they had acquired. Therefore, the university created *Honos Civicus*, an honors society for graduating students to recognize their completion of exemplary work in the curriculum and co-curriculum. Since its establishment in 2009, over 600 undergraduate, graduate, and professional schools students have gained admission to *Honos Civicus*. Just as students who excel in their academic studies can quality to graduate with honors, they now can graduate with civic honors and list this achievement on their resumés. The *Honos Civicus* approach started with undergraduates in Arts and Sciences, and Engineering, and now has been adopted by graduate schools in Medicine, Veterinary Medicine, Dental Medicine, and Nutrition Science and Policy.

The earliest plans for our university-wide college focused almost entirely on U.S. and local aspects and expressions of active citizenship—local volunteering and U.S.-oriented applied research. Early critical input from the Board of Trustees steered our effort toward greater attention to the international dimensions of active citizenship. Because Tufts has long-standing strengths in international relations both at the undergraduate and graduate level, this is a particularly important part of Tisch College's work to date and of its future as well. Our graduates are heading to careers that include substantial international as well as domestic leadership roles. Therefore, our institution has a special opportunity and obligation to be sensitive to, and to address strategically, how international cultures, economies and politics impact civic values and competencies. Since one-half of undergraduate students do at least a semester of academic work abroad, we have worked with the Office of Study Abroad to grow the opportunities for students to incorporate community service in their periods of Study Abroad. An interdisciplinary major in International Relations is one of the most popular majors for undergraduates, and therefore, integration of active citizenship in the courses that they take is an important priority. Furthermore, the Talloires Network is an important vehicle for Tufts to exchange and collaborate with universities around the world that share our commitment to civic engagement and social responsibility. We initiated the Talloires Network in order to both learn from institutions of higher education in other parts of the globe, to share our experience with them, and to work together on selected civic education and research projects. For example, a major current project of the Talloires Network is the Youth Economic Participation Initiative, a partnership with The MasterCard Foundation that supports demonstration projects of eight TN member institutions that are innovating in the preparation of their students to be "transformative entrepreneurs"—economic entrepreneurs who also are effective leaders for community change.

Given Tufts' major investment in civic education and its status as a research university, it is essential that the institution evaluate the impacts of these activities on Tufts students. The ultimate test of a commitment to educating students for lifetimes of active citizenship is, of course, their actual civic behavior after they graduate. Are they more civically active? If so, in what ways and how did their experiences at Tufts contribute to those behaviors? To what extent can these behaviors be attributed accurately to what they did as university students? The daunting methodological obstacles to such assessment include controlling for self-selection and prior experience. Short of studying the behavior of alumni, it would be informative to study students' perceptions of their civic values and skills, before and at the conclusion of their Tufts studies. Therefore, early in the development of the College, it initiated a longitudinal study of the impacts of varying levels of participation on undergraduate students who reported both lower and higher levels of pre-university community service experience. Preliminary results were encouraging. Students' levels of involvement in civic activities at Tufts correlated positively with their viewpoints on: self-efficacy, the value of personal involvement in addressing social problems, their levels of knowledge about community and national issues, their interest and sophistication with respect to the causes of social problems, and their confidence in developing solutions to societal challenges (Wilson et al. 2006).

5.4.2 *Faculty Support and Capacity-Building*

Integration of civic skills in the academic curriculum of course requires full participation by professors in diverse disciplines. Therefore, support and building the capabilities of professors has been a major focus for Tisch College. We first made a series of curriculum grants to individual faculty members. They all strengthened active citizenship in their teaching, but this one-by-one approach did not achieve the broad "ripple effect" that was needed. Therefore, an early adjustment in our programming was to institute a Faculty Fellows program which each year chooses and supports professors from all schools to undertake curriculum development and research projects. The Faculty Fellows meet monthly, and receive staff and financial support for their projects. Here are just a few examples of Faculty Fellows projects. The chair of the Department of Civil and Environmental Engineering conducted a curriculum review and development process to raise up the department's teaching of active citizenship. A professor of nutrition science and policy developed a long-term initiative to combat childhood obesity in one of Tufts' host communities. A professor of child development studied the impact of students' participation in designing a virtual community on their civic values and skills. A public health professor orga-nized a program to broker collaborative research projects between Tufts faculty members and community partners. His effort developed into an ongoing Community Research Center. The over 100 colleagues who have been Tisch Faculty Fellows since 2002 have become a vibrant community of citizen scholars. They are invited to apply for secondary academic appointments in Tisch College to symbolize and to support their ongoing civic education and research roles. This expanding cadre of professors are the faculty of Tisch College. A five-member Faculty Executive Committee advises Tisch College on its program directions and policies.

5.4.3 Research

Tisch College's expanding research activities develop new knowledge about how young people develop civic and political values and skills, and actively apply this knowledge to strengthen efforts to improve civic participation throughout the U.S. and internationally. The Center for information and Research about Civic Learning and Engagement is the leading source of authoritative research on the civic and political engagement of young people in the U.S. It is both a primary producer of fresh research on this topic and also a major source of support and collaboration with many youth-serving organizations. CIRCLE is an influential contributor to public dialogue and to policy policy-setting to advance democratic participation. Each year CIRCLE offers a two-week intensive seminar, the Summer Institute of Civic Studies, for doctoral students from multiple disciplines and advanced prac-titioners. Over the past several years over 100 graduate students, professors and practitioners from the U.S. and around the world have participated in the Institute, which has become a significant national and global vehicle for elevating the civic engagement skills of new and future professors. Also at Tisch, the Institute for Democracy and Higher Education works with a consortium of over 800 institutions of higher education to help them to elevate their political education activities. With its mission to strengthen democracy and advance social and political equity, the Institute is a primary source of research, training, and advocacy for political learning and engagement.

The Tisch Community Research Center mentioned above is governed by a board of both faculty members and community partners. The Center explores potential joint projects and provides seed grants for incipient collaborative projects that seem promising. Community-based research at Tufts and in higher education more broadly has been encouraged by two major federal government agencies, the National Science Foundation and the National Institutes of Health, which have allocated funds for community-collaborative research and that credit community collaboration in their assessment of research grant applications. The Community Research Center has generated several million dollars of support for projects, including a multiple year study of the negative health impacts generated by air pollution from a highway that runs through one of the University's host communities.

5.4.4   Community Partnerships

Tufts has invested significantly in strengthening and sustaining partnerships with community organizations and governmental agencies. Tisch College partners with over 80 local community-based organizations, public schools, and local city agencies. These relationships are concentrated in those communities where the universities' campuses are located because we believe that the university has a special responsibility to support those communities and also in order to facilitate travel by Tufts faculty and students and community partners to and from Tufts campuses. We strive to plan, conduct and manage our activities in full collaboration with community partners, "to take into consideration the impressive assets of local communities as well as the problems and challenges that they face" (Tisch College of Civic Life 2016). The College maintains long-term collaborations and to involve community partners in setting priorities with respect to student volunteering, service learning projects, and community-engaged research. Each year staff of Tisch College survey community partners to gather their assessment of the quality and value of students' voluntary service and their priorities for the coming period. Another important mechanism of accountability is that representatives of Tufts host communities serve on the Tisch College Board of Advisors. As was noted above, each year the Tufts President convenes a symposium at which community partners, students and professors reflect on the quality and impacts of our community partnerships and identify opportunities for improvement.

5.4.5   Institutional Social Responsibility

During the past fifteen years that the University has worked to strengthen its civic teaching, research and service activities, it also has taken new initiatives with respect to the social responsibility dimensions of its non-academic policies and practices, and has sought to manage these efforts in a fashion that is consistent with its commitment to active citizenship. Although there has not been an explicit link or direct coordination between the university's active citizenship teaching and research and its corporate social responsibility, since 2000 two examples of corporate social responsibility stand out, and at least indirectly reinforce the university's active citizenship initiative. One is a dramatic instance of social responsibility-oriented investment of a portion of the university's endowment, and the second is an extensive commitment to environmental and sustainability goals in the institution's services and facilities.

In 2005 Pierre and Pamela Omidyar, who generously supported what is now known as Tisch College, gave Tufts a $100 million endowment gift with the proviso that it be used entirely to support microfinance projects. Although Tufts does not use a formal social responsibility screen in managing its endowment, for the past twelve years it has managed this portion of its endowment as what is by definition a social responsibility endeavor. Administered separately from the rest of the Tufts endowment, the Omidyar-Tufts Microfinance Fund has supported microfinance programs in over 50 developing countries. Income from the Fund is used for a variety of purposes, including to support the Tufts Loan Repayment Assistance Fund that helps Tufts graduates to repay their student loans if they are working in lower-paying public service jobs.

During the same period that the University has expanded and strengthened its environmental education and research programs, it has sought to elevate how it manages its core business practices consistently with principles of environmental sustainability. An Office of Sustainability serves as resource, catalyst and advocate to promote sustainability in all aspects of the University's operations. In 1999 Tufts pledged to meet or beat the Kyoto Protocol of the U.N. Framework Convention on Climate Change. It created the Tufts Climate Initiative with the goal of reducing greenhouse gas emissions from Tufts campuses to 7% below the 1990 levels by 2012. The University continues to strive for sustainability in its practices with respect to building design and maintenance, energy and water use, recycling, food procurement, and transportation.

5.5   Future Opportunities and Issues

In its first decade and a half of existence, Tisch College of Civic Life is both well established, and in academic time, is still young. What will the future hold for Tufts' ambitious commitment to civic education? We are optimistic that the University's strong efforts in this realm will be sustained, and that they will achieve deepening impact and also continue to evolve. The fact that this area of endeavor at Tufts is so deeply rooted in its history is reason for optimism, as is its success to date (positive results will encourage staying the course). The recent innovations developed by the current leaders of Tisch College and of the university as a whole suggest that the future could hold further change—as subsequent leaders and stakeholders sustain the same core vision and mission, and develop new ways to address it and to respond to changes in the higher education landscape and local context.

When the organizers of Tisch College reported on this effort a decade ago, we anticipated three future challenges. Each of these remains a significant challenge: (1) Will Tisch College maintain its focus on infusion or become another silo? Ten years ago we wrote, "Even though our across-the-curriculum strategy is working, there inevitably will be pressures to move away from the infusion model. It may be easier to promote infusion in early stages of the College than it is to sustain it. It is easier to develop separate academic programs than to change many existing ones. In an institution of silos, there will be pressures for us to become another silo (Hollister et al. 2006)." So far, a new generation of Tufts leaders have resisted such pressures; they have stayed true to the across-the-curriculum and across-the-institution founding principle and invented new ways to use it. (2) What long-term impacts will be achieved? To revisit again our earlier reflections, "In ten, twenty, and thirty years, will greater numbers of Tufts graduates be more effective leaders for community change? Will our democracy reflect the benefit of increased citizen participation? (Hollister et al. 2006)" The answer after ten years is a resounding yes. (3) "To what extent will active citizenship become a lasting part of Tufts academic programs, culture and institutional identity? (Hollister et al. 2006)" A promising indicator on this last point is that the financial foundation of Tisch College continues to become more solid, with the raising of additional financial endowment, and with steady growth in support by all stakeholders, which in the realm of organizational dynamics is another powerful form of endowment.

An enduring challenge for all universities that are deeply committed to civic engagement and social responsibility is to demonstrate that these programs can be a route to higher quality teaching and research. Our collective opportunity is to counter the skepticism about the academic rigor of engaged teaching and research by reframing these activities as a path to excellence, and to generate a growing body of examples that prove the point. Each year community-engaged teaching and research at Tufts is adding evidence to the case for academic quality.

How will future external pressures and trends—financial pressures, globalization, and technological changes—influence the future of Tufts' model? The inexorable trend toward greater globalization means that the international dimensions of civic education and research will become increasingly important. All the more reason to further combine Tufts' distinctive strengths in international relations and in civic life. All the more reason for the university to participate vigorously in international forums for exchange and collaboration, including the Talloires Network and the University Social Responsibility Network.

References

Ehrlich, T. (2000). *Civic responsibility and higher education*. Phoenix: Oryx.

Hollister, R. M. (2002, February 7). *Lives of active citizenship*. John DiBiaggio Chair Inaugural Lecture, Tufts University.

Hollister, R. M., Mead, M., & Wilson, N. (2006). Infusing active citizenship throughout a research university: The Tisch College of Citizenship and Public Service at Tufts University. *Metropolitan Universities, 17*(3), 38–55.

Hollister, R. M., Pollock, J. P., Gearan, M., Stroud, S., Reid, J., & Babcock, E. (2012). The Talloires network: A global coalition of engaged universities. *Journal of Higher Education Outreach and Engagement, 16*(4), 82–100.

Hollister, R. M., Wilson, N., & Levine, P. (2008). Educating students to foster active citizenship. *Peer Review, 10*(2/3), 18–21.

Hoyt, L. M., & Hollister, R. M. (2014). Strategies for advancing global trends in university civic engagement—The Talloires network, a global coalition of engaged universities. *All Ireland Journal of Teaching and Learning in Higher Education, 6*(1), 16916–16919.

Musil, C. M. (2009). Educating students for personal and social responsibility. In B. Jacoby et al. (Eds.), *Civic engagement in higher education: Concepts and practices* (pp. 49–68). San Francisco: Jossey-Bass.

Ostrander, S. M., & Portney, K. E. (Eds.). (2007). *Acting civically: From urban neighborhoods to higher education*. Hanover, NH: University Press of New England/Tufts University Press.

Tisch College of Civic Life, Tufts University. (2016). *Tisch College strategic plan*, Tufts University. http://activecitizen.tufts.edu/strategicplan/. Accessed 1 Jan 2016.

Watson, D., Hollister, R. M., Stroud, S. E., & Babcock, E. (2011). *The engaged university: International perspectives on civic engagement*. New York and London: Routledge.

Wilson, N., Terkla, D. G., & O'Leary, L. S. (2006). *University College of Citizenship and Public Service Outcomes Study presentation*, Tisch College of Citizenship and Public Service.

Youniss, J., & Levine, P. (Eds.). (2009). *Engaging young people in civic life*. Nashville: Vanderbilt University Press.

Chapter 6
University Social Responsibility as Civic Learning: Outcomes Assessment and Community Partnership

Matthew Bakko and Amanda Moore McBride

Abstract This chapter addresses the challenges and opportunities regarding student civic learning frameworks, outcomes, and assessment tools in the context of university civic renewal, engagement, and partnership. Recently, a wide variety of conceptualizations of civic learning and corresponding student learning outcomes and assessments have been created, offering colleges and universities both the challenge and opportunity of choosing from a plethora of avenues through which to actualize student civic learning as part of their civic missions. Largely missing from this advance is the pedagogy of teaching and realizing authentic, mutually beneficial community partnership as essential for civic learning, and then assessing the outcomes of such pedagogy. An exploration of civic learning frameworks and a case study of Washington University in St. Louis bring into conversation a partnership-focused strategy for civic renewal with other civic engagement literature within the diverse landscape of student civic learning assessment. Grounding the ongoing development of civic learning frameworks and outcomes in the practice of partnership provides the opportunity to build the capacity of students to engage intentionally in the forms of partnership that can transform civic life.

Keywords Civic learning · Service learning · Civic learning assessment · Integrative assessment approach · The United States

6.1 Introduction

University Social Responsibility is emerging as a field worldwide (Millican and Bourner 2011; Vasilescu et al. 2010). This is occurring at a time when higher education institutions in the United States are reaffirming a commitment to their

M. Bakko (✉)
Washington University, St. Louis, USA
e-mail: matthewbakko@wustl.edu

A.M. McBride
University of Denver, Denver, USA

© Springer Nature Singapore Pte Ltd. 2017
D.T.L. Shek and R.M. Hollister (eds.), *University Social Responsibility and Quality of Life*, Quality of Life in Asia 8,
DOI 10.1007/978-981-10-3877-8_6

civic mission (Boyer 1996; Saltmarsh 2005; The National Task Force on Civic Learning and Democratic Engagement 2012). This commitment includes educating students for civic and community engagement. Within the last decade, a broad representation of scholars and leaders in American higher education has recognized personal and social responsibility as one of four essential learning outcomes for students, under which civic knowledge and engagement is a core component (National Leadership Council for Liberal Education and America's Promise 2007). The Association of American Colleges and Universities made a clarion call for resources, research and assessment, and thought leadership to develop students who, among other things, "contribut[e] to a larger community" (AAC&U 2014b). This movement is occurring in tandem with an increased push for universities to be better partners with their communities at home and abroad (Saltmarsh and Hartley 2011; The National Task Force on Civic Learning and Democratic Engagement 2012). This chapter specifically addresses the challenges and opportunities regarding student civic learning constructs, outcomes, and assessment tools in the context of institutional change and community partnership.

A recent watershed moment for civic and community engagement in higher education occurred with the publication of *A Crucible Moment: College Learning and Democracy's Future* (The National Task Force on Civic Learning and Democratic Engagement 2012). This report is a strategic call to action to renew the civic mission of higher education institutions, develop and promote a civic engagement and learning framework to enact this mission, and cultivate partnerships for societal civic transformation. Supporting this call, a wide variety of conceptualizations of civic learning and corresponding student learning outcomes and assessments have been created, offering colleges and universities both the challenge and opportunity of choosing from a plethora of avenues through which to actualize student civic learning as part of their civic missions (Reason and Hemer 2015; Simons 2015; Torney-Purta et al. 2015). Largely missing from this advance is the pedagogy of teaching and realizing authentic, mutually beneficial community partnership as essential for civic learning, and then assessing the outcomes of such pedagogy.

In this chapter, the field of civic learning is discussed broadly and specifically, through the use of examples of civic and community engagement at Washington University in St. Louis, led by its Gephardt Institute for Civic and Community Engagement. While the Gephardt Institute implements its own student civic learning activities and partnership development, it is also in service to the wider university by building the capacity of others through promotion of and training on effective civic engagement practices, assessing the cross-institutional outcomes of these practices, and fostering mutually beneficial and reciprocal partnerships between community, the university, and its various actors. Thus, this chapter brings into conversation the partnership-focused strategy for civic renewal of *The Crucible Moment* with other civic engagement literature within the diverse landscape of student civic learning assessment.

6.2   Community Engagement and Civic Learning: Toward Partnership

Higher education institutions in the United States have been newly challenged since 2014 by students, faculty, staff, local community stakeholders, as well as the broader public to act toward a more just and equitable society (Eagan et al. 2015; Wilson 2015; Wong and Green 2016). Part of the challenge has been about diversity and inclusion, but it has also been about the practices of colleges and universities that continue to reinforce negative dynamics of power and privilege. In the context of civic learning, for example, practices that prioritize student learning above the impacts on the community entity engaging in the partnership are in question. When the partner gives more than they may receive from the engagement, or when they are not even acknowledged for their role in contributing to students' learning through providing access to their community, organization, or expertise, then higher education institutions diminish students' civic learning that happens through partnership. How we approach and involve community in our educational practices should exemplify the civic knowledge, skills, and behaviors that we expect our students to learn.

Washington University in St. Louis acknowledged these challenges and has acted on this moment to renew the civic charge of the newly constituted Gephardt Institute for Civic and Community Engagement in 2015. While the original Institute was founded in 2005 to further develop the next generation of civic leaders, its recently expanded purpose is to support the entire university in effective community engagement by embracing a problem-solving, partnership-based approach. The university seeks to understand and benefit societal conditions by leveraging expertise and capacity across the academy, but to do so in partnership with community. The Institute has been charged to sponsor a range of initiatives that ensure that the development of reciprocal, mutually-beneficial partnerships are central to any community engagement effort at the university. The renewed Institute underscores the larger difference in approach—from "for" to "with," from quantity to quality, from short-term to long-term partnership.

Critically, the Institute now emphasizes education and critical analysis with students before, during, and after they engage in the community. Student initiatives incorporate pedagogy that teach students, and allow them to practice, how to assess and develop reciprocal partnerships, appropriately enter and exit communities, address power dynamics, use skills involved in engaging responsibly such as cultural humility, evaluate outcomes in regards to mutual benefit and shared goals, and reflect on their identity and personal growth in the partnership context. The Institute is also growing resources and technical assistance for training all campus stakeholders, including faculty who want to connect their classroom content to community for students' real-world learning. The goal is that it should be done in partnership with community partners serving as co-educators. Now, we seek to develop concrete learning outcomes for effective partnership and assess the impacts of Washington University's community engagement through research with students, faculty, and community partners. Below, a review of the status of civic learning assessment is presented and the case study continues with an example of the Institute's attempt to measure the impact of this approach to civic engagement that emphasizes community engagement.

6.3 Civic Learning: Issues in Constructs, Outcomes, and Assessments

Student learning outcomes, operationalized indicators, and their related programs and activities vary greatly according to how civic learning is conceptualized as a construct across different higher education institutions. Torney-Purta et al. (2015) identified over 30 civic-related constructs from approximately 15 recent civic frameworks in use in the United States and internationally. "Civic" is often the prefix in these constructs, being placed before such terms as literacy, action, identity, mindedness, knowledge, and responsibility. Other utilized constructs include citizenship, democratic participation skills, ethical and social responsibility in a diverse world, and active citizenship.

Different values, motivations, knowledge, skills, and behaviors are common elements of these constructs' stated definitions, all of which are emblematic of an oft used definition of civic engagement (AAC&U 2014a; American Democracy Project, n.d.) by Ehrlich (2000, p. vi):

> Civic engagement means working to make a difference in the civic life of our communities and developing the combination of knowledge, skills, values and motivation to make that difference. It means promoting the quality of life in a community, through both political and non-political processes.

Whether as a simultaneous activity of civic engagement, or as a precursor to it, this definition makes clear that engagement is also the process of "civic learning," a term best encapsulated by Saltmarsh (2005, p. 53) as the "development of a capacity for engagement." While this provides a guidepost in forming civic constructs, it also leaves plenty of space for divergent operationalization, meaning how a given college or university may aim to develop that capacity differs greatly. On the positive side, this allows institutions to frame civic engagement and learning in ways that make sense to their specific institutional, as well as social, economic, and political contexts. However, when the development, implementation, and evaluation of civic learning courses, programs, and activities is based upon vastly diverse constructs and intended outcomes, the development of and generalizability of a body of evidence-based knowledge and effective practices in student civic engagement and learning is put into question (Finley 2012; Torney-Purta et al. 2015).

This is particularly salient in the case of service learning, as much of the literature on the outcomes of student civic engagement practices is based on it (Finley 2011). For example, three meta-analyses of literature on service learning outcomes conceive student learning quite differently. While one examines literature for service learning's effects on primarily academic achievement outcomes (Warren 2012), another compares academic outcomes with a much broader set of personal, social, and citizenship outcomes (Conway et al. 2009). The third meta-analysis diverges from the others by analyzing service learning in terms of the outcomes of "understanding social issues," "personal insight," and "cognitive development" (Yorio and Ye 2012, p. 11). And although many civic engagement practices, such as reflection and greater interaction with community, are associated with achieving student learning outcomes through both service learning and many other, less-studied forms of civic engagement (Finley 2011), the diversity of selected outcomes in the literature makes for a confusing conceptual landscape and difficult comparison across forms.

This diversity of concepts and outcomes is matched by an array of student civic engagement and learning assessment tools. Researchers can find dozens of instruments that focus on one to a few outcomes of civic-related learning, but most come short of incorporating the broader range of civic knowledge, skills, values, behaviors, and motivation outcomes essential to effective civic engagement. Examples of these outcomes often isolated in various tools include service involvement preference, personal values, pluralistic orientation, civil society knowledge, national identity, and activism orientation. However, recent meta-analyses of civic engagement and learning assessment tools can assist practitioners in selecting a tool that best fits the constructs and outcomes around which they organize their civic engagement initiatives (Reason and Hemer 2015; Simons 2015; Torney-Purta et al. 2015). Of particular note is Simons' (2015) list of assessment resources, which were selected in terms of their evidence of psychometric validity and reliability. Still, the lack of coherence across civic learning outcome measures and assessment research, and the use of divergent instruments by researchers and practitioners, presents an issue of internal validity that makes precarious the task of comparing civic learning practices for their effectiveness (Finley 2011).

A community partnership approach is absent from civic learning frameworks, outcomes, and assessment tools. While a number of these assess students for various community-oriented attitudes, values, and behaviors, they do not navigate this from the model of mutuality, reciprocation, or other frames relevant to the transformative partnership approach advocated for by *A Crucible Moment* (The National Task Force on Civic Learning and Democratic Engagement 2012). For example, frameworks and tools assess students for their belief in civic responsibility (National Association of Student Personnel Administrators and the American College Personnel Association 2004), value for community involvement (Higher Education Research Institute 2015), ability to work across difference (National Survey of Student Engagement 2013), or involvement in community problem solving (Lopez et al. 2006), but do not assess student's in regards to the overarching partnership approach they take with community. Further, the Personal and Social Responsibility Inventory (AAC&U 2011, p. 19) includes an 18 item dimension for "contributing to a larger community" that "includes recognizing and acting on one's responsibility to your campus community, the local community, and wider society, both nationally and globally. It also includes contributing to the greater good and an ability to accurately respond to the needs of others." This focus on responsibility and student's self-perceived ability to act on it is emblematic of current civic learning frameworks, and comes short of reflecting the partnership approach being fostered in today's higher education climate.

Beyond the conceptual domain, analysis of the assessment tools available to civic engagement and learning researchers illuminates several other limitations. First, few assessment tools have been validated with psychometric tests (Simons 2015; Torney-Purta et al. 2015). Out of the 21 psychometrically-validated measures of service learning found by Simons (2015), only about half of these were analyzed for advanced evidence, such as through confirmatory factor analysis. As discussed above, the conceptualizations of civic learning are numerous, and researchers must be careful in selecting tools that accurately reflect the intended constructs under study. Furthermore, psychometric validation is crucial in light of most tools relying upon participant self-report (Torney-Purta et al. 2015). Research participants may view the achievement of civic learning outcomes as socially desirable, resulting in inaccurate measurement. Some assessments have been validated against social desirability bias, such as the Civic Minded Graduate Scale (Steinberg et al. 2011) discussed below.

Another major issue in civic learning assessment is in regard to research design and analysis and comparison of subgroups. Most data on civic learning is available only at the aggregate level, masking the effects that identities, such as race, sex, or cultural background, and other moderating experiences, such as academic discipline or civic engagement experiences outside the scope of a singular study, have on civic engagement outcomes (Reason and Hemer 2015). Without a body of literature regarding group difference, it may be more difficult for developers of assessment tools to ascertain how outcomes and indicators are more or less salient to some potential research participants than others. This is especially important to consider for an international audience, as most assessment tools are constructed in the context of the global west (Torney-Purta et al. 2015). Researchers should consider the use of both demographic variables and institutional tracking of other moderators (such as through a common marker like Student ID numbers) to better understand subgroup difference.

6.4 Integrative Assessment Approaches

There are, however, several recent promising frameworks and/or tools that offer a more robust and integrative approach to assessing change across outcomes of civic knowledge, skills, values, motivations, and behaviors, that are pertinent to various civic engagement approaches and activities. Notable ones include the Civic Learning Spiral (Musil 2009), the civic engagement VALUE Rubric (AAC&U 2014a), and the Civic-Minded Graduate model (Steinberg et al. 2011), the latter of

Table 6.1 Comparison of civic engagement assessment approaches

Model	Description	Constructs/outcomes	Instruments
Civic learning spiral (Musil 2009)	Six civic learning principles that occur and develop simultaneously	Self Communities and culture Knowledge Skills Values Public action	No formal instrument, but outcome measures from Cooperative Institutional Research Program (CIRP) surveys have been mapped onto constructs (see Hurtado et al. 2012b)
Civic engagement VALUE (valid assessment of learning in undergraduate education) rubric (AAC&U 2014a)	Progressive and adaptable benchmarks for developing and tracking student civic engagement	Diversity of community and culture Analysis of knowledge Civic identity and commitment Civic communication Civic action and reflection Civic contexts/structures	No instruments, but a guide for institutions to assess student civic learning milestones across activities and assignments
Civic-minded graduate (Steinberg et al. 2011)	Integration of a student's identity with their educational and civic experiences	Knowledge (volunteer opportunities, academic knowledge and technical skills, contemporary social issues) Skills (listening, diversity, consensus-building) Dispositions (valuing community engagement, self-efficacy, social trustee of knowledge) Behavioral intentions	Scale: 30-item self-report Narrative prompt and rubric: written reflection connecting civic mindedness to educational and civic experiences Interview protocol and rubric: semi-structured interview on educational experiences, specific civic-minded outcomes, and response to a community-based scenario

which is currently used at Washington University (see Table 6.1 for a snapshot comparison of the approaches).

Civic Learning Spiral. Inspired by AAC&U's (2014b) core commitment to social and personal responsibility, the Civic Learning Spiral was developed through blending aspects of the major educational reform movements of diversity, global learning, and civic engagement, towards their common goal of lifelong engagement. The symbolic spiral is a relational integration and synthesis of six 'braids,' representing core principles of civic learning that occur simultaneously, rather than in linear progression. These include: self, communities and culture, knowledge, skills, values, and public action. These braids provide a conceptual framework for a student's lifelong civic learning, and learning outcomes related to each of the six are offered for informing institutional strategy around integrating the Spiral throughout curricular and co-curricular experiences (Musil 2009).

While the Spiral is not officially paired with an operationalized assessment tool, it was utilized as a guiding paradigm by Hurtado et al. (2012a, b) in studying predictors of service learning. The authors layered nine outcome measures, most of which were psychometrically validated, from four Cooperative Institutional Research Program (CIRP) surveys onto the braids of the Spiral. For example, a process of "conceptual mapping" (Hurtado et al. 2012b) found that the "values" braid could be sufficiently measured through a single tool designed to measure "social agency," while the "knowledge" braid required two measures to capture its intent: one scale on "civic awareness" and another on "integration of learning." These measures were used to analyze outcomes of several existing study samples, in which the researchers found predictors of civic learning across the multiple dimensions of the Spiral, including service learning participation, engaging with others of different races and ethnicities, and political participation, such as voting in campus elections (Hurtado et al. 2012b). The integration of mostly validated measures provides a compelling case for the capacity of the Civic Learning Spiral to address the psychometric limitations present in much of the student civic learning assessment field.

VALUE Rubric. Most colleges and universities do not have an institution-wide civic engagement and learning assessment strategy (Hatcher 2011). In order to assist institutions in this task, experts were convened by the Association of American Colleges and Universities to develop a series of VALUE (Valid Assessment of Learning in Undergraduate Education) rubrics that provide adaptable benchmarks for student learning across a range of outcomes. The rubrics can help inform the content of courses and other educational activities, but "were developed as 'metarubrics' to be used at the institutional or programmatic levels in order to assess student learning overall and over time, not for specific assignments" (Rhodes and Finley 2013, p. 6). Rubrics come in the form of developmental charts with progressive milestones for student learning. As such, they act as a both a guide of student expectations that can inform the development of courses and programs and a mirror against which student learning can be compared. Rubrics have been assessed for reliability, face validity, and content validity through institutional case studies and calibration across disciplines, and therefore provide a useful means for higher education administrators and researchers to compare institutional outcomes. Since their development in 2010, over 3000 higher education institutions around the world have considered or utilized VALUE rubrics (Rhodes and Finley 2013).

Influenced by the Civic Learning Spiral framework, civic engagement is one of 15 outcome areas for which a VALUE rubric was created. It integrates behavioral benchmarks related to civic knowledge, values, skills, and motivation across six overarching learning outcomes areas: (1) Diversity of communities and cultures; (2) Analysis of knowledge (connects and integrates disciplinary knowledge to civic engagement; (3) Civic identity and commitment; (4) Civic communications; (5) Civic action and reflection; and (6) Civic contexts/structures (collaboration within and across communities). Of note, benchmarks subsumed under one outcome are not achieved in isolation of other outcomes. For example, the capstone benchmark for civic communication is that a student "tailors communication strategies to effectively express, listen, and adapt to others to establish relationships to further civic action," illustrating resonance with "civic action and reflection" and "civic contexts/structures" (AAC&U 2014a).

Universities have found success in utilizing and adapting the civic engagement VALUE rubric. Daemon College uses the rubric to align course content with the broader goals of degree programs. Civic benchmark areas from the rubric are applied to major courses of study and used to create course content that reflects that application. The rubric is also used as a guide in the process of creating and assessing proposed curricular changes (Morace and Hibschweiler 2011). At Loyola University Chicago, civic engagement is a core curricular requirement. Students submit course assignments, which are informed by the VALUE rubric, to an e-portfolio system where they are assessed against the rubric's overarching benchmarks. This portfolio approach allows faculty and staff to have an integrative view of a student's learning across all courses, which reflects the integrative approach of the rubric itself (Green and Kehoe 2011).

Civic-Minded Graduate Model. One other civic learning framework of note has gained significant traction in the field, particularly because it prompted the creation of rigorously validated assessment tools: The Civic-Minded Graduate model, developed by the Center for Service and Learning at Indiana University – Purdue University Indianapolis (IUPUI). The model is framed around the concept of "civic-mindedness," which is "a person's inclination or disposition to be knowledgeable of and involved in the community, and to have a commitment to act upon a sense of responsibility as a member of that community" (Pike et al. 2014, p. 93).

The civic-minded graduate is an individual who has experienced a tripartite integration across the dimensions of: (1) sense of self or identity; (2) educational experiences; and (3) civic experiences. This manifests as a student whose sense of self is attached to their educational and civic experiences, as in turn, these experiences have cultivated an identity deeply related to their education and civic engagement (Bringle et al. 2011; Steinberg et al. 2011). To achieve this integration, IUPUI identified ten learning areas subsumed under four broader civic learning outcomes:

1. *Knowledge*: Volunteer opportunities; Academic Knowledge and Technical Skills; Contemporary Social Issues
2. *Skills*: Communication and listening; Diversity; Consensus-building
3. *Dispositions*: Valuing community engagement; Self-efficacy; Social trustee of knowledge
4. *Behavioral intentions*: Intent to be involved in future community service (Steinberg et al. 2011).

These learning outcomes were developed through literature searches and focus groups with scholars and civic engagement professionals (Pike et al. 2014).

The framework utilizes three complimentary instruments to measure student civic mindedness. The first, the Civic-Minded Graduate Scale, is a quantitative, cross-sectional, and self-report survey of 30 operationalized questions across the ten learning areas described above. The second is a narrative prompt that allows students to do a written self-reflection regarding their civic-mindedness. The final instrument is a qualitative semi-structured interview where students are prompted to discuss their educational experiences, speak to specific civic-minded outcomes, and envision their response to a community issue-related scenario. These instruments and the overarching civic-minded construct itself have strong psychometric reliability and validity, and the scale has been tested for social desirability bias (Steinberg et al. 2011).

The Civic-Minded Graduate model and associated assessment tools can be implemented by educators and researchers to assess civic-mindedness and related outcomes before, during, or after specific programs, courses, activities, or to evaluate a student's overall comprehensive educational experience (Steinberg et al. 2011). Assessment results can be used to ascertain predictors, or "pathways," most effective towards engendering civic-mindedness (Steinberg and Norris 2011) and guide programmatic changes related to civic engagement and learning. On a broader level, the Civic-Minded Graduate model has been used as a beacon that can guide institutional strategy and the development of programs and services (Bringle et al. 2011).

6.5 The Civic Minded Graduate Model at Washington University in St. Louis

The Civic-Minded Graduate model has been a valuable framework for the Gephardt Institute for Civic and Community Engagement at Washington University in St. Louis. Staff and stakeholders view the model as aligning well with the Institute's mission of cultivating informed and actively engaged citizens through community partnership. Thus the model is a reflective node for the Institute, influencing thinking around desired learning outcomes across all Institute programs.

In practice, the model's tools have been used for the purposes of specific program evaluation. For example, the "Civic Scholars" signature program is ideal for a civic-minded evaluation as staff of the Institute view this program as best aligning with the essence of the Civic-Minded Graduate models integration of identity, educational experiences, and civic experiences through cultivating civic knowledge, skills, dispositions, and behavioral intentions. Civic Scholars is a two-year curricular program that provides undergraduate students with skills and knowledge to foster lifelong civic engagement. A highly competitive program, undergraduate sophomores are selected who best exemplify potential for civic leadership and show commitment to community service and civic engagement. The program blends scholarly content, reflective practice, sustained mentorship, and the development of a cohort-based learning community, and each Civic Scholar receives a scholarship of $5,000 to support a substantial civic or community-based project during the summer between the two years of the program.

Due to alignment between the Civic-Minded Graduate model and the Gephardt Institute's mission, the Civic-Minded Graduate Scale has been used to assess students in the program, which has helped Institute staff and university stakeholders understand the efficacy of the program. Through utilizing the Scale as a retrospective pre-test, researchers found consistent growth across nearly all indicators of civic-mindedness embedded in the instrument. While this confirmed the tangible learning outcomes of the program, using the Scale did not provide information regarding which program components (i.e. predictors) led to this program success. To discover this, researchers used the qualitative Civic-Minded Graduate tools as inspiration to implement a series of focus groups with current Civic Scholars and alumni in order to ascertain the key elements of the program. Consistent with student civic engagement literature (Finley 2011), the duration and intensity of the program, the focus on reflection, and high levels of interaction with external community were found to be crucial indicators of programmatic success.

The Civic-Minded Graduate Scale is also a tool that most closely incorporates assessment of learning outcomes deemed crucial to the Institute's focus on community partnership. This includes skills such as listening and understanding others' perspectives, resolving problems through consensus, and empathy (Steinberg et al. 2011). However, the scale is missing crucial language on and indicators of partnership relevant to the Institute's initiatives. A more suitable tool in this vein would also include assessments of students' values around mutuality and reciprocity, knowledge of different forms of partnerships and skills to cultivate them, and behaviors that demonstrate an appropriate engagement in and conclusion of relationships with community partners. Such learning areas should inform future assessment tools that integrate the partnership-focused civic mission of higher education with other civic learning outcomes, or be used to generate a supplementary tool that would align with an already useful framework like the Civic-Minded Graduate model.

As the Gephardt Institute works to build the capacity of others on campus to cultivate civic-mindedness in students, the Civic-Minded Graduate model can be utilized as a common institutional goal and point of reference. Combining the Scale with both subgroup demographic variables and tracking information concerning students' differential experiences at the university (e.g., number and type of service learning courses, civic-related co-curricular involvement, etc.) will allow for a better understanding of which students are developing civic-minded attributes and how. While the model may not speak to all possible measures of civic learning that higher education institutions may find relevant, such as Washington University's focus on developing knowledge and skills for cultivating reciprocal community partnership, the Gephardt Institute views it as a model that currently offers one of the best integrations of the knowledge, skill, value, behavior, and motivation outcomes central to conceptualizations of civic learning and engagement.

No matter how integrative or functional though, no framework or assessment tool exists that speaks to all the various ways civic engagement and learning have been conceptualized. Perhaps a single framework does not need to do this, but we are in a time when some scholars are calling for the development of a new generation of assessment that better synthesizes current thinking in student civic learning and engagement outcomes (Torney-Purta et al. 2015). Indeed, *A Crucible Moment* calls for not only the increased dissemination and use of current civic engagement assessment frameworks, but the establishment of standards in civic learning (The National Task Force on Civic Learning and Democratic Engagement 2012). It is encouraging that approximately half of the member institutions of the Association of American Colleges and Universities have embraced civic engagement learning outcomes for all their students (Hart Research Associates 2015), yet the literature demonstrates that frameworks, concepts, and methods are diverse. An opportunity exists for the field of civic engagement and learning in higher education to continue robust discussion on outcomes and assessment. As suggested, the practice, teaching, and assessment of transformative partnership is a crucial topic for this discussion.

6.6 Toward Assessing Civic Learning for Community Partnership

The National Task Force on Civic Learning and Democratic Engagement (2012) makes clear in *A Crucible Moment* its prescription that higher education institutions should form "collaborative, generative partnerships and alliances" (p. 64). In tandem, it also emphasizes the values of reciprocation, mutuality, and collective problem-solving in civic learning. "Model(ing) institutional citizenship" (p. 33) could provide a powerful lesson for students developing their civic agency, and transformative partnerships offer a conduit through which students can learn how to engage with, in, and alongside community. However, institutions can go further than modeling university-community partnerships for the purposes of civic learning, and capitalize upon the unique and expansive learning opportunity that presents itself when students participate in any kind of community partnership.

As proposed in the case study above, institutions have the opportunity to make institutional strategy and practice regarding community partnership an intentional and direct student civic learning outcome. As mutual and reciprocal community partnerships facilitate student civic learning, they also engender a learning opportunity regarding that partnership. Through pedagogy on the knowledge and skills of partnership, students can do more than engage *through* partnership; they can consciously observe and critically reflect on their own practice in the context of a broader institutional strategy of transformational community partnership in which they are participating and contributing positively or negatively. Students are then consciously advancing a university mission around effective partnership, while also learning the practice of partnership that they can use for a lifetime of civic engagement.

Some existing civic learning models and related assessment tools do address certain knowledge and skills related to doing work effectively in and with community, but not explicitly within the broader approach of transformational, reciprocal, and mutual partnership called for in *A Crucible Moment*. For example, the Civic-Minded Graduate model has outcomes related to a students' valuing of community engagement, knowledge regarding social issues, and skills to build consensus (Steinberg et al. 2011), all of which would augment learning outcomes related to transformative partnership. However, as with other frameworks, this does not adequately convince that the model's assessment tools are useful in assessing a student's understanding of and ability to foster different forms of partnership *within a transformative partnership approach*.

What these learning outcomes related to partnership would look like is open to discussion. A likely candidate for inspiration moving forward is the work of Bringle, Clayton, and their colleagues, which has heavily influenced Washington University's understanding, language, and action regarding partnership. The scholars employ a relationships continuum to illustrate the differences between exploitive, transactional, and transformational (see Fig. 6.1) community partnerships (Bringle et al. 2009; see also Enos and Morton 2003). This model is aided by the SOFAR (Students, Organizations, Faculty, Administrators, and Residents) framework, utilized for understanding the practical dynamics that can characterize each of the three partnerships along the continuum (Bringle et al. 2009), and the Transformation Relationship Evaluation Scale (TRES), used for systematically evaluating the exploitive, transactional, and/or transformational characteristics that may be present in any university-community relationship (Clayton et al. 2010). As students gain tangible partnership-related skills through community-engaged experiences, the latter evaluation scale could be adapted as a helpful instructional tool for teaching students detailed aspects of community relationships and partnerships, such as power, conflict, benefit, decision-making, and resources. It could also be bolstered with other work that describes effective practices for aiding in the development of effective university-community partnerships (Bringle and Hatcher 2002).

Institutional case studies of effective practices can inform the development of systematized learning outcomes as well. What do members of higher education institutions learn and teach each other in order to advance transformative partnerships with community? And what are the best methods for that learning or

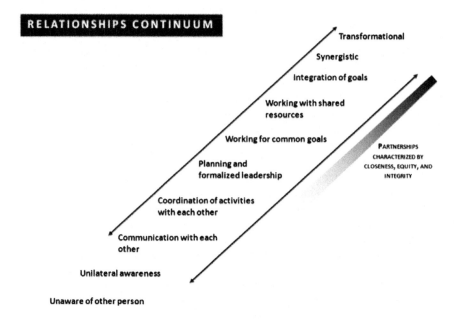

Fig. 6.1 Different types of relationships among participants in service learning and civic engagement partnerships (Bringle et al 2009, p. 4)

teaching? Cases like Washington University provide inductive evidence that opportunities for informed action and critical analysis of self through deep reflection, and of others through intentional dialogue, can foster the values of mutuality and reciprocity, the skills to enter and exit communities responsibly, the knowledge of power dynamics and university-community relations, and the motivation to engage in social issues affecting communities.

Washington University is also a useful case study for thinking through the institutional difficulties in advancing the practice, teaching, and assessment of transformative partnership. For example, the university's highly decentralized administrative and decision-making structure can lead to a plethora of disjointed partnerships across different units. This frequently fosters an environment where strategic priorities are difficult to align, partnership is not adequately tracked or communicated, and the community experiences a wide range of positive and negative interactions with the university. Naturally, the development and implementation of cross-cutting learning outcomes and assessment regarding partnership is a difficult undertaking in this environment, and student learning of partnership often lacks quality control.

Moreover, the last two years has seen an increase in student protests on university campuses in the United States, which are often directed towards university practices (e.g., diversity and inclusion in recruitment and retention, investment portfolios, etc.) and affiliations. The development and implementation of, as well as reflection on, these protests present rich civic learning opportunities. However, faculty or staff who work with students to understand and explore their civic motivations and actions are often viewed as culpable. Washington University has not been immune to student protests, nor has it directly addressed the confusion and frustration experienced by faculty and staff in their foundational role to promote student learning. Furthering university social responsibility will demand that we be clear on faculty and staff responsibilities.

A common and established framework can provide guidance in managing some of the institutional barriers present in practicing and teaching partnership toward effective student learning. As the learning of partnership is often done through the practice of it, a helpful pedagogical framework is found in Kolb's (2015) experiential learning model, which is familiar to those immersed in service learning pedagogy. In having concrete civic engagement experiences through university-community partnership, students can simultaneously observe and critically reflect on the partnership itself, their role in it, and the civic learning gained. Instructors can then help students generalize their experience towards application in the future. For this to be effective, however, there must be clear understanding of the specific civic learning outcomes related to partnership.

6.7   Conclusion

This chapter has discussed the field of civic learning as an approach to fostering university social responsibility, specifically through practicing, teaching, and assessing transformative partnership with community. It has discussed some of the constructs, outcomes, and assessment tools embedded in current civic learning frameworks, while discussing their challenges towards advancing and teaching mutually beneficial and reciprocal partnership. Washington University and its Gephardt Institute for Civic and Community Engagement offer an example of progress towards a civic learning framework and practice that emphasizes community engagement and partnership.

Higher education institutions are answering the call to engage in transformative partnerships. At the same time, civic engagement leaders and researchers are developing more integrated and robust civic learning frameworks, outcomes, and assessment tools. Marrying new thinking and practices of community partnership with the ongoing development of civic learning outcomes provides the opportunity to build the capacity of students to engage intentionally in the forms of partnership that can transform civic life. Partnership then becomes another crucial form of civic learning fostered at the university, extending the reach of University Social Responsibility far past graduation.

Appendix

See Table 6.1; Fig. 6.1.

References

AAC&U. (2011). *2014 personal and social responsibility inventory student survey.* Retrieved from http://www.psri.hs.iastate.edu/documents/2014_PSRI_Stu_Sample.pdf

AAC&U. (2014a). *Civic engagement VALUE rubric.* Retrieved from https://www.aacu.org/civic-engagement-value-rubric

AAC&U. (2014b). *Core commitments: Educating students for personal and social responsibility.* Retrieved from https://www.aacu.org/core_commitments

American Democracy Project. (n.d.). *Civic engagement.* Retrieved from http://www.fgcu.edu/ADP/CivicEngagement.html

Boyer, E. L. (1996). The scholarship of engagement. *Bulletin of the American Academy of Arts and Sciences, 49*(7), 18–33.

Bringle, R. G., Clayton, P. H., & Price, M. (2009). Partnerships in service learning and civic engagement. *Partnerships: A Journal of Service Learning & Civic Engagement, 1*(1), 1–20.

Bringle, R. G., & Hatcher, J. A. (2002). Campus–community partnerships: The terms of engagement. *Journal of Social Issues, 58*(3), 503–516.

Bringle, R. G., Studer, M., Wilson, J., Clayton, P. H., & Steinberg, K. S. (2011). Designingprograms with a purpose: To promote civic engagement for life. *Journal of Academic Ethics, 9*(2), 149–164.

Clayton, P. H., Bringle, R. G., Senor, B., Huq, J., & Morrison, M. (2010). Differentiating and assessing relationships in service-learning and civic engagement: Exploitative, transactional, or transformational. *Michigan Journal of Community Service Learning, 16*(2), 5–22.

Conway, J. M., Amel, E. L., & Gerwien, D. P. (2009). Teaching and learning in the social context: A meta-analysis of service learning's effects on academic, personal, social, and citizenship outcomes. *Teaching of Psychology, 36*(4), 233–245.

Eagan, K., Stolzenberg, E. B., Bates, A. K., Aragon, M. C., Suchard, M. R., & Rios-Aguilar, C. (2015). *The American freshman: National norms fall 2015.* Los Angeles: Higher Education Research Institute, UCLA.

Ehrlich, T. (2000). *Civic responsibility and higher education.* Phoenix, Arizona: Oryx.

Enos, S., & Morton, K. (2003). Developing a theory and practice of campus-community partnerships. In B. Jacoby & Associates (Eds.), *Building partnerships for servicelearning* (pp. 20–41). San Francisco, California: Jossey-Bass.

Finley, A. (2011). *Civic learning and democratic engagements: A review of the literature oncivic engagement in post-secondary education.* Washington DC: Association of American Colleges and Universities.

Finley, A. (2012). Civic-perspective narrative. In D. W. Harward (Ed.), *Civic provocations* (p. XVI). Washington, DC: Bringing Theory to Practice.

Green, P. M., & Kehoe, A. (2011). *Adapting VALUE rubrics in experiential learning courses.* Retrieved from https://www.aacu.org/sites/default/files/files/VALUE/loyolachicago.pdf

Hart Research Associates. (2015, December 17). *Trends in learning outcomes assessment: Key findings from a survey among administrators at AAC&U member institutions.* Retrieved from https://www.aacu.org/publications-research/publications/trends-learning-outcomes-assessment-key-findings-survey-among

Hatcher, J. A. (2011). Assessing civic knowledge and engagement. *New Directions for Institutional Research, 2011*(149), 81–92.

Higher Education Research Institute. (2015). *2016 diverse learning environments—Core survey.* Retrieved from http://heri.ucla.edu/PDFs/surveyAdmin/dle/2016/DLE-2016-Core-Instrument. pdf

Hurtado, S., Ruiz, A., & Whang, H. (2012a). Advancing and assessing civic learning: New results from the diverse learning environments survey. *Diversity and Democracy, 15*(3), 10–12.

Hurtado, S., Ruiz, A., & Whang, H. (2012b). *Assessing students' social responsibility and civic learning.* Paper presented at Annual Forum of the Association for Institutional Research, New Orleans, Louisiana. Retrieved fromhttp://heri.ucla.edu/pub/AssessCivicLearning.pdf

Kolb, D. A. (2015). *Experiential learning: Experience as the source of learning and development.* Upper Saddle River, New Jersey: Pearson Education.

Lopez, M. H., Levine, P., Both, D., Kiesa, A., Kirby, E., Marcelo, K., & Williams, D. (2006). The 2006 civic and political health of the nation. *The Center for Information and Research on Civic Learning and Engagement.* Retrieved from http://www.civicyouth.org/PopUps/2006_CPHS_ Report_update.pdf

National Association of Student Personnel Administrators and the American College Personnel Association. (2004). *Learning reconsidered: A campus-wide focus on the student experience.* Washington, DC.

National Leadership Council for Liberal Education and America's Promise. (2007). *College learning for the new global century.* Retrieved from https://www.aacu.org/sites/default/files/ files/LEAP/GlobalCentury_final.pdf

National Survey of Student Engagement. (2013). *Topical module: Civic engagement.* Retrieved from http://nsse.indiana.edu/pdf/modules/2015/NSSE%202015%20Civic%20Engagement% 20Module.pdf

Millican, J., & Bourner, T. (2011). Student-community engagement and the changing role and context of higher education. *Education + Training, 53*(2/3), 89–99.

Morace, R., & Hibschweiler, I. (2011). *Daemon college and the use of VALUE rubrics.* Retrieved from https://www.aacu.org/sites/default/files/files/VALUE/daemen.pdf

Musil, C. M. (2009). Educating students for personal and social responsibility. In B. Jacoby and Associates (Eds.), *Civic engagement in higher education: Concepts and practices* (pp. 49–68). San Francisco, California: Jossey-Bass.

Pike, G. R., Bringle, R. G., & Hatcher, J. A. (2014). Assessing civic engagement at Indiana University–Purdue University Indianapolis. *New Directions for Institutional Research, 2014* (162), 87–97.

Reason, R. D., & Hemer, K. (2015). *Civic learning and engagement: A review of the literature on civic learning, assessment, and instruments.* Retrieved from https://www.aacu.org/sites/default/ files/files/qc/CivicLearningLiteratureReviewRev1-26-15.pdf

Rhodes, T. L., & Finley, A. (2013). *Using the VALUE rubrics for improvement of learning and authentic assessments.* Washington DC: Association of American Colleges and Universities.

Saltmarsh, J. (2005). The civic promise of service learning. *Liberal Education, 91*(2), 50–55.

Saltmarsh, J., & Hartley, M. (2011). Democratic engagement. In J. Saltmarsh & M. Hartley (Eds.), *To serve a larger purpose: Engagement for democracy and the transformation of higher education* (pp. 14–26). Philadelphia, Pennsylvania: Temple University Press.

Simons, L. (2015). Measuring service-learning and civic engagement. In R. S. Jhangiani, J. D. Troisi, B. Fleck, A. M. Legg & H. D. Hussey (Eds.), *A compendium of scales for use in the scholarship of teaching and learning* (pp. 102–122). Retrieved from http://teachpsych.org/ Resources/Documents/ebooks/compscalesstl.pdf

Steinberg, K. S., Hatcher, J. A., & Bringle, R. G. (2011). Civic-minded graduate: A north star. *Michigan Journal of Community Service Learning, 18*(1), 19–33.

Steinberg, K., & Norris, K. (2011). Assessing civic mindedness. *Diversity & Democracy: Civic Learning for Shared Futures, 14*(3), 12–14.

The National Task Force on Civic Learning and Democratic Engagement. (2012). *A crucible moment: College learning and democracy's future.* Washington, DC: Association of American Colleges and Universities.

Torney-Purta, J., Cabrera, J. C., Roohr, K. C., Liu, O. L., & Rios, J. A. (2015). Assessing civic competency and engagement in higher education: Research background, frameworks, and directions for next-generation assessment. *ETS Research Report Series, 2015*(2), 1–48.

Vasilescu, R., Barna, C., Epure, M., & Baicu, C. (2010). Developing university social responsibility: A model for the challenges of the new civil society. *Procedia-Social and Behavioral Sciences, 2*(2), 4177–4182.

Warren, J. L. (2012). Does service-learning increase student learning? A meta-analysis. *Michigan Journal of Community Service Learning, 18*(2), 56–61.

Wilson, J. (2015, December 31). How black lives matters saved higher education. *Al Jazeera America*. Retrieved from http://america.aljazeera.com/opinions/2015/12/how-black-lives-matter-saved-higher-education.html

Wong, A., & Green, A. (2016, April 4). Campus politics: A cheat sheet. *The Atlantic*. Retrieved from http://www.theatlantic.com/education/archive/2016/03/campus-protest-roundup/417570/

Yorio, P. L., & Ye, F. (2012). A meta-analysis on the effects of service-learning on the social, personal, and cognitive outcomes of learning. *Academy of Management Learning & Education, 11*(1), 9–27.

Chapter 7
Connecting Research with Social Responsibility: Developing 'Age-Friendly' Communities in Manchester, UK

Tine Buffel, Julian Skyrme and Chris Phillipson

Abstract This chapter aims to explore ways of addressing the goals of 'university social responsibility' through research activities. It develops the argument that research can play a dual role in producing findings which are beneficial to society but which also empower individuals and local communities through their direct involvement in the research process. The chapter starts with setting out how the University of Manchester defines and approaches 'social responsibility'. Second, it presents a research project which illustrates this approach. The study has been identified by the World Health Organization (WHO) as a best practice example of involving older people as co-investigators in researching and developing what it terms 'age-friendly' cities. The chapter then discusses the objectives of the study, the process of involving and training older people to become co-researchers, the research outcomes, and the impact of the research. Finally, the chapter concludes with a discussion of the lessons learned from the project, and suggests ways forward for (re-) connecting research with the goal of social responsibility.

Keywords Social responsibility · Research impact · Population ageing · Urbanisation · Age-friendly

T. Buffel (✉) · C. Phillipson
School of Social Sciences, ESRC Future Leader Researcher,
The University of Manchester, Humanities Bridgeford Street-2.13 v,
Manchester M13 9PL, UK
e-mail: tine.buffel@manchester.ac.uk

C. Phillipson
e-mail: chris.phillipson@manchester.ac.uk

J. Skyrme
The University of Manchester, 186 Waterloo Place, Oxford Road,
Manchester M13 9PL, UK
e-mail: Julian.Skyrme@manchester.ac.uk

© Springer Nature Singapore Pte Ltd. 2017
D.T.L. Shek and R.M. Hollister (eds.), *University Social Responsibility
and Quality of Life*, Quality of Life in Asia 8,
DOI 10.1007/978-981-10-3877-8_7

7.1 Introduction

'University social responsibility' reflects the aspirations of universities to transform the communities of which they are an essential part. This can occur through who and how they educate, the creation and application of knowledge to solve societal problems, and a range of 'third mission' activities such as public and civic engagement, internationalism and responsible operational management. Of these, research can play a vital role in highlighting the way in which universities can demonstrate economic, social and cultural benefits for a variety of groups. This chapter aims to explore ways of addressing the goals of university social responsibility through research activities, taking the example of engagement with local communities disadvantaged in some way or who have limited access to university resources. The last of these has been identified as a key strategy for the University of Manchester, which aims to contribute to the social and economic success of communities: 'by using our expertise and knowledge to find solutions to the major challenges of the 21st century' (The University of Manchester 2012). 'Population ageing,' alongside other themes such as global inequalities, sustainability and energy, represents an important challenge the university is addressing through high-quality research activity, interdisciplinary collaboration and cross-sector partnerships.

A key argument of this chapter is that research can play a dual role in producing findings which are beneficial to society but which also empower individuals and local communities through their direct involvement in the research process. The chapter is organised in three parts: first, it sets out how the University of Manchester defines and approaches 'social responsibility,' and addresses the question of how universities more generally can help bridge the gap between academic research, policy and practice. Second, it presents a research project that illustrates Manchester's approach to social responsibility. The study has been identified by the World Health Organization (WHO) as a best practice example of involving older people as co-investigators in researching and developing what it terms 'age-friendly' cities. The chapter then discusses the objectives of the study, the process of involving and training older people to become co-researchers, the research outcomes, and the impact of the study. Finally, the chapter concludes with a discussion of the lessons learned from the project, and suggests ways forward for (re-) connecting research with the goal of social responsibility.

7.2 Social Responsibility at the University of Manchester

Whilst a substantial literature exists on corporate social responsibility (Friedman 1962; Epstein and Roy 2001; Crane et al. 2013), there have been relatively fewer attempts to define *university social responsibility* (USR). This is despite the fact that universities have been in existence and contributing to society since the eleventh century. Across the world today, a number of universities are more explicitly defining their mission and activities in relation to social responsibility, as reflected in international networks such as the USR and Talloires Networks.

The University of Manchester is the UK's largest university, with more than 38,000 students. It is ranked fifth in the UK and 35th in the world for the quality of its research (Academic Ranking of World Universities 2016) and has 25 Nobel Prize winners amongst current and former staff and students. Significantly, Manchester was the first of England's 'civic universities.' These universities emerged in the 19th century in major cities outside of London, with an explicit mission to serve their regional economies and culture and to link their research with their teaching activities (Jones 1988). The origins of the University were therefore closely linked to Manchester's development as the world's first industrial city: key regional figures established the University to improve people's lives in Manchester and across the world through the advancement of knowledge and scholarship in healthcare, engineering and the liberal arts.

Building on this longstanding heritage of social engagement, the University of Manchester is the first university in the UK to position social responsibility as a core strategic goal. Forming part of a three-goal strategy, social responsibility sits equally alongside the University's more longstanding aims to deliver world-class research and outstanding learning. Social responsibility is defined by the University as 'making a difference to the social and environmental well-being of our communities and wider society through our teaching, research, engagement and operations' (The University of Manchester 2012). The University sees its first two goals of research and teaching as asking the question 'what are we good *at*?' Social responsibility, in contrast, is seen to ask the more fundamental question 'what are we good *for*?' (The University of Manchester 2012). The University addresses this question through a five-point plan for implementing social responsibility as outlined in Fig. 7.1.

- **Goal 1: Research with impact**: where the University's research and discovery makes a positive difference to society.
- **Goal 2: Socially-responsible graduates**: where the University's students and graduates learn to exercise important social and environmental responsibilities.
- **Goal 3: Engaging our communities**: where the University engages with people and organisations to make a difference in local communities and wider society.
- **Goal 4: Responsible processes**: where the University's 'business processes' and policies balance efficiency with opportunities for creating social benefit.
- **Goal 5: Environmental sustainability**: where the University's research, teaching and activities are guided by our commitment to environmental sustainability.

Figure 7.1 conceptualises the different ways a university might approach the global challenge of ageing societies. This can be met in a variety of ways through the goal of social responsibility. Knowledge creation and research, the main subject of this chapter (Goal 1), are important vehicles towards this end. However, the

Fig. 7.1 The University of
Manchester Strategic
framework for social
responsibility. *Source* www.
socialresponsibility.
manchester.ac.uk

University of Manchester also aims to deliver informed and skilled graduates able
to respond to issues of ageing societies as professionals and future citizens, through
exposure to curricular and extra-curricula experiences (Goal 2). Additionally, we
engage older residents through pioneering outreach and in-reach programmes at the
University's museum and art gallery, with a particular focus on health and well-
being (Goal 3) (see e.g., Allen et al. 2015). And the University's human resource
policies have allowed staff the time to engage in training significant numbers of
staff, students and the public to become '*Dementia Friends*' (Alzheimer's Society
n.d.)—a major UK initiative to change people's perceptions of dementia (Goal 4).
Key to providing leadership and coordination across these different dimensions to
social responsibility is the University's Manchester Institute for Collaborative
Research on Ageing (MICRA). MICRA promotes interdisciplinary research on all
aspects of ageing, emphasising the importance of healthy and active ageing. The
Institute brings together over 2000 academics, practitioners, policy makers and
older people and helps bridge the gap between academic research and policies in
order to make a difference to the lives of older people, especially those living in the
University's local communities. The next section focuses on how researching
ageing societies can make a positive contribution to society—both from the perspective of traditional 'research impact' emanating from knowledge creation, but
also through careful selection of research methodologies that can include, empower
and involve members of the local communities in which universities are located.

7.3 Global Ageing and Social Responsibility

Addressing grand societal challenges through research and engaging local communities are key ways in which the University of Manchester is implementing its approach to social responsibility. As noted above, **population ageing** and **urbanisation** have been highlighted as important issues facing both the global north and south. **Population ageing** is taking place across all countries of the world, albeit at varying levels of intensity. The proportion of those 60 years and over in the global north increased from 12% in 1950 to 23% in 2013, and is expected to reach 32% in 2050. In the global south, the share of older persons increased slowly between 1950 and 2013, from 6 to 9%, but this is expected to accelerate in the coming decades, reaching 19% in 2050 (United Nations 2014a). Of equal importance has been the spread of **urbanisation**, with over half of the world's population (54%) now living in urban areas, with this expected to increase to around two-thirds by 2050 (United Nations 2014b). Understanding the relationship between population ageing and urban change has become a major issue for public policy. The case for such work is especially strong given that cities are where the majority of people (of all ages) now live and where they will spend their old age. A report from the Organisation of Economic Cooperation and Development (OECD) (2015) makes the point that:

> Designing policies that address ageing issues requires a deep understanding of local circumstances, including communities' economic assets, history and culture. The spatially heterogeneous nature of ageing trends makes it important to *approach ageing from an urban perspective*. Cities need to pay more attention to local circumstances to understand ageing, and its impact. They are especially well equipped to address the issue, given their long experience of working with local communities and profound understanding of local problems.

This argument raises an important challenge for policies relating to ageing and urban environments. One significant policy response has come from the WHO, through its approach to developing what has been termed 'age-friendly cities and communities.' This model will be further explored in the next section of this chapter.

7.4 Researching and Developing "Age-Friendly" Cities

Developing 'age-friendly' cities has become a key issue driving policies aimed at older people (see Buffel et al. 2012). City regions across the world will need to plan ahead for ageing populations with more people living into their 80s, 90s and beyond. The WHO (2002) defines an age-friendly city as one that is: '…an inclusive and accessible urban environment that promotes active ageing…' The notion of 'active' refers to the idea that older people should be able to continue to participate in social, cultural, spiritual, economic and civic matters, i.e., not just the ability to participate in the labour market or to be physically active (WHO 2002). This idea was taken further in 2007, when the WHO launched the 'Global Age-friendly Cities' project. In 33 cities around the world, focus groups with older people, caregivers, and service providers were conducted in order to identify those factors that make urban environments 'age-friendly.' A resulting checklist of action points addressed aspects of service provision (e.g., health services, transportation), as well as dimensions of the built environment (e.g., housing, outdoor spaces and buildings), and social aspects (e.g., civic and social participation) (WHO 2007) (see Fig. 7.2). This work concluded that progress in developing these action points should make cities 'friendly for all ages' and not just 'elder-friendly': 'it should be normal in an age-friendly city for the natural and built environment to anticipate users with different capacities instead of designing for the mythical 'average' (i.e. young) person' (WHO 2007).

In 2010, the WHO launched the 'Global Network of Age-friendly Cities and Communities', in an attempt to encourage implementation of policy recommendations from the 2007 project. The network has a membership of 380 cities and communities across countries in the Global North and South (2017 figures) (see, further, WHO n.d.).

The Age-friendly Cities (AFC) approach has been highly influential in raising awareness about the need to adapt urban environments to the demands of an ageing population. However, research is needed that examines the wide range of approaches required to develop age-friendly communities across different localities (Fitzgerald and Caro 2016). Applied research, for example, could help us to identify relationships and interactions between the age-friendly domains, with the practical goal of influencing change across all levels of urban life. Realising the potential of AFC will require major initiatives at national, regional and local government level,

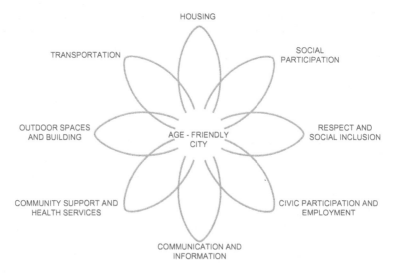

Fig. 7.2 The eight domains of an Age-Friendly community

across all of the major dimensions identified by the WHO. **However, a key argument of this chapter is that such work will not itself deliver age-friendly environments without the direct involvement of older people themselves**, for two main reasons: first, older people are the best group for reporting on the benefits as well as frustrations experienced through living in a particular area. Second, whilst progress has been made in identifying some key policies for age-friendly work, there has been much less success in terms of making older people themselves central to the development of policies and research. The next section discusses an example of a participatory research project which prioritised the social role of universities in engaging older people and local community stakeholders in producing research and developing plans to improve the age-friendliness of their neighbourhood.

7.5 Research and Partnership Building

The study discussed in this section illustrates the ways in which university research can play an important civic role in empowering individuals and local communities. In this project, older people, local stakeholders, community organisations and researchers work together not only to examine the opportunities and constraints of their neighbourhood, but also to identify actions and strategies to improve the physical and social environment. The focus of the research was on examining how older residents perceive their neighbourhood and how it might influence active ageing.

The specific objectives of the research project were to:

- Identify the issues older residents themselves viewed as important in developing the age-friendliness of their neighbourhood
- Understand how older people experience, use, negotiate and appropriate their immediate living environment
- Involve older people, not only as the research target group, but also as experts and actors in the planning, design, development and implementation of the study
- Promote evidence-based policy-making and practice at the local level

7.6 Studying the Lives of Older People

Using research as way of empowering neighbouring communities is an important dimension of the University's social responsibility agenda. However, successful engagement with local communities requires the application of particular research methods. The work described here drew on participant observation, focus groups, in-depth interviews, training and community action. More generally, the study used an **ethnographic approach** (O'Reilly 2012) involving direct and sustained contact with older people in the context of their daily lives. Participant observation was used to gain an understanding of the physical, social, cultural and economic context in which study participants live; the relationships among and between people; their neighbourhood, ideas, norms, and events; and people's behaviours and activities. This method was especially useful in developing an understanding of the quality of older people's lives in the three research neighbourhoods.

The project uses a method of '**coproduction**', i.e., a collaborative process of research, training and action towards social transformation, in this case to improve the age-friendliness of the areas (Kindon et al. 2007; Sanz et al. 2015). To provide a sounding board for the overall planning of the research, a Research Advisory Board and an Age-Friendly Steering Group (a lay Advisory Committee) were formed by the University of Manchester.

Three contrasting research areas (based on social characteristics, patterns of deprivation, ethnic composition) were selected, all located across the University's local communities in the city of Manchester. Each of these neighbourhoods illustrated a range of challenges to ageing in place, with older people experiencing different forms of social exclusion.

The **research activities** can be summarised as follows:

- **Participant observation** in particular places in the three research areas (parks, pubs, local shops, bus stops) and key community meetings and events
- **15 semi-structured interviews with city-wide key informants** about the age-friendly approach in Manchester
- **Participatory mapping exercises** with attendees of community events to identify local opportunities and challenges
- **14 focus groups with a total of 123 representatives of community organisations and older residents** across the three neighbourhoods
- **3 training sessions** for older people to become co-researchers
- **68 semi-structured interviews with 'hard-to-reach' older people** conducted by the co-researchers
- **4 reflection meetings with the co-researchers**
- **Co-development of summary leaflets presenting key findings** with co-researchers
- **3 dissemination workshops** bringing together older people, community organisations and different stakeholders

As reflected in the activities listed above, **participation** was central to the project: older residents in the University's neighbouring communities acted as **co-investigators** at all stages of the process, including planning, design and implementation. A second feature shaping the research was **collaboration**: a range of university partners—local government, third sector, NGOs—acted as advisors or contributed via focus groups, interviews and ongoing partnership work. A third feature was **action:** recommendations have been generated for urban design, regeneration, community engagement and policy implementation. This has resulted in insights from the work being fed directly into social programmes and initiatives, within Manchester and beyond. The next section will reflect on the process of participatory research with older people, including the associated opportunities and challenges.

7.7 The Research Process: Involving Older People as Co-investigators

An ethnically diverse group of eighteen local older residents, aged between fifty-eight and seventy-four, were recruited and trained as co-investigators. Recruitment took place through advertising and information and public events held in the local research areas. The study used a volunteer profile including various criteria for the recruitment of the co-researchers. They participated in two training sessions, with the aim of ensuring that every co-researcher had a thorough understanding of the different phases involved in conducting a participatory research project. The training provided an overview of the different elements of the research process, for example designing the research materials, interviewing techniques, data analysis and translating findings into practice. The training sessions were structured around these topics, but were interactive and flexible at the same time, following the pace and issues raised by the group. Special attention was given to the design of the research and the research materials, to ensure that it was particularly sensitive to marginalized voices within the community. A full description of the project, including practicalities such as insurance, remuneration, training sessions and training certificates, can be found in the following guide: *"Researching age-friendly communities. Stories from older people as co-investigators"* (Buffel 2015).

7.7.1 Improving the Wellbeing of Socially Disadvantaged Groups of Older People

Most studies on ageing tend to have an over-representation of people who are socially active in the community and/or already well connected. However, the project reported here aimed to involve socially isolated groups of older people, with the aim of promoting healthy and active ageing. The co-researchers received targeted training focused on recruiting older people experiencing isolation and/or exclusion. All co-researchers lived locally and used their networks to find individuals who met the selection criteria.

7.7.2 Interviews Conducted by the Co-researchers

The co-researchers conducted sixty-eight interviews, across the three research areas, with older people who were experiencing social exclusion, isolation, poverty or health problems. The interviews focused on ways of improving the quality of life for older people living in urban communities. The interview questions and topic guide used during the interviews were developed in partnership with the co-researchers, and focused on a range of issues, including: residential histories; feelings about ageing in the neighbourhood; future plans/desires in terms of residential locations and housing; neighbourhood change; safety; daily activities; use of amenities and services; community support and health services; access to food; mobility and transportation; opportunities for social/cultural/political participation; communication and information; and ideas on how to improve the neighbourhood to age well. All interviews were transcribed word-for-word for analysis.

7.7.3 Reflection Meetings with Co-researchers

In addition to the training sessions, the co-researchers and research team participated in four reflection meetings. The purpose of these was to encourage interactive and joint learning through discussion, analysis and critical reflection. For example, co-researchers exchanged ideas on how to recruit socially isolated older people; discussed and refined the interview schedule; reflected on their role of researcher and looked at whether there were any reported issues that needed signposting. Other meetings involved data analysis sessions in order to develop a joint framework for the interpretation of the qualitative data. Together with the co-researchers, the different steps of qualitative data analysis and coding were discussed and applied to the data.

7.7.4 Community Events and Dissemination Events

Throughout the research process, the University undertook a range of public engagement activities and events across the three research areas. These included events such as history group meetings, social gatherings and neighbourhood festivals. The research process and preliminary findings were presented at these events by the co-researchers to increase awareness about the project and strengthen links between the project partners and community organisations in the research neighbourhoods.

Dissemination workshops were held in each of the research areas bringing together different stakeholders (e.g., older residents, local government departments, voluntary organisations, health and care services, urban planners, fire services and local businesses). The purpose of these workshops was to: reflect on the research findings and their activities in relation to older people; discuss how organisations can work in partnership with older people; and identify indicators to monitor the impact of these actions. The co-researchers were involved in the organisation of these events and have presented the research findings alongside the research team. Summary leaflets presenting the key findings of the project to community and policy stakeholders were also produced.

7.8   Advantages of Using Coproduction Methods

The participatory approach in this project is about radically rethinking who *initiates* and *undertakes* the research process, and who *learns* or *benefits* from findings produced by universities. The coproduction method used has several advantages for the different stakeholder groups involved. What follows are some of the findings arising from the reflection meetings with the co-researchers, highlighting advantages for older people themselves, the communities in which they live, and policy-makers with an interest in creating age-friendly neighbourhoods. After presenting the key advantages for each group, these will be illustrated with quotes coming from the co-researchers and stakeholders who participated in the reflection meetings as part of the project.

7.8.1   Recognising Older People as Active Citizens

Participants identified the following advantages associated with the coproduction approach involving older people as co-researchers:

- Older people feel heard and recognized as peers in the development of the research
- It counteracts stereotypes of older people by emphasising and making their involvement and participation visible
- It demonstrates the central role older people can play in the creation and development of policies and practices
- Older people are enabled to develop new skills, knowledge and relationships which may increase confidence and enhance life chances

Some of the above advantages regarding older people's recognition and influence were especially evident in the way co-researchers talked about their motivations and reasons to participate in this project:

> I value and enjoy working together with older people, we learn a lot from each other. Together we can influence the planning and development of services, locally and nationally. I welcomed the opportunity to learn from others in this project, and to learn new skills, and to have my contributions valued. (74-year-old woman, co-researcher)

Similar points were made by some of the community development workers involved in the project who felt that the work had the potential to make positive changes to the communities in which older people reside:

> The age-friendly research project has had a big impact in the area in the sense that it has encouraged participation and given a lot of older people the opportunity to be actively involved and to be heard. It is empowering to contribute to something that will be used to benefit others. (Neighbourhood community worker)

As the above suggests, research can make a difference to communities not only through the findings which are generated but also a result of methodological processes that empower individuals and communities. 'Success' in such participatory forms of university research can therefore be seen to rest not only on the quality of information produced, but also on the extent to which skills, knowledge and participants' capacities and networks are developed through the research experience (Kesby et al. 2005). The co-investigators identified a number of skills they felt were nurtured throughout the project, including: improved communication, presentation and listening skills; improved abilities to conduct interviews respecting different views; better knowledge about data analysis and reporting research findings; and improved competence in working with different social and ethnic groups of older people. Training sessions and reflection meetings were found to be especially helpful. The practical exercises, such as interviewing each other, and conducting data analysis, were especially valued. A typical comment was:

> The training we received gave confidence… to embark on the project… During the training, I improved my listening and communication skills. I see myself already using these skills in my other areas of work. (70-year-old woman, co-researcher)

7.8.2   Older People as Experts in Contributing to High Quality Research

- Older co-researchers have extensive knowledge about ageing themselves, and can help shape the research design and provide valuable learning
- Older co-researchers greatly assist with the recruitment of hard-to-reach research participants, providing opportunities to get some of the most 'unheard' voices
- It generates a sense of 'ownership' of the research which stimulates the participation and advocacy of older citizens
- Older residents who act as co-researchers are able to develop relationships of trust, rapport and empathy with older interviewees
- Supportive and relaxed interview situations with peers enhance high quality data

Many co-researchers and stakeholders reflected on the benefits (and challenges, see below) of involving older people as leaders of the project. The closeness in age, as well as the familiarity between co-researchers and interviewees as a result of living in the same area, was seen as a major advantage in accessing and recruiting hard-to-reach groups of older people:

> I think that engaging older residents to interview older residents has been extremely successful. There seemed far less barriers to communication with closeness in age. We were all able to have quite deep and meaningful conversations. (63 year-old woman, co-researcher)

Other advantages of involving older people as co-researchers included: a better understanding of the actual concerns of older people; the collection of rich in-depth interview data based on a trusting relationship between interviewer and interviewee; the development of new partnerships with community organisations; and preventative initiatives targeting particular groups of older people, such as those who are socially isolated. For example:

> Our local community organisations have been seeking ways and means of engaging with older people, to assess their needs and to prevent their isolation in their homes. Visiting people in the comfort of their homes makes them relaxed and confident to discuss and express their fears and concerns. (59-year-old man, co-researcher)

7.8.3 Building Better Connected Communities

- The project is collaborative at every stage, involving discussion, learning, pooling skills and resources and working together with different community stakeholders
- The project provides opportunities to signpost older people to services and activities in line with their needs
- The involvement of older people and community stakeholders in research is seen as an incentive for organisations to disseminate the research findings and improve their practices
- The project has generated a wide range of initiatives and suggestions aimed at improving the neighbourhoods in which older people live

Reflecting the above, comments were made about how the project had contributed to the development of a sense of community:

> Already, people are demonstrating that they feel more connected by getting involved with other projects and using the skills and abilities gained as part of this project in other areas: taking on more active roles as volunteers, and the engagement that has taken place between the co-researchers and the people they have interviewed. [...] Projects like this empower older people and communities into realising they have a voice. (Community Development Worker)

The co-investigators and community stakeholders also made numerous suggestions to improve the age-friendliness of their neighbourhoods on the basis of the interview findings. Alongside ideas for improving the age-friendliness of local business, shops and transport, many of the suggestions were aimed at promoting relationships between different groups within the community:

One idea is to think more closely about the demographics of neighbourhoods. The Irish community, for example, and that is certainly true of West Indian people and certain Asian communities have got a lot of skills in gardening. A lot of people living in this area have come from rural areas. We need to tap into these skills. They could use those skills in community allotments for example. (58-year-old man, co-researcher)

Other ideas included: improving signage to social meeting places, information centres and health services; promoting 'joined-up' services which enable adequate support for people living in their own homes; and considering whether existing projects and activities could be made intergenerational, involving different groups of residents. Partnerships between different community stakeholders, social groups and local councilors were seen as key to achieving those.

7.8.4 Policy Makers Can Take Better Decisions

- Policy makers can benefit from the knowledge, experience and potential of older people
- Participatory projects can better understand the needs of older people and adjust policies and strategies to the changing needs of citizens at different ages
- They can build a broad consensus and achieve long-term support for their reforms
- Coproduction is a more democratic alternative to designing policies which may be better suited to cope with the increasingly complex challenges associated with population ageing and urbanization

The above points are reflected in the following quote from a senior manager from Manchester City Council:

The involvement of local residents in this study, as co-researchers, is a significant contribution to the city's Age-Friendly Manchester programme. The approach recognises the centrality of older people as active citizens in the Age-Friendly approach and gives a unique voice to many of the most excluded older people in central and south Manchester. Moreover, the findings of this work will play a direct role in the development of the city's plans for the neighbourhoods in which the research has been conducted. (Senior Strategy Manager, Age-Friendly Manchester)

7.8.5 Universities Can Demonstrate Their Commitment to Social Responsibility

Universities can demonstrate their commitment to responsibility through:

- Increasing the impact of their research
- Extending the interaction between the University and its neighbouring communities

- Increasing the confidence and skills of disadvantaged groups
- Enhancing civic relationships between the University and other policy stakeholders
- Sharing knowledge between the academy and the community

Given its collaborative nature, the project has provided opportunities for science, policy, practice and older people to interact and develop a better understanding of each other's interests and approaches to developing age-friendly communities. On the one side, the project can be seen as a forum for meaningful social engagement and mutual learning exchange, mobilising older people's expertise and knowledge to stimulate creative ideas and initiatives around the age-friendliness agenda. On the other hand, a number of challenges are also associated with the coproduction approach, and these will be explored in the following section.

7.9 Challenges of Using Coproduction Methods

The approach of this project, involving older residents as co-researchers, also raises a number of methodological, practical, political and ethical challenges. A key challenge is that a participatory project requires *time, energy and commitment* from university research teams, local residents, and a range of community and policy stakeholders. It also involves *coordination* by universities of these players as well as multiple *partnerships*. One challenge linked to this is the need for negotiating *power* relationships between different stakeholders, such as those between policy makers and practitioners, or between university and community-researchers. Ray (2007) for example suggests that older people who are able to participate in training to develop research projects as co-researchers are likely to have access to more resources than other older people, be in good health and feel they have space from other responsibilities. This may create power imbalances and potential tensions between the 'successfully ageing' *older co-researcher* on the one side and the *research participant* who may need assistance and support on the other. The empowerment of citizens through community participation therefore has to be understood in the context of a critical and ethical perspective concerning issues of justice between social groups (Ziegler and Scharf 2013).

Another issue to be considered when using coproduction methods is that such work *raises expectations*. The act of a university asking older people and community stakeholders to define problems in their neighbourhood and participate in the search for a solution can raise expectations about what solutions should be implemented. Coproduction methods are therefore most appropriate where there are opportunities for long-term engagement by universities with stakeholder groups so that demands and expectations can be addressed in a collaborative way. At the same time, it is important not to create false hopes with interview participants, and to discuss the scope and limits of the project:

It raises expectations—don't get me wrong I think the project should try to raise expectations. But if they are not realistic—because the older people haven't been kept informed about the scope of the project or constraints from key organisations, then this could lead to disillusion. And the next time someone tries to do similar work it will be harder to engage older people. (58 year old man, co-researcher)

Other challenges faced by universities are linked to the issue of conducting research with community researchers. Through multiple training sessions and reflection meetings, the co-researchers in this project were supported when they faced difficulties during the research process. For example, some co-researchers had technological problems with the recording of the interviews. Others encountered emotional stories and experiences, especially amongst older people who could be described as vulnerable in the context of experiencing social exclusion. This man, a 62 year-old co-researcher, who conducted interviews with older people with Asian backgrounds, for example, said:

The most difficult thing is to hear things that are painful and have been ignored. Painful stories among some of the Asian older people I interviewed were about their children who ignored their parents or undervalued their role in the family as elders.

The challenges associated with coproduction methods warrant serious consideration from all the partners involved. Participatory research engages multiple actors at all stages, to design with them their role throughout the process, to take into account their needs and concerns throughout the project, to carefully encourage, recruit, support and train them, as well as involve them in the sharing and implementation of research findings (Shura et al. 2010). This implies the need for sufficient resources for universities engaged in such methods of research, not only in terms of research funding, but also in terms of human support, resources, training, energy and commitment if this is to be successful.

7.10 Impact of the Study

Developing and supporting 'research with impact' is an important dimension of the University's approach to social responsibility. Research Councils UK (RCUK) defines research impact as 'the demonstrable contribution that excellent research makes to society and the economy'. In recent years, the UK government and research councils have placed increasing emphasis on the need for evidence of economic and social returns from its investment in research. Universities are challenged to increase the visibility of their research not only to demonstrate the contribution they make to society, but also to improve their chances in the competition for government research funding. One way to achieve this is through positioning themselves to work with policy, industry or third sector partners. In this project, a wide range of stakeholders were involved in getting the study findings known, disseminated and used. Research impact was realised with the major end user groups of the study, including policy-makers, practitioners, communities and older people.

Local political actors and policy stakeholders were involved from the start of the project, and helped develop the aims of the study as well as a dissemination strategy that translated research findings from policy *implications* to policy *impact*. The project findings were of particular interest to the *World Health Organization's Global Network of Age-Friendly Cities and Communities*. The idea of co-research 'with' and 'by' older people is viewed by the WHO as key to developing urban environments responsive to demographic change. However, systematic guidance is lacking about how to develop such work. This project, and its *Participatory Guide to Developing Age-Friendly Communities* (Buffel 2015), builds upon policy priorities identified by the WHO, and fills an important gap in knowledge around how universities can undertake co-research projects with older people. It has also been publicised as a best practice example of co-production by organisations such as the *United Nations, Age Platform Europe,* and the *World Health Organization*. The work has also been presented at a number of policy conferences such as the UN open-ended Working Group on Ageing and at the Thematic Network on Innovation for Age-Friendly Environments meeting.

Following this, the *World Report on Ageing and Health* (WHO 2015) has identified the issue of 'creating age-friendly environments' as a key priority area for action to improve healthy ageing, and the study presented here is seen as instrumental in moving this agenda forward. Commenting on the 'research *with*, not just *for* older people' in Manchester, the WHO (2015) states that:

> Taken as a whole, this study represents a significant methodological step forward in developing new models for community engagement. Interventions such as those used in the study represent excellent sources of data, valuable exercises in community engagement for all participants, and cost-effective mechanisms for producing informed policy in times of austerity.

The study has also influenced a number of **UK local authorities.** For example, *Manchester City Council* has used the project findings to further develop its strategy for the Age-Friendly Manchester Programme. It has provided the City Council with an evidence-base for the strategic commissioning of services that have an impact on older people's quality of life. The City Council has played a major role in supporting the coproduction approach taken by the study:

> This project breaks new ground in working with older people as co-producers of research and policy. It throws down an exciting challenge to those shaping public policies to support older people. (Senior manager for Age-Friendly Manchester)

The project builds on the idea of 'evidence-based practice', using research findings to inform the work of **practitioners and community stakeholders**. One of the community developers, for example, made the point that:

> The research enables us to look at ways of moving forward with future initiatives taking the research findings into account and utilising the expertise and experiences of our local co-researchers. The project will also be beneficial to other areas across Manchester as a

good example/resource for identifying priorities of residents and examining the definition of an age-friendly neighbourhood.

However, the potential of the project will only be fully realised if the research proves to have a positive impact on the lives of **older people, their families and communities** living in the city. As mentioned above, the training workshops and public events have been beneficial in terms of identifying community assets and resources that can be used to improve the quality of community life. Co-researchers and community stakeholders have been able to develop new skills, knowledge and relationships which all can be employed as *on-the-ground* assets to examine community needs and establish priorities. Through developing new collaborative partnerships, the research project has been able to inspire innovative approaches to engaging older residents as leaders and visionaries in developing age-friendly projects. For example, one of the issues in relation to older people living alone is to ensure healthy eating and good nutrition. Arising from this, the co-researchers, together with local stakeholders, have set up a community-based project where older people who enjoy cooking provide a fresh meal for a socially isolated neighbor, e.g., someone who recently experienced bereavement or had financial difficulties.

The co-researchers have now formed a permanent group and are applying for funding for age-friendly initiatives in partnership with the University. This is likely to produce a number of new projects targeted at health and wellbeing concerns experienced by older people. Further evaluation and research will be needed to track the impact of initiatives designed to improve the quality of life of older people.

The novel features of the work were acknowledged in the **'Engage' prize** for best partnership initiative from the **National Coordinating Centre for Public Engagement** and a **'Making a Difference Award'** for outstanding local community collaboration at the **University of Manchester** (The University of Manchester n.d.). At the award ceremony, the director of the Manchester Institute for Collaborative Research on Ageing identified the study as an outstanding example of how research can contribute the University's social responsibility agenda:

> It is a fine example of the work that can be done drawing together different groups and illustrates a great partnership between the researchers and the City Council which has been of great benefit to older people and to the University.

The University's **Manchester Institute for Collaborative Research on Ageing** (MICRA) has played a key role in developing and supporting **partnerships with community organisations and policy stakeholders** for the project. Many of the co-researchers took part in MICRA's public engagement events which explore key themes in ageing by engaging with academics, care providers, older people, and the voluntary and the private sector. Three local co-researchers also presented the project at a university seminar exploring the ways in which urban environments can contribute to 'healthy' and 'active' ageing. The seminar formed part of a Festival of Social Science which aimed to illustrate *how social science research can contribute to creating age-friendly environments from the perspective of older people, policy* *makers and business* (MICRA). The day was well attended (over 150 participants from different sectors and disciplines) and generated many ideas for pushing the age-friendly agenda forward.

Finally, the impact of research can be illustrated through a study's outcomes and publications, aimed at both academic as well as policy and community audiences. The project has led to various outputs, including a **Participatory Guide to Developing Age-Friendly Communities** (Buffel 2015) (ISBN: 978-0-9576682-2-5), a short **film** with over 4200 views on Youtube, (Buffel and Hewson 2015) a **policy blog** (Manchester Policy Blogs 2014), and a number of **papers** in academic journals and books (Buffel et al. 2013, 2014; Buffel and Hewson 2015; Buffel and Phillipson 2016). The research team has also been able to attract additional **University funding** to continue the impact work with the co-researchers and community stakeholders involved in the project. For the University, it is strategically important to invest in this type of work, because it brings together two of its core goals: 'world-class research' and 'social responsibility' (*Manchester 2020: The University of Manchester's Strategic Plan*, The University of Manchester 2012). This is illustrated in the short film presenting the research beacons of the University, including the issue of 'addressing global inequalities' (The University of Manchester 2017) in which this project also features.

7.11 Coproduction for University Social Responsibility Agenda: Lessons Learned

A number of lessons can be drawn from the project, these including the importance of developing collaborative partnerships; the need for negotiating power relationships; and the importance of further experimentation with methods of coproduction in producing 'socially responsible' research and policy change.

On the first of these, the strong rapport between the university and a range of community stakeholders, practitioners and older residents has been crucial in applying the coproduction approach at a community level. Participatory research engages multiple actors at all stages, to design with them their role throughout the process, to take into account their needs and concerns throughout the project, to carefully encourage, recruit, support and train them, as well as involve them in the sharing and implementation of research findings (Shura et al. 2010). This implies the need for sufficient resources by universities, not only in terms of research funding, but also in terms of human support, resources, energy and commitment.

Second, whilst seeking to democratise knowledge production and fostering opportunities for those involved, participatory research nevertheless constitutes a form of power and carries the risk of reproducing the very inequalities it seeks to address. Power relationships may exist between professional university researchers and co-researchers, but also between co-researchers, who are often relatively highly educated, on the one hand and marginalised groups of older interviewees on the other.

This raises a number of questions in terms of defining what counts as a 'community' and potential tensions between (co-) researchers, the researched and community activists. Resolving these issues will need a high degree of self-awareness amongst the individuals and groups involved. One way of addressing this is through maximising the heterogeneity of older people represented in age-friendly research, in terms of for example age, gender, class, ethnicity, and cognitive and physical abilities.

Third, the project suggests that universities employing participatory research approaches can potentially engage local residents in the research process in ways that can benefit them as individuals, the communities in which they live, and through the process of developing beneficial policy outcomes, such as creating more age-friendly cities. The extent to which universities can engage local communities in their research can have a direct influence on policy and practices aimed at improving the quality of life in old age.

7.12   Conclusion

The University of Manchester was the first university in the UK to position 'social responsibility' as a core strategic goal, alongside more longstanding aims to deliver 'world-class research' and 'outstanding learning'. Social responsibility is defined by the University as '*making a difference to the social and environmental well-being of our communities and wider society through our teaching, research, engagement and operations*'. Research can contribute to the university's social responsibility agenda in two main ways: by producing knowledge and findings which can improve the quality of life of groups such as older people; and by empowering local communities through their direct involvement in the research process.

The study presented in this chapter firstly demonstrates the potential to generate significant research impact, in terms of academic as well as social impact. The study highlighted a number of innovative solutions about how cities can adapt their structures and services to the needs of people as they grow old, and these have been crucial in influencing the development of 'age-friendly' policies and service provision in Manchester and beyond. A second way in which research can contribute to the University's social responsibility goals is through engaging with people and organisations to make a difference to the local communities of which the university is a part. The study used a method of '*coproduction*', defined as a collaborative process of research, training and community action towards social transformation, in this case to improve the age-friendliness of its local neighbourhoods. Older residents were trained by the University as co-researchers and were involved as experts in the planning and implementation of the study. This produced a more collaborative approach to university research based upon a process of mutual education that recognises the value of both *scholarly* knowledge and *community-based* knowledge. This point has been developed by Marsh (1985) in the following way:

> Only when a broader section of society can have a say in research agendas, can have access to the apparatus of social research and can have some control over the means of information dissemination will the subjects of research really be accorded citizenship status. […] For a real democratisation of social research to occur, there will have to be changes not just in the status of the researched, but also in the right to be a researcher.

As the study suggests, the success of communities in becoming more age-friendly will, to a large extent, depend on whether older people, including those facing social exclusion, will be involved as key actors in setting the agenda for future urban development. This will require a shift in the balance of power between older residents and other urban stakeholder (Kindon et al. 2007; Shura et al. 2010). Although the results of this project are promising, further research using similar approaches are needed to test whether these results could be replicated in other settings. A further implication of this work concerns its relevance for research within universities, especially that focused around the search for new treatments in relation to the needs of an ageing population. Much of this work will depend on close cooperation with older people themselves, for example in relation to clinical trials and involvement in patient advisory groups. The findings of this study suggest that the ongoing development and experimentation with coproduction methods may continue to inspire new understandings and possibilities for engaging older residents and community stakeholders. Universities can play a significant role in supporting this type of work by promoting the 'public role' of academics who, through their choice of research programmes and methods, can have an empowering role for different groups in society.

Acknowledgements The authors would like to express their gratitude to the School of Social Sciences at the University of Manchester; the Age-Friendly Manchester team at the City Council, Chorlton Good Neighbours, Whalley Range Community Forum, the Manchester Institute for Collaborative Research on Ageing and all of the co-researchers and participants in the study.

References

Academic Ranking of World Universities. (2016). *ARWU World University Rankings 2016*. Retrieved from http://www.shanghairanking.com/ARWU2016.html

Allen, P., Brown, A., Camic, P.M., Cutler, D., Harvey, L., Parsons, M.P, Sweeney, R., Ward, E., & Zeilig, H. (2015). *Becoming a dementia-friendly arts venue: A practical guide*. Retrieved from http://www.alzheimers.org.uk/dementiafriendlycommunities

Alzheimer's Society. (n.d.). *Dementia Friends*. Retrieved from https://www.dementiafriends.org.uk/

Buffel, T., Phillipson, C., & Scharf, T. (2012). Ageing in urban environments: Developing age-friendly cities. *Critical Social Policy, 32*(4), 597–617.

Buffel, T., Phillipson, C., & Scharf, T. (2013). Experiences of neighbourhood exclusion and inclusion among older people living in deprived inner-city areas in Belgium and England. *Ageing & Society, 33*(1), 89–109.

Buffel, T., McGarry, P., Phillipson, C., De Donder, L., Dury, S., De Witte, N., et al. (2014). Developing age-friendly cities: Case studies from Brussels and Manchester and implications for policy and practice. *Journal of Aging & Social Policy, 26*(1–2), 52–72.

Buffel, T. (Ed.). (2015). *Researching age-friendly communities. Stories from older people as co-investigators*. Manchester: The University of Manchester Library.

Buffel, T., & Hewson, C. (2015). *Researching age-friendly cities. A film funded by the school of social sciences, The University of Manchester.* Retrieved from https://www.youtube.com/watch?v=WXELgwHQ34o

Buffel, T., & Phillipson, C. (2016). Can global cities be 'age-friendly cities'? Urban development and ageing populations. *Cities, 55,* 94–100.

Crane, A., Matten, D., & Spence, L. J. (2013). *Corporate social responsibility: Readings and cases in a global context.* Abingdon: Routledge.

Epstein, M. J., & Roy, M. J. (2001). Sustainability in action: Identifying and measuring the key performance drivers. *Long Range Planning, 34*(5), 585–604.

Fitzgerald, K. G., & Caro, F. G. (Eds.). (2016). *International perspectives on age-friendly cities.* New York: Routledge.

Friedman, M. (1962). *Capitalism and freedom.* Chicago: University of Chicago Press.

Jones, D. R. (1988). *The origins of civic universities: Manchester, Leeds, Liverpool.* London: Routledge.

Kesby, M., Kindon, S., & Pain, R. (2005). Participatory research. In R. Flowerdew & M. Martin (Eds.), *Methods in human geography* (pp. 144–166). London: Pearson.

Kindon, S., Pain, R., & Kesby, M. (2007). *Participatory action research approaches and methods. Connecting people, participation and place.* London, New York: Routledge.

Marsh, C. (1985). Informants, respondents and citizens. In M. Bulmer (Ed.), *Essays on the history of British sociological research.* London: Cambridge University Press.

Manchester Policy Blogs. (2014). *How can we make our towns and cities more age-friendly?* Retrieved from http://blog.policy.manchester.ac.uk/featured/2014/06/strategy-and-creativity-the-key-to-making-the-uk-more-age-friendly/

OECD. (2015). *Ageing in cities.* Paris: OECD. doi:10.1787/9789264231160-en.

O'Reilly, K. (2012). *Ethnographic methods.* Oxon: Routledge.

Ray, M. (2007). Redressing the balance? The participation of older people in research. In M. Bernard & T. Scharf (Eds.), *Critical perspectives on ageing societies* (pp. 73–88). Bristol: Policy Press.

Sanz, M. F., Ferrer, J. G., Figueroa, C. V., Ferrandis, E. D., & Rigia, F. R. (2015). *Guidelines for coproducing age-friendly environments with older people.* Brussel: AFE-INNOVNET.

Shura, R., Siders, R. A., & Dannefer, D. (2010). Culture change in long-term care: Participatory action research and the role of the resident. *The Gerontologist, 51*(12), 212–225.

The University of Manchester. (2012). Manchester 2020. The University of Manchester's strategic plan. Retrieved from http://documents.manchester.ac.uk/display.aspx?DocID=25548

The University of Manchester. (n.d.). *Outstanding local community collaboration - Dr Tine Buffel.* Retrieved from https://www.youtube.com/watch?v=fRZfYTZwVKU

The University of Manchester. (2017). *Addressing global inequalities.* Retrieved from https://www.manchester.ac.uk/research/beacons/global-inequalities/

United Nations. (2014a). *Concise report on the world population situation in 2014.* New York: UN Department of Economic and Social Affairs Population Division.

United Nations. (2014b). *World urbanization prospects.* New York: UN Department of Economic and Social Affairs.

World Health Organization. (2002). *Active aging: A policy framework.* Geneva: WHO.

World Health Organization. (2007). *Global age-friendly cities: A guide.* Geneva: WHO.

World Health Organization. (2015). *World report on ageing and health.* Geneva: WHO.

World Health Organization. (n.d.). *Age-friendly world - Adding life to years.* Retrieved from https://extranet.who.int/agefriendlyworld/

Ziegler, F., & Scharf, T. (2013). Community-based participatory action research: Opportunities and challenges for critical gerontology. In J. Baars, J. Dohmen, A. Grenier, & C. Phillipson (Eds.) *Ageing, meaning and social structure. Connecting critical and humanistic gerontology* (pp. 157–180). Bristol: Policy Press.

Chapter 8
Nurturing University Students to Be Socially Responsible Citizens: An Examination of Two Approaches to Volunteering

Ann Jardine

Abstract This chapter discusses two different approaches to developing socially responsible students through volunteering within the university framework. Both sit outside the academic curriculum and provide very different opportunities. The first program is an integral part of a wide reaching outreach program which works with students within disadvantaged communities: in New South Wales, Australia, from Kindergarten to the end of schooling in Year 12. The second program sits within the co-curricular space and offers university students opportunities to work within the not for profit sector. Each approach provides a rich opportunity for students to engage with disadvantaged communities and for personal growth. The chapter explores each approach. It also examines some of the learnings and outcomes for students, the university and the wider community.

Keywords Community engagement · Leadership program · New south wales · Social responsibility · Volunteering

8.1 Introduction

In 2015, UNSW Sydney (The University of New South Wales) set about developing a new strategic plan. Driven by the new Vice Chancellor Professor Ian Jacobs, the process involved wide consultation with all members of the UNSW community including staff, students, the University Council and Alumni. It was an ambitious task. Over the course of six months involving many consultations, a discussion paper was developed and subsequently, a paper of strategic intent. The final outcome of this widespread consultation is the UNSW 2025 Strategy (www. 2025.unsw.edu.au). This has given clear direction on what the University views as its priorities over the next ten years.

A. Jardine (✉)
University of New South Wales, Goodsell Building F20, Sydney, NSW 2052, Australia
e-mail: a.jardine@unsw.edu.au

© Springer Nature Singapore Pte Ltd. 2017   121
D.T.L. Shek and R.M. Hollister (eds.), *University Social Responsibility and Quality of Life*, Quality of Life in Asia 8,
DOI 10.1007/978-981-10-3877-8_8

A strong discourse that ran though all consultative phases with staff and students was a commitment to social justice and social responsibility. This commitment of the UNSW community has emerged across the 2025 Strategy with the result that, in the words of Professor Jacobs, *'It outlines an innovative, ambitious and altruistic agenda'* (p. 4). An agenda has been established to make a difference to the lives of people in Australia and globally. The importance that the University places on social responsibility is laid out in two major strategic priorities within the overall 2025 Strategy. The first is that of social engagement. The second is the global impact of the University. Within those priorities are two key themes of 'a just society' and 'our contribution to disadvantaged and marginalised communities'. The first theme sets out to position UNSW as an international exemplar in equity, diversity and inclusion, while the second theme espouses the strong commitment to working with marginalised and disadvantaged communities. These two themes provide a strong framework for the focus of UNSW social responsibility over the next ten years.

The 2025 Strategy provides a clear road map for promoting and embedding university social responsibility. An organisational structure has also been put in place to further promote and embed within UNSW. This includes a senior DVC position which has carriage of key parts of the Strategy including those described above and the theme of 'leading the debate on grand challenges' which sits under social engagement strategic priority. Academic leads will push these strategic agendas as the 2025 Strategy moves forward, thus providing not only a focus but also a public face for promoting the Strategy both within and external to the organisation.

However, much already exists that comfortably sits within the strategic framework which demonstrates university social responsibility. Within the research sphere, centres focusing on human rights, Indigenous health, refugee research and major environmental issues such as climate change and tackling greenhouse gases are already adding to the global knowledge of major issues. Within the teaching and learning sphere there is a clear acknowledgement of social responsibility embedded within the graduate capabilities, one of which focuses on producing global citizens who are capable of acting in a socially just and responsible way.

This graduate capability recognises that students can be significant catalysts for social change for the future. However, strategies for developing such a graduate capability do not only lie within the academic framework of the University. This chapter explores how two established but different approaches sitting outside the curriculum have utilised student volunteering to nurture students to be socially responsible citizens and in doing so, support the strategic intent of UNSW in its commitment to university social responsibility.

The UNSW Leadership Program and UNSW ASPIRE are two avenues where social responsibility is nurtured in the student body. Both were established prior to the development of the 2025 Strategy. Initiated and driven by the professional staff of the University, the two programs incorporate student volunteering as a key component, but approach it within very different frameworks. One approach enables breadth in that it can reach and potentially appeal to more of the student body. The other enables depth in that it can provide a more sustained and potentially richer volunteering experience but in doing so cannot involve as many of the student body.

8.2 Social Responsibility Through a Co-curricular Framework

The UNSW Leadership Program (https://student.unsw.edu.au/leadership) sets out to develop leadership capabilities through a socially responsible co-curricular framework. It has its genesis in the service learning approach established in universities in the United States (USA) since the 1990s. Petkus's (2000) description of service learning as 'a pedagogical process whereby students participate in course-relevant community service to enhance their learning experience' (p. 64) aptly applies to the Leadership Program. Broadly shaped and informed by a service learning framework, the program sets out to provide an experiential educative approach. The experience is framed around three key components. The first component focuses on learning through workshops. The second component provides the student with the opportunity to enhance, enrich and apply their learning through community engagement in an environment that is meaningful to them as an individual. The third component of reflective practice enables the student to learn about self, and apply their knowledge and skills to their personal development.

Unlike service learning which sits in the curricular space and results in academic credit, the Leadership Program sitting as it does in the co-curricular space does not count as part of a degree load. However, it is regarded as a valuable part of the student experience at UNSW and as such is recognised through UNSW Advantage. UNSW Advantage (www.student.unsw.edu.au/advantage) is the vehicle through which the University recognises and accredits extra-curricular and co-curricular activities. Such accreditation promotes the importance of learning in the non-academic space, particularly through student engagement in professional development and volunteering. Accredited activities are recorded on the Australian Higher Education Graduation Statement (AHEGS) received by all students graduating from an Australian university. AHEGS enables both academic and other achievements of the student to be recorded in one statement. The aim is to help both the mobility and professional recognition of Australian graduates within an increasingly global marketplace.

UNSW Advantage provides the student with a tangible record of their participation in the Leadership Program. The Program encourages students to engage through its marketing. It is marketed as a tool for personal and professional development, and as a means to enhance employability through supporting the development of the soft skills involved in effective leadership. However, the underlying philosophy and one that emerges more strongly in the course of the

Program is that leadership involves social responsibility and bringing about social change.

As in service learning courses, the Leadership Program provides a structured experience to develop and hone learning (in this case soft skills). As it does not sit within the structure of a degree, the Program can be offered with flexibility. It can be entered and completed at any time during a student's enrolment (undergraduate or postgraduate), and stepped through at the individual's pace. In total, the Program encompasses 30 h of time commitment for all components, 20 h of which must be volunteer work within the wider community.

The teaching component of the Program focuses on a menu of workshops which enable knowledge and skill acquisition. As more is learnt about the value of different workshops to the overall experience of the student, the menu of offerings is adapted accordingly. The majority of these workshops are taught by the professional staff of the University rather than the academic staff. The range of professional skills embodied across a large group of staff are utilised to present workshops of value. Presenters volunteer their expertise and the resultant workload is absorbed into their normal activities. Workshops are interactive and practical. Four electives can be chosen based on the interest of the student. The topics range from handling conflict effectively, to understanding personality using tools such as MBTI, to the practical exploration of design thinking and entrepreneurship. One workshop 'The Introduction to the UNSW Leadership Program' is regarded as core and must be completed by all participants. As part of the flexible nature of the Program, this compulsory workshop is offered online.

As with service learning, reflective practice is an important part of the learning experience of the student. Within the curricular space, the use of reflective practice is not confined to service learning. It is common within many degrees, particularly within education, medicine and allied health. In this co-curricular space, participants are led through a structured self-reflection practice. At the start of the Program students reflect on their understanding of leadership and those they regard as leaders. At the end of the Program they have the opportunity to reflect on their own journey across the Program. Sometimes part of that journey is a realisation of how valuable self-reflection can be.

> I know we all groan when it comes to self-reflection but something I have learnt in my study is how crucial it is to your own development and being able to respond well to others.

> Participating student 2014

The final component of the Leadership Program is designed to foster the sense of social responsibility in participants, through the opportunity of meaningful community engagement (often termed civic engagement in the USA). Students are required to set up their own volunteering placements. This is a deliberate strategy to enable students to consolidate some of the soft skills they have been developing in workshops. As an offshoot, it also means that there is no need for a significant university infrastructure to manage the placements. Chosen placements can be in external not for profit organisations or supporting the socially responsible work in the University. In order to make the volunteering experience meaningful, students are encouraged to identify social causes or issues that they care about. While students find their own placements, there is structure and support for the process. Part of structuring the experience was the development of a community engagement action plan template to guide students in securing a placement. Students are also given support in having meaningful dialogue with organisations about their placements.

The reach of the Leadership Program throughout the wider community has been extensive. Since 2012 students have undertaken over 9500 volunteering hours and have engaged with 233 not for profit organisations. Many of these organisations are working with the most vulnerable members of Australian society addressing local, national and indeed global needs. Volunteering has found UNSW students working in aged care, community and welfare, environmental and conservation agencies, health, human rights, with people with disabilities and with children experiencing educational disadvantage.

It is evident from the feedback from students that it is the volunteering experience that has the most impact. Not only does it enable students to enhance and expand new skills and knowledge but it also enhances personal learning and growth. In some cases, it brings about life changing decisions.

> It's really good that it (the Program) gets people giving back to the community and realising they were more of a leader than they thought they were, and that they have the potential to enact change whether on a large scale or not.
>
> Participating student 2014

> Firstly, attending the many Leadership workshops led me to reflect upon the fulfilment and enjoyment I found in life. This contemplation led me to realise that I was not enjoying my Architectural education as much as the experience I was gaining as a mentor in the primary school. The connections I formed with the children while volunteering gave me such enjoyment and fulfilment that upon finishing my Bachelor of Architecture I decided that instead of pursuing an architecture career, I would find work as a Teacher's Aide. I am now thoroughly enjoying my work in a school and am strongly considering pursuing a teaching degree.
>
> Participating student 2015

For UNSW, the community organisations providing opportunities are very much seen as valued partners in nurturing socially responsible students. It is also evident that there is reciprocal benefits from the volunteering with, as indicated below, the organisations gaining from taking on the student volunteers.

> The partnership with UNSW has been an asset to our organisation. Through the Leadership Program we have had some fantastic volunteers come on board.

> The partnership with the Program has had significant benefits. We have been able to tap into a body of engaged volunteers through a very easy process.
>
> Community not for profit partners

The UNSW Leadership Program has proved to be a successful and cost-effective strategy in engaging students in a way that is mutually beneficial to the University, students and the wider community. Over 2500 participants across the student profile of the University are currently enrolled. The Program is popular with international students (25% of all program enrolments) and undergraduate students (85% of enrolments). The gender breakdown broadly reflects the UNSW profile with 55% of enrolments from female students. In many instances students have remained volunteering after the conclusion of their 20 h.

> I am continuing to volunteer at the organisation where I did my community engagement hours. I think the Leadership Program is a fantastic way of making UNSW students more community minded and confident in their leadership abilities.
>
> Participating student 2014

This supports the evidence from the USA suggesting that such community engagement enhances an ongoing sense of social responsibility. The Leadership Program itself supports the notion that structured opportunities for such community engagement do not need to lie solely in the curricular space.

8.3 Social Responsibility Through Student Volunteering Within the UNSW ASPIRE Outreach Program

The second strategy discussed in this chapter takes a very different approach to nurturing social responsibility. It takes the approach of engaging students as volunteers within a university program whose mandate is addressing social injustice and working towards a just society. A long standing and strong partnership between student volunteers and a program that exemplifies the social responsibility of the University has been developed within the ASPIRE outreach program (www.aspire.unsw.edu.au).

ASPIRE works with a number of schools within communities in the state of New South Wales (NSW) that have been identified as disadvantaged in socio-economic terms. These communities traditionally have low progression rates to university overall, and particularly low progression rates to the research intensive Group of Eight (GO8) universities of which UNSW is a member. The aims of ASPIRE are to work within these communities to enable aspirations, raise awareness and support academic attainment in order that students can make university education a choice for them. The program has grown from two Sydney high schools in 2007 to over 50 primary, high and central (educating students from Kindergarten to the end of senior school in Year 12) schools in 2016 situated across Sydney and rural and remote NSW.

Outside Sydney the program works with students from Kindergarten through the whole school lifecycle. In Sydney the focus is primarily on high school students. In working with these students, ASPIRE has implemented a longitudinal and sustained approach. The program partners with the same schools over a number of years, in order to work with the students year on year. An educational framework is employed where activities build on the work undertaken in the previous year. The school students are given multiple opportunities to engage with the University with activities taking place on campus, in school and in the wider community.

As with the Leadership Program, the approach taken by ASPIRE has been grounded in an evidence base. Its development has been particularly informed by the Aimhigher program that ran for a number of years in England until 2011. What flowed from Aimhigher was a wealth of practitioner-led experience and evidence. Some of that evidence related to the use of university students in programs setting out to widen access to university in disadvantaged communities. A scan of the literature flowing from the practice of others in engaging university students in outreach programs informed ASPIRE in several ways. A major consideration was the benefits to the school students. These included interacting with university students who acted as role models to change negative perceptions about university (Porter 2010; Church 2011). They also included these students having a valuable source of information about university culture and processes (Church 2011; Thompson 2010). This source of 'hot knowledge' negated to a certain extent the lack of relevant family social capital. The flow-on effects from interactions raised motivation and led to academic success (Roberts and Weston 2011).

In light of the research, involving university students was regarded as a crucial part of the ASPIRE program. The decision in 2009 to engage on a voluntary level rather than the model of offering paid positions preferred within the English context was in part due to funding (up until 2016, ASPIRE has been largely funded from uncertain external sources) but was largely driven as a result of discussions with UNSW students themselves. There was a recognition that a university education and attending a GO8 university in particular gave them a place of privilege. Students wanted opportunities to engage differently with the university and to 'give back' to society more broadly.

As a result, the ASPIRE Ambassador program was developed. As with the Leadership Program, the ASPIRE program can be regarded as sitting within the co-curricular space. Student participation is accredited through UNSW Advantage and appears on AHEGS. University students engage with school students across the breadth of the program activities both in schools and on campus. Engagement may be in the form of leading activities, providing case studies of their own learning journeys, starring in videos on ASPIRE themes, working one on one with school students or working in the ASPIRE communities—in Homework Clubs for example. More recently, Ambassadors have assisted in fundraising activities to support the work of ASPIRE.

Over the years since ASPIRE Ambassadors were established, much has been learnt of the value of the scheme from both the school student perspective and, equally importantly, the UNSW student perspective. There have also been learnings for the ASPIRE team in managing the student volunteers.

The value of enabling school students with a lack of relevant social capital regarding university education to engage with ASPIRE Ambassadors has supported the international evidence. In a detailed evaluation of the program conducted with the partner schools in 2014, one of the major themes to emerge was the positive effect of the Ambassadors. Teachers identified two key benefits. Firstly, the 'hot knowledge' that passed between Ambassadors and school students. This exchange which often occurred in incidental conversations was aided by the level of comfort school students felt in asking questions of someone close in age and actually living the experience. Secondly, teachers highlighted the practical help in navigating university admissions processes and forms from those who had just experienced it. Qualitative feedback through interviews with teachers in Sydney partner schools included the following:

> Having those Ambassadors as well, that really makes a difference, having young people that look like them and are able to talk to them about uni.
>
> They're always friendly, they're always delightful. I think they love coming to our school. Yeah, very friendly; they want to engage.
>
> Having students interact with the Ambassadors that come out to the school. When it is another voice other than ourselves giving the students opportunity to reflect on their future I think the students listen more.
>
> Sydney school teachers 2014

Feedback from school students suggests that they do not consciously tap into the value of the Ambassadors at the time, with the majority of feedback centring on the fun they have had interacting with Ambassadors. The transfer of 'hot knowledge' is something teachers verbalise rather than the students. In a few cases, the role of the university student has been in the forefront of the school student experience, and encouragingly, some school students have expressed a wish to become an Ambassador in the future.

> It was really good that we had the chance to interact with the students from the uni because we got to ask questions about the campus and what they do.
>
> I want to be an ambassador when I am in uni.
>
> If I get to go to UNSW, I want to be an ASPIRE Ambassador when I am there.
>
> ASPIRE school students 2015

The value of the volunteering experience expressed by ASPIRE Ambassadors has been interesting. In the 2014 evaluation, Ambassadors were surveyed as part of the process. The data indicated the major reasons for initially becoming an ASPIRE Ambassador centred on self and in particular, personal development and improving career prospects. However, when asked an open-ended question on what they liked most about being an Ambassador, what emerged was a strong theme of altruism. This sense of social responsibility, which was also seen as an outcome in the structured Leadership Program, may be the reason why ASPIRE has a high percentage of returning volunteers across the life of their degree.

> The best thing about being an Ambassador is seeing students' attitudes change after we speak with them about university. It's so rewarding to have them come in, quite unsure of

university and with many questions, and then to have them finish, being much more likely to consider university as an achievable option for future study.

I like being able to interact with school students and share my knowledge and experiences to them. It is a very warm and happy feeling knowing I have made an impact in another person's life and their choices for the future.

I like being able to interact with students whose position I was once in. Being in a position in which I can make some sort of difference is really rewarding.

Being able to help school students with their questions about university and post-school study. In particular, giving them hope and setting straight the facts about what types of students can make it to university. The most rewarding thing about being an ASPIRE Ambassador is giving recounts of one's own experiences about university and later high school, the student who once never thought about the idea of going to university has a renewed sense of optimism about university and seriously considering it as an option for the future.

ASPIRE Ambassadors 2014

The initial focus on self may in part be influenced by the background of the Ambassadors completing the survey. While approximately 50% were first in family to attend university, the vast majority had gone to schools where there was a high level of social capital. With students who attended ASPIRE partner schools (and therefore received their education in a context of disadvantage), the sense of altruism appears to emerge as a driver for becoming an Ambassador.

I wanted to be an ASPIRE Ambassador to act as a role model for other school students. To show them they can go to uni too, just like me.

Once I found out I could volunteer for ASPIRE I was really excited as I always wanted to give back because I was so thankful for the Ambassadors who came when I was in high school because they inspired me.

I would like to share my story and tell people I was in the same shoes as them because I feel that it is not that effective when someone who isn't as disadvantaged as you comes and says you can do it but when you know someone who was exactly where you are ends up going where you want to go it makes it a lot easier and helps build that bridge.

ASPIRE Ambassadors 2015

Another reason why the UNSW students often return to volunteer in ASPIRE may lie in the soft skills that they recognise they develop through participation. These skills in particular relate to communication, team building, problem solving and leaderships skills. They mirror many that are taught in the Leadership Program, and support the notion that the experience of volunteering itself is a valuable learning tool.

It brings me out of my shell and makes me more confident.

I have better communication and leadership skills through doing various workshops and events and I have been able to learn strategies which work well when working with young people.

I don't even know where to begin. Being an ASPIRE Ambassador has definitely taught me some new skills and just opened my eyes to the wider community especially after interacting with such a wide variety of students from different schools, cultures, etc. I've learnt new leadership and team work skills.

Developed better communication skills, good teamwork skills working with other Ambassadors, leadership skills when leading your group, pushed me out of my comfort zone a bit, good improvisation/problem solving skills when faced with a challenge, and has also widened my view on the world through allowing me to experience and observe different cultures and low socio-economic areas and has helped me to understand the challenges they face and how real they actually are. In a way, has also been a very humbling experience and has been in line with my passion for helping other people.

ASPIRE Ambassadors 2014/2015

The involvement of student volunteers within ASPIRE has had demonstrable benefits to the overall success of the program. The commitment and dedication of UNSW students to the program over the years has been hugely encouraging to all involved. Each year ASPIRE works with between 150 and 200 volunteers. Since 2010 the number of students wishing to be volunteers has outweighed the number that can be accommodated within the program. Ambassadors have volunteered over 20,000 h of their time both during semester and during holidays. There have been over 3000 instances of Ambassador participation in activities in that period. The students who are volunteering are high achievers, often in double degrees or in prestige degrees such as Medicine and Law. It is recognised that the demographics of Ambassadors do reflect the domestic student profile of the University quite well, particularly in the gender split (with 60% being female) but there is a lack of representation from certain ethnic cohorts that are heavily represented in partner schools. International students are also less likely to volunteer in the program. Strategies to encourage underrepresented cohorts to volunteer are being examined.

What has been most encouraging has been the number of students who return to volunteer over the life of their degree and the increase in the number of Ambassadors who attended ASPIRE schools, went through the program and are now acting as very tangible role models, giving back to their school communities. This thread of personal connection that now runs through ASPIRE has helped build a growing sense of community around the outreach being undertaken as part of the University strategy to work towards a just society.

One major difference between student volunteering within the Leadership Program and ASPIRE is that in the first instance the organisation where they gain a placement manages the volunteers. In the case of ASPIRE, the volunteers are managed through the program itself. Since 2010, a number of learnings about managing a large force of student volunteers to successfully work in potentially sensitive communities have occurred for the ASPIRE team in how to manage a large group of student volunteers. Not least has been a clear recognition of the reciprocal nature of the volunteering so that the needs of all parties in the process are met.

Early on, the need for a selection and training process was recognised and put in place. This was to give some rigour and validity to participation and to ensure Ambassadors were set up for success. This approach is backed up by the evidence of others in the sector (Sanders and Higham 2012). The process has been refined over the years as more experience of managing volunteers within this outreach space has been gained. Applicants are provided with a job description and are required to address the following set of selection criteria through an online process:

- Willingness to participate in at least two ASPIRE activities per semester (ASPIRE activities are usually 4–6 h long)
- Belief in the potential of all school students regardless of personal circumstance
- The ability to relate to young people and be a positive role model
- The ability to communicate sensitively to students and community members from Indigenous and diverse cultural backgrounds
- Willingness to share experiences of university life
- A good understanding of the barriers that can prevent young people from low socio-economic backgrounds from accessing higher education.

Potential Ambassadors are then invited to attend a group interview and activity followed by successful applicants receiving training. This process has ensured that Ambassadors have a very good understanding of their role. Roles are further clarified and explored at briefings prior to major activities. It is evident from evaluation that the training is successful and that the volunteers perceive their role as intended by the program team.

> From an Ambassador's point of view, I believe we give school students a better perspective of what university is and more importantly the type of people that go to university. This especially clarifies the misconception that to go to uni you have to be a nerd or always having to get 99/100, thus in turn giving hope to some school students and making them see that university is not completely out of their reach as they might have thought. In addition to this, the other main role I believe we have is to provide school students with general information about tertiary study and the various options available while giving more in-depth details about university study based on my own experiences.
>
> ASPIRE Ambassador 2014

The role of Ambassadors has also expanded over time to recognise the unique skills of the university students and to provide deliberate opportunities for their personal development. As a result of feedback, Ambassadors are now provided with more opportunities to take lead roles in the running of activities both in school and on campus. Opportunities are also provided for them to develop and run subject-specific workshops in their areas of expertise. These academic enrichment activities have mutual benefits for both the volunteers and the partner schools. The Ambassadors are able to develop and display a range of skills to impart knowledge. School students are able to access learning not available through the normal curriculum.

Probably the biggest learning has been how to successfully manage a changing group of volunteers to maximise participation and to promote a win-win environment for both the volunteers and the program. One of the keys has been to have a member of the team responsible for the management of the volunteers. This is not only from the practical aspect of managing participation but also in the building of relationships and identifying non-monetary ways of rewarding participants. During

2015 the volunteer coordinator put on several social activities to bring Ambassadors together with each other and the wider ASPIRE team. Recognition was provided through the offering of professional development opportunities related to the outreach work. This included a cultural humility workshop aimed at increasing awareness when working in the many multicultural ASPIRE schools. The combination of events have in turn created a stronger sense of community articulated by the Ambassadors as highly valued.

> I really enjoy the fact we get to meet lots of people who are also Ambassadors and this is definitely a highlight. I have made many friends along the journey and thoroughly enjoy every moment of volunteering.

ASPIRE Ambassador 2014

A surprising result from teacher feedback on the value of the Ambassadors was the importance placed on the Ambassadors working with students in the school itself. It had been thought that the greatest value was involvement in the on-campus events. Given this feedback, one obstacle that remains for the ASPIRE program is how Ambassadors can be linked into the classroom in rural and remote partner schools. Schools range from between 350 and 720 km from UNSW. The travel to the furthest school requires a plane trip and a four hours' drive. Engaging in regional or remote schools involves being away from the university for up to five days. This time commitment means that over 95% of Ambassadors cannot be involved in rural and remote school activities. An option being explored and will be evaluated is to use video conferencing. This does have some obstacles of its own, including the reliability of internet connections in rural areas and the engagement of students through this medium. Currently a small scale pilot is being run as a value-add to the main ASPIRE program, where Ambassadors are reading to students in Year 2 via video conferencing. A further option under consideration is to tap into postgraduate research students who are likely to have more flexibility of time. Currently, most volunteers have come from the undergraduate ranks although more students who are moving into fulltime postgraduate studies are remaining as Ambassadors.

8.4   Conclusion

As mentioned at the start of this chapter the UNSW Leadership Program and ASPIRE employ very different approaches to nurturing socially responsible students. One approach enables breadth in that it can reach and potentially appeal to more of the student body. The other enables depth in that it can provide a more sustained and potentially richer volunteering experience but in doing so cannot involve as many of the student body. It is evident though, whether the structured approach or less structured approach is taken, that the outcomes for the volunteers, partners and UNSW are positive.

Student volunteering does not always create a win win win situation (Brewis et al. 2010) but the evidence indicates that for both of these programs, it is the case.

Multiple benefits have emerged for and been identified by the student volunteers. The wider community, whether schools or nonprofit organisations, have clearly articulated how they value the commitment and skills of UNSW students who have given their time. For UNSW, these are two successful examples of the 2025 Strategy and university social responsibility in action. For those involved in both programs there is the joy and satisfaction of seeing UNSW students embarking on what is hopefully a life long journey to actively work towards a just society.

One story exemplifies this journey. The journey of one student took her from an ASPIRE partner school, to being an ASPIRE Ambassador working back in her school, to becoming a member of the ASPIRE team managing the student volunteers. The journey did not end there. In 2016, it took her to Pakistan, her country of origin, to work for a nonprofit organisation in the challenging area of education for women and girls. Social responsibility is in action.

References

Brewis, G., Russell, J., & Holdsworth, C. (2010). *Bursting the Bubble: Students, Volunteering and the Community Research Summary*. Retrieved from the National Co-ordinating Centre for Public Engagement: https://www.publicengagement.ac.uk/sites/default/files/publication/bursting_the_bubble_summary_report.pdf

Church, E. (2011). *An Evaluation of the Aimhigher Northamptonshire Vocational Programme*. Retrieved from Higher Education Academy: https://www.heacademy.ac.uk/system/files/ahnorthants-evaluation_of_vocational_programme.pdf

Petkus, E. (2000). A theoretical and practical framework for service learning in marketing: Kolb's experiential learning cycle. *Journal of Marketing Education, 22*(1), 64–70.

Porter, S. (2010). *A sporting chance: Boys into higher education using a football project (Report of the second phase evaluation)*. Retrieved from Higher Education Academy: https://www.heacademy.ac.uk/system/files/ahleics-boys_into_he_using_football_project.doc

Roberts A., & Weston, K. (2011). *Making a difference through mentoring: An evaluation of the impact of mentoring practices undertaken through the Aimhigher programme in Hertfordshire schools*. Retrieved from Higher Education Academy: https://www.heacademy.ac.uk/system/files/herts_making_difference_through_mentoring.pdf

Sanders, J., & Higham, L. (2012). *The role of higher education students in widening access, retention and success. A literature synthesis of the Widening Access, Student Retention and Success National Programmes Archive*. Retrieved from Higher Education Academy: https://www.heacademy.ac.uk/system/files/wasrs_sanders.pdf

Thompson, M. (2010). *Birmingham & Solihull Associates Scheme Evaluation Report 2009-2010: "Working together to make a difference..."*. Retrieved from Higher Education Academy: https://www.heacademy.ac.uk/system/files/ahbs-working_together_to_make_a_difference.pdf

UNSW. (n.d.). Retrieved from http://student.unsw.edu.au/leadership

UNSW. (n.d.). Retrieved from www.2025.unsw.edu.au

UNSW. (2015). UNSW 2025 strategy: Our strategic proprieties and themes.[Online Brochure]. Retrieved from http://www.smh.com.au/cqstatic/gkdrkt/unsw_2025strategy%20(1).pdf

UNSW Advantage (n.d.). Retrieved from http://student.unsw.edu.au/advantage

UNSW Aspire. (n.d.). Retrieved from http://www.aspire.unsw.edu.au/

Chapter 9
The Paradoxical Fabric of Hope in Academy-Community Partnerships: Challenging Binary Constructions of Conflict-Cooperation

Dassi Postan Aizik, Roni Strier and Faisal Azaiza

Abstract The global interest in University Community Partnerships (UCP's) has made the study of these initiatives an important field of research. Studies show that the increased number of UCP's stems from the fact that both parties see in these shared ventures an opportunity to achieve reciprocal goals. Universities perceive them as a way to show their social commitment to the community, while simultaneously expanding the scope of academic activities and goals. Communities for their part, look at these projects as ways to promote their own social agendas and prioritize critical issues. However, along with these expected mutual gains, studies have also recognized these partnerships as highly complex, often conflictive enterprises, which may generate multiple internal tensions due to competing interests and power disputes. In many cases, the complex nature of these partnerships may severely challenge the chances for their success and sustainability to the extent that studies portray the contested nature of these partnerships as dysfunctional. This chapter challenges this theoretical perspective and offers an alternative theoretical framework to re-examine the binary construction of cooperation-conflict. Using the Organizational Paradox Theory and based on a comprehensive UCP established in the University of Haifa, Israel, this chapter analyses four areas of paradox that illustrate the complexity of UCP. The first part of the chapter will present a review of current research on UCP's and briefly introduces the Organizational Paradox theoretical framework. The second part describes the methodology of the study. Based on our case study, the third part examines four cases that exemplify paradoxes in UCP. In the discussion section, we elaborate on the contribution of Organizational Paradox Theory to the understanding of

D.P. Aizik · R. Strier (✉) · F. Azaiza
University of Haifa, Haifa, Israel
e-mail: rstrier@univ.haifa.ac.il

D.P. Aizik
e-mail: dpostan@univ.haifa.ac.il

F. Azaiza
e-mail: azaiza@univ.haifa.ac.il

© Springer Nature Singapore Pte Ltd. 2017
D.T.L. Shek and R.M. Hollister (eds.), *University Social Responsibility and Quality of Life*, Quality of Life in Asia 8,
DOI 10.1007/978-981-10-3877-8_9

academic-community partnerships, culminating with recommendations for both research and practice.

Keywords Academy-community partnership · Community partnership · Social responsibility · Organizational Paradox Theory · Civic engagement

9.1 Theoretical Background

9.1.1 University-Community Partnerships

UCP is a broad and vague concept that covers a wide variety of initiatives, actions, and programs carried out in cooperation between academic institutions and communities. These collaborative endeavors may include action research projects, learning activities and in-service training of students in social services, joint programs in academia and community educational institutions, and even community-based training programs (Russell and Flynn 2001). The vagueness of the term UCP derives from several reasons. First, these partnerships are characterized by different types of involvement, various forms of action models, differing scopes of activity and levels of commitment. Second, the concept of "community" in itself is a complex and dynamic construction that is subject to diverse interpretations. A community may be represented by individuals (residents), institutions (school or community agencies), or social groups (geographic, functional or virtual communities). As a result, different representations of community may generate multiple perceptions regarding the concept of academy-community partnership. Lastly, the concept of "partnership" is not less complex and is subject to different interpretations. A private initiative by a researcher to conduct a study using participatory research methods in the community may be perceived as an academy-community partnership, while at the other end of the spectrum academy-community partnership can be defined as a joint, long-term, comprehensive, strategic and systematic effort carried on by academic institutions and communities. For example, Butcher et al. (2011) distinguish between "transactional partnerships" and "transformational partnerships". Transactional partnerships are based on the achievement of individual or institutional interests through a process of exchange. Although both parties may benefit from this process, the scope of the partnership is very limited. In contrast, a transformational partnership may have many dimensions, including ideological, ethical, social, and organizational dimensions in which both parties aspire towards a common goal, applying their abilities and assets to deal with complex social issues. These transformational partnerships are characterized by multiple factors such as shared planning, management and evaluation, reciprocity, long-term commitment, strong leadership support, and a significant involvement of the University in the process of building up the community's capability. In this chapter, we refer to transformational UCP's in the second and broader sense of the term as an institutional partnership built up over time between academic institutions and communities.

The multiplying number of partnerships between academia and the community in recent decades is a response to large-scale changes in societal, economic and institutional settings. These changes affected the organizational and academic culture of research institutions of higher education (Brown-Luthango 2013; Carlton et al. 2009; Fisher et al. 2005). Many research universities have responded positively to the call to expand the traditional concept of academic scholarship beyond academic research, through programs and activities that promoted a new type of "engaged scholarship" (Boyer 1990, 1996). Governments and various financial institutions also contributed to this process by supporting academic-community initiatives around the world. In this way, research universities have begun to deal with pressing social issues through innovative alliances and long-term relationships with communities (Amey and Brown 2005; Arches and Aponte-Pares 2005).

This development has made UCP's into an important subject for research. Studies cover many diverse topics including, but not limited to their impact on academic institutions and community (D'Augelli 2006; Dulmus and Cristalli 2012; Buys and Bursnall 2007), knowledge creation and development of teaching methods (Farquhar and Dobson 2004; Johnson Butterfield and Soska 2005; Suarez-Balcazar and Kinney 2006), the impact of academy-community partnerships on creating social capital (Feagan and Rossiter 2011; Gronski and Pigg 2000; Mulroy 2008), the role of academic-community partnerships in the process of advocacy and promotion of social rights (Mulroy 2004), characteristics of successful partnerships and effective tools (Stewart and Alrutz 2012; Taylor et al. 2004), and the study of the partnership versus conflict paradigm (Jarvis-Selinger et al. 2008; Kaufman 2004). These studies have shown that the construction of UCP's is a very complex process, which includes various tensions and conflicts (Strier 2011, 2014).

Research indicates numerous barriers that impede the creation of cooperation and mutuality between universities and communities (Cobb and Rubin 2006; Maurrasse 2002). These difficulties relate to the hierarchical and bureaucratic institutional structure of universities as opposed to the more informal and loose structures of communities as well as the nature of the relationship between them (Gronski and Pigg 2000; Huxham and Vangen 2000). In light of this complexity, it is clear that the continuous organizational efforts required to maintain the viability and vitality of these partnerships are inevitable. One of the major sources of conflict in such partnerships relates to the fundamental unequal power relations existing between the parties (Gray 2003, 2004), wherein inequality in power relations between the academic researchers, residents and community agencies damages the level of trust, and raises feelings of exploitation and lack of mutuality (Dantnow 1998). Research shows that academic institutions tend to benefit more from long-term partnerships than do local communities, an element which generates negative feelings and distrust towards academia (Perkins et al. 2004). These studies indicate that the development of significant partnerships is affected by organizational tensions, conflicts of interest, bureaucratic constraints, defects in planning and implementation of projects, lack of an ongoing evaluation process, competition for resources and recognition, diverse knowledge from various stakeholders, a clash of values, and mistrust and uncertainty about the feasibility of the results (Altman 2005; Maginn 2007). While these issues are seen in most studies as barriers to cooperation, this article suggests an alternative theoretical framework, which challenges the binary concept presenting cooperation and conflict as opposing concepts. This perspective highlights the relationship between cooperation and conflict as inherent to the development of powerful and meaningful partnerships.

9.1.2   Paradox and Partnership

Paradox situations refer to a state in which opposing factors coexist at the same time (Strier 2014). Various studies indicate partnerships to be complex organizational entities characterized by situations of simultaneous conflict and cooperation, namely the coexistence of mutually exclusive elements (Luscher et al. 2006). The concept of paradox contains two main components. The first is underlying tension. Or, elements, that seem to make sense when presented independently, but appear unrelated, or inappropriate when joined together. The second component relates to the strategies and coping mechanisms employed by partners to deal with the tensions, which arise from the existence of the opposing factors (Smith and Lewis 2011). Partnerships are inherently complex organizational operations in that they are specifically designed to face complex missions by balancing between competing interests and demands in varied environments (Luscher and Lewis 2008). Desivilla and Palgi (2011), describe partnerships as entities found in a dialectical discourse. They are created to allow cooperation in the realization of common goals, which would have not been achieved by any one of the parties, had they acted independently. However, in a contradictory way, partnerships encourage each of the parties to emphasize their own goals and advocate for their own interests, often at the expense of other partners. Even though balancing these tensions may help overcome small obstacles and improve short-term results, from a paradox theory perspective, in order for the partnership to be sustainable, organizations must constantly strive to cope with multiple, different, and oftentimes contradictory demands. The paradox perspective allows integration of collaboration and conflict in that it shows duality, uncertainty and ambiguity as structured characteristics of healthy organizational complexity (Lewis 2000).

9.2   Methodology

This research is based on case study methodology (Yin 2013; Stake and Savolainen 1995). A case study is an in-depth examination of the particular, where researchers seek to increase their understanding of the phenomena studied. The underlying assumption of this method is that case studies are essential for the development of social sciences (Feagin et al. 1991; Flyvbjerg 2006). A case study is the main study design used by researchers to study complex phenomena (Richardson, 1994), and is useful for both generating and testing hypotheses (Flyvbjerg 2006).

The methodology of case studies raises controversy concerning its scientific validity. Flyvbjerg (2006) describes five common assumptions among scholars who question the scientific validity of the methodology: theoretical knowledge is more valuable than practical information, which results from the use of case study; a single case cannot be used to generalize, therefore case studies do not contribute to the development of the social sciences; a case study is an appropriate methodology for the development of new research hypotheses, but not to test research hypotheses or for the development of a theory; verification of case study findings is difficult; and it is difficult to collect specific case studies and incorporate their findings into a theory about broader phenomenon. Despite the general consensus that they find in some circles, Flyvbjerg (2006) argues that these assumptions are incorrect and that the development of social sciences will suffer and even lose its unique contribution without the use of primary and in-depth case studies.

Sabar (2001), characterizes case study as inductive because it presents the data of the situation regardless of hypotheses, allows for the expression of a lot of sensitivity, the ability to diagnose and express complex situations from different points of view and its content is mostly descriptive. Dayan (2003) argues that a system of case studies is preferred when investigating contemporary phenomenon in their natural environment and when the boundaries between phenomenon and context are not entirely clear. It is possible to distinguish between three types of case study: an internal case study that serves as a way to become deeply acquainted with the specific case in order to stand on its nature and understand it better; an instrumental case study is carried out not only to understand the case itself, but also to gain more insight about a specific topic; and a collective case study which gathers a number of specific cases, by which general insights are revealed. This study uses an instrumental case study to facilitate a deeper understanding of complex interactions in UCP's.

9.3 Case Study: The University of Haifa "Flagship Program: Facing Social Exclusion Promoting Solidarity"

The University of Haifa "Flagship program" is an UCP between the university and excluded communities in western Haifa, Israel. The program's long-term goals are threefold: to reduce the level of polarization, to promote solidarity between the various groups comprising Israeli society, and to encourage the integration of excluded groups into mainstream society. The "Flagship Program" is an interdisciplinary institutional initiative supported by the top university's management levels (i.e. provost and president's offices), which encompasses all of the university's faculties. Thus, it enables faculty, students and administrative staff from all departments of the institution to take part in community efforts within the campus and outside with the local community. The "Flagship program" aims to create a sustainable partnership with the local authorities, community centers, NGO's, and residents from excluded communities and groups.

The program began operating in 2011 with the support of the Planning and Budgeting Committee of the Israeli Council for Higher Education (ICHE). The ICHE encourages universities and colleges in Israel to establish institutional academic-community partnerships, and develop civic engagement courses. Such courses combine an academic curriculum of student's fieldwork with people from underprivileged groups. The University of Haifa is located in the city of Haifa in the north of Israel. Once an industrial city off the coastline, today Haifa is a modern metropolis composed of a variety of groups, facing the challenges of a post-industrial city in a multi-cultural environment. Jewish residents living closely together with Arab Muslims and Christian residents as well as other minorities comprise the city's diverse population. This creates a rich fabric, but at the same time, one that poses great challenges to co-existence and inclusion. The University campus reflects this wide diversity, attracting the variety of different groups living in and around Haifa as well as students and faculty from other parts of the country. In this regard, the city and the University of Haifa are excellent fields for the development of socially inclusive academic projects.

The Flagship partnership was designed to express the uniqueness of the University in promoting innovation and excellence in the study of Israeli society, enhancing values of multiculturalism and community involvement. Its model combines four areas of activities: the first are civic engagement courses that combine academic classes and fieldwork. These courses offer students community activities with academic training in various departments such as social work, the-ater, music, law and education. The second area of activity is devised in order to widen the accessibility of academic knowledge to the community through the development of a unique program called "Academia in the Community". Through "Academia in the Community", the University's faculty joins the community in planning and running multi-disciplinary courses held for residents and agencies in local community centers. These courses are based on community needs as expressed by activists and professionals from local services. Courses are action-oriented to support the conversion of academic knowledge into social change practices. The third area of the program is a community project greenhouse. To help neighborhoods develop their own community entrepreneurships, researchers from the University of Haifa provide academic support to community projects that fight exclusion in various aspects or promote inclusion of diverse groups in society. Residents and community agencies, together with researchers and students all take part in a range of projects aimed at creating positive change for people and groups who face social exclusion, such as immigrants from Ethiopia, partnerships of Arab and Jewish residents, elderly people with cognitive disabilities, children with spe-cial needs etc. The fourth channel, which accompanies all projects, is aimed at developing knowledge that can exert change. To reach that goal a unique research center, The Interdisciplinary Center for the Study of Poverty and Social Exclusion was established. The center promotes interdisciplinary, action-research projects in the field.

Although all parties involved are highly committed to the success of the program, the development and implementation of this complex mosaic uncovered many tensions within the university and between academy and community. The following section will present four cases using Paradox Theory as a unifying theme for analysis of such complexities.

9.4 Academy-Community Partnerships- Areas of Paradox

This section presents four areas of paradox that characterize academic-community partnerships. These areas of paradox relate to tensions built into the establishment, management and development of these initiatives (Andriopoulos and Lewis 2009). The case studies presented are based on personal interviews with program staff members and community partners. Examples are presented at length in order to provide a rich description of the case and reflect in detail the areas of paradox; however, some details were presented more vaguely in order to maintain confidentiality and anonymity of participants.

9.4.1 Top-Down Work Versus Bottom-Up Work

One of the most common goals of academic-community partnerships is to promote social change (Werkmeister Rozas and Negroni 2008). However, such change necessarily involves actions of political significance that may be highly politically sensitive (Cherry and Shefner 2004). Therefore, it is not surprising that academy-community partnerships may take actions that create conflicts with well-anchored political and economic interests (Davies et al. 2007). Such actions may create tensions with local or government authorities, which in turn might harm future university's fundraising from private or public sources (Arches and Apontes-Pares 2005). In light of the potential risk of political tensions a partnership that aims at promoting social change is likely to create, clear and firm top-down management support and backup on the part of University leadership is needed. The university's highest institutional levels must be involved and committed to change.

On the other hand, a transformational, egalitarian and strong partnership between academia and community requires a more participative, emancipatory, and grassroots orientation. A bottom-up, collaborative orientation develops as part of a learning culture of consulting with local professionals and activists. It demands an attitude that prefers non-hierarchical experiences and equal access to decision making. In order to adapt itself to the community empowerment approach, the organizational culture of academy-community partnerships should reflect a participative and democratic nature. Only by creating an open organizational environment, which is non-bureaucratic and empowering to the community, can universities offer an equal, mutually beneficial partnership. However, in order to achieve this, the University authorities must agree to intentionally give up to a great degree of organizational control in the management of the partnership and be ready to delegate power from the managerial level to professionals and members of the community in the field.

A top-down vs. bottom-up paradox involves dealing with aspects of control and decision making as partnership members try to maintain institutional control as part of the necessary top-down approach, while still striving to uphold an egalitarian distribution of control with the community, as part of the bottom-up approach. Because it involves the core issues of the joint process in terms of planning and funding, this paradox is perhaps the most significant source of tension in UCP's. These tensions may occur due to disagreement between academic authorities with decisions and actions carried out by members of community, faculty or students at the field level. In other cases, tensions may be a result of claims made by different parties due to decisions taken by the academic authorities without their involvement.

From its inception, the "Flagship Program" was trying to work towards a more equitable approach to decision making. Therefore, instead of creating a full intervention program based on academic knowledge, it was decided to start the process from the bottom-up through the mapping and identification of needs among residents and agencies in the region. This move was designed with the aim of identifying significant issues for the population in the area where the program operates, one where the residents comprise a diverse group of Israeli society, many of whom deal with social exclusion: Arab-Palestinians and Jews, immigrants from the former USSR, immigrants from Ethiopia, an aging population, people living in poverty, parents of children with special needs and more. As part of the partnership principle, residents and professionals were asked to take part in focus groups that gather information about the area. These groups also promoted joint brainstorming regarding core issues of the program, courses of action, target populations, nature of partnerships and other issues related to the implementation of the partnership. The idea was to collaborate with community activists and professionals without what might become the manipulation of power of academy over disenfranchised communities. Consequently, the aim was to create a nonhierarchical dynamics in order to generate action and research from the bottom-up in a way that reflects the needs of the area and not necessarily the research agenda or other aspirations of the academy.

Contrary to initial belief, the mapping out process was much more complex than expected. Most of the professionals in the community were happy about the future involvement of the University, but they expressed their concerns regarding the University's interference in local community affairs. Against this background, it was precisely the fear of mapping out processes and testing the needs of the community that stood out. Some of the professionals claimed there was no need for such an analysis since their many years of experience in the community gave them ample knowledge of all the needs and priorities for intervention. Other professionals explained that going out into the field and testing for these variables would likely trigger many expectations on the part of residents. People living in excluded neighborhoods, who have had their fill of promises to improve their situation from countless organizations, tend to distrust the system. Representatives of the social agencies in the region suggested that raising new expectations would raise social unrest when eventually the University would not be able to satisfy the needs. At that point, the residents' anger and further mistrust would be directed towards them— the same agencies and professionals who are already coping with a difficult reality, would have to buffer the frustration and pain likely to be caused by the academic intervention as well. In addition, other concerns raised were that the process would be too long and use too many resources at the expense of actually implementing the projects successfully. In this way, and contradictory to what might be expected, what was designed as a participatory egalitarian process was met with much hesitation and suspicion from both the professional and the community lay leadership. This understandable apprehension by those who are usually at the bottom end of the planning process, delayed the University's direct access to the community due to other professional considerations. Thus a paradoxical situation is created in which the academy dictates from top what is supposed to be a bottom-up working plan.

A similar paradox existed in the give-and-take that characterized the relationship within the University institutions involved with the partnership program. Various administrative staff members had difficulty dealing with the ambiguity and loss of control derived from organizational practices dictated by fluctuating community needs. Administrative departments of the University are naturally used to working within clear timelines, and well planned and budgeting. Working from the bottom-up, however, does not allow for total control of all elements of planning. Such a dynamics requires a high level of flexibility to deal with uncertainty and change associated with the characteristics of community level work. In order to adapt to local changes in the field, especially within marginalized communities suffering from many aspects of exclusion, one must allow projects to develop in accordance with community needs and not according to the hierarchical structure. Dealing with this complexity requires the UCP's leadership to submit project plans and budget activities that are planned in advance and at the same time receive the support of the administration of the institution and a great deal of confidence in the process from the faculty and administrative authorities.

In the planning process of the program the various stakeholders—management, staff, professionals and community agencies, were forced to reexamine the limits of uncertainty and control when dealing with the ambiguity of community oriented development within the structured boundaries of a large academic institutions. The paradox between management and control from the top-down and the parallel growth from the field upwards took place at different levels: between professionals and the neighborhood residents, local agency staff to university and academic partners in program management, and between Flagship program staff and university administration.

While defining a clear method of planning and operation might have resolved some of the tensions, understanding the paradox is beneficial for the project itself and for its stakeholders. The University, for its part, started to rely on its relationship with the local community as a means to stay relevant to diverse groups and society's most urgent problems. Such connections also give the University a way to encourage students to gain experience in a variety of professional, research areas, and the educational opportunity for personal development as active citizens. The community benefits from the significant contribution of academy to social issues, which are of great importance to them. By virtue of the joint work, they also experience empowerment and equitable work relations with the academy. It should be noted, however, that the bottom-up vs. top-bottom paradox poses exciting challenges to project management that must simultaneously maintain control and decentralization, and a relatively high level of ambiguity in cumbersome decision-making processes.

9.4.2 Organizational Relationships Versus Organizational Effectiveness

Academy-community partnerships usually create a coalition of diversity, an associations of partners who would typically not be working together in the absence of a common agenda. Members of these partnerships belong to different organizations, and more often than not, they come from different social classes, ethnic, cultural and educational backgrounds as well as different political perceptions (Sandy and Holland 2006). Baum argues that the greater the diversity of the member's backgrounds, the greater the complexity of the partnership (Baum 2000). This complexity requires continuous investment in maintaining and nurturing the quality of the relationship between the partners, as it promotes connections between different groups and the creation of a climate of acceptance, which opens a channel for understanding and resolving conflicts (Strand et al. 2003). At the same time, it is important to remember that the effectiveness of the UCP is measured by the output it generates, especially by evaluating measurable goals and visibility of results in the field. These achievements require diverting the energies of the partnership in this direction (Rogge and Rocha 2004). This suggests that a partnership that is targeted towards the achievement of defined objectives will be more effective (Nocon et al. 2004). Since shaky internal relations can lead to stagnation and neutralize partners ability to act in coordination with each other due to internal conflicts (Ostrander and Chapin-Hogue 2011), UCP's require an investment of significant resources with internal maintenance, which inevitably reduces the resources invested towards achieving external goals (Wiewel and Lieber 1998).

This dynamic creates a constant tension between investment in processes and investment in output.

The establishment of a "Flagship program" and its implementation required investment of considerable resources to build a partnership between the university and community agencies and residents. This partnership, along with the constant strive to produce tangible and visible outputs, are the basis for continued sustainability of the program. The paradox between organizational relationships and organizational effectiveness was evident in one of the flagship program's projects, which deals with the prevention of the cultural exclusion of immigrants of Ethiopian descent. One of Israel's most marginalized ethnic Jewish groups, this community is confronted by racism and deep rooted social exclusion. This project emerged from the needs of the community as recognized by the initial mapping process collectively conducted by the programs staff and faculty with residents from the Ethiopian community. Ethiopian members of the community, faced with the reality of cultural exclusion of their heritage, voiced their need to be heard. They argued that cultural exclusion affects young people of the community who are not exposed to their heritage and feel shame in it. As a result, they distance themselves from their parents' and detach from their native culture and narratives. Moreover, cultural exclusion distances the legacy of Ethiopian Jewry from Israel's central discourse in educational institutions, cultural events and other arenas of public interest. At the local level, activists raise the need for a "home for the Ethiopian culture", a place where they can display their heritage and celebrate holidays and events of joy and grief. One of the mothers interviewed spoke of her disappointment when she discovered that public kindergartens had no dark-skinned dolls. She shared her frustration knowing her children were being educated in a school system that does not include stories of the Ethiopian community or the story of their heroic immigration. During the many conversations held with members of the community it was evident that members feel oppressed and excluded from dominant culture, their voices silenced, and their Ethiopian heritage reduced to local folkloristic elements.

This request prompted the Flagship Program staff to start up a new project, in collaboration with the Dov Noy Folktale Archives at the University of Haifa and community partners. The project plan defined clear outputs, which were achievable in a limited period, and required the cooperation of the University administration, community agencies and residents. In this new initiative, an academic researcher trained students of Ethiopian origin to collect folk tales and traditional narratives from Ethiopian community members. With the researcher's guidance, they planned to gather stories, which would later be incorporated along with photographs and other documentation into a book and exhibition to preserve Ethiopian tradition and culture in the local community and in Israel. After they were documented, the stories and other cultural artifacts would be transformed into an innovative educational program for the general population and for members of the Ethiopian community. Although all stakeholders approved the project, after having received its budget, the project raised several significant disputes and tensions between partners. One of the agencies involved stressed that the oppression and discrimination faced by the community were more serious than cultural issues. They were convinced that the project should deal with what they felt were more acute problems like unemployment, health or welfare issues, before turning to engage in matters of culture and symbolic capital. Others feared that immigration stories might awaken traumatic experiences, open wounds, and raise 'demons from the past'. Some partners who initially agreed with the projects' goals expressed opposition to the process. Differences between stakeholders threatened the relationship to the point of dismantling the project. Tentative support from some partners and complete lack of support from others delayed projects execution and completely hampered establishment of a steering committee, which was integral to project implementation.

In order to respond effectively to the needs raised by the local Ethiopian community, and at the same time to acknowledge the conflicting viewpoints of different agencies working with the Ethiopian community, it was imperative to strengthen the ties between the partners and improve internal coordination between partners, especially with those who opposed the project. At the same time, rapid progress was needed to advocate for changes in the educational system, as requested by activists from the Ethiopian community. In addition, differences between partners endangered its continued funding. In practice, the lack of good communication between all partners damaged the effectiveness of the entire project.

Management of this paradox means understanding that in situations of tension between partners the effective choice is not necessarily a one-solution preference, such as nurturing relationships as preferred over another solution, namely the achievement of outputs. Instead, the perspective of a paradox highlights movement toward an understanding of each other's solution (Jules and Good 2014). In the case described, the project activity continued towards achieving its goals, as many resources were invested alongside the creation of a steering committee that included representatives of all the partners and many community activists in order to nurture the partnership. At the same time, goals were redefined in a process, which enabled a display of intermediate results promoting community change and recognized the complexity of the project as an effort to promote cultural and social inclusion.

9.4.3   Egalitarian Approach Versus Hierarchical Structures

UCP's are collaborative efforts carried out by organizational entities characterized by dissimilar organizational cultures, sometimes even diametrically opposed. Naturally, differences in organizational cultures create many tensions and conflicts. One paradox we discovered in our case relates to the need for egalitarian approaches while acknowledging hierarchical structures. The existence of open channels of communication between the University and the community is a necessary condition for the development of healthy partnerships (Barnes et al. 2009). Specifically, this climate allows an informal and flexible framework for reflexive learning among partnership members. On the other hand, this same egalitarian and informal approach, which characterizes some UCP's, may create tensions and conflicts within the institutional structures of partners that are often based on formal and hierarchical relationships. This tendency to foster open and egalitarian relationships within a hierarchical system of power relations such as academic and governmental institutions may be the source of tensions linked to threats to formal hierarchies and power relations in organizations (Cox 2000). In other words, an egalitarian approach seems to be simultaneously a required precondition for meaningful partnerships, and at the same time, it might also be a serious threat to its very existence.

Transformative partnerships based on the principles of mutuality and equality, such as the "Flagship Program", generate grey areas that are "blind" to hierarchical structures. Areas where relationships that are more egalitarian exist between groups that are usually associated with more hierarchical patterns. These areas exist outside of the organizational parameters that the partners came from, in the meeting place between academia and community. However, they can also be found within the boundaries of the university itself. In the field, one can observe "deviant" norms in the management of power relations. For example, in one of the annual closure events held at the University, community activists surprised faculty and university administration when they decided to honor them by giving them community diplomas. By doing so, community representatives adopted an academic practice, changing power relations—whereby usually the academic authorities award diplomas to students. In this case, the community took control and distributed diplomas to the faculty, including the Provost, turning the hierarchical pyramid of academy upside down. The use of social media also contributed to the progressive dismantling of the hierarchical pyramid and the rapid transition from the formal domain to the non-formal, as academic faculty and administration staff involved in the "Flagship program" became "friends" with students, residents, activists, NGO's members, and professionals from social services in the community. Sometimes the encounter between professors, students and activists working together in the field, far from the hierarchical structures of campus challenged formal relationships. As a result, even in the classroom itself, the gap is narrowed by making learning a mutual process that gives greater appreciation to knowledge gained from field experience than that of theory. At the same time, community and students empowerment, so common to transformative partnerships, may contest rigid academic structures and require faculty and administrative levels willingness to adapt a dynamic, evolving organizational structure. Egalitarian practices create multiple challenges to existing power relations and raise new dilemmas, not only in the relationship between academy and community, but also in the relationship between faculty, students and administration staff within the University.

9.4.4 Forging a Common Vision Versus Celebrating Multiple Identities

As described earlier, the success of an UCP depends largely upon its internal cohesion (Nation et al. 2011). This cohesion is achieved through a variety of activities aimed at creating a sense of "togetherness", a common identity that can hold the initiative as an alliance between all its members. This sense of belonging helps partners work together, find common solutions to complex issues, and overcome internal disagreements. In other words, cohesion is essential to morale and the creation of a shared vision. On the other hand, UCP's are often perceived by minority and excluded groups as an effective means to achieve recognition for their silenced voices and identities, an opportunity to both show and tell their stories and raise their own claims. Thus, even in the preliminary stages of formulating a common vision for action, an emphasis must be placed on identity issues of the community partners. In other words, maintaining internal cohesion means respecting diversity. In the same vein, consolidating a shared vision requires paying attention to their different needs and identities (Strier 2013).

The "Flagship Program" works with marginalized communities in multicultural neighborhoods. The recognition of the multiple identities of marginalized groups is a central theme when working with excluded communities. This theme was particularly evident in one of the "flagship Program" projects, which operates in a neighborhood in which Arabs and Jews live together. The projects' goal is to promote a joint tourist community economic enterprise that would bring in tourists, while moving in new private and public investments to the area. The University of Haifa committed to provide academic guidance for the project through the Geography Department, which helped to develop a tourist plan for the project. However, in the process of creating a shared vision for the project, Jewish and Arab resident discovered huge differences regarding their respective historical narratives of the neighborhood. Jewish residents tended to stress the very ancient historical background of the region, while the Arab residents referred to the Palestinian narrative and recent history of the neighborhood until the creation of the Jewish state in 1948. Jewish residents called this seaside neighborhood 'Ein Haym' (Eye of the Sea) in Hebrew, whereas Arab resident used the former name 'Wadi El Jamal' (Valley of Camels), referring to its history as a passageway to merchants riding upon camels. These tensions are bound to the paradox between striving to support a shared vision and the need for recognition of differences between participants. Dealing with this paradox requires maintaining an ongoing, open and honest dialogue between all parties, and understanding that actualization of this shared vision is conditioned upon expression of different identities in the process of collaborative work. This process, which recognizes the different identities, is likely to create separation and conflict in a group that is supposed to work together diligently towards a shared goal.

9.5   Discussion

This chapter offers an innovative theoretical prism for academy-community partnerships. While most studies show the relationship between partners on a continuum of cooperation and conflict or stress conflict as a sign of system failure, we suggest an alternative way to look at partnerships as "fields of paradox" that allow for the coexistence of opposites at the same time. This concept is based on the Organizational Paradox Theory, which re-examines the binary construction of cooperation-conflict as essentialist opposition. Four common paradoxes in academic-community partnerships are presented through case studies that show how seemingly contradictory events can not only coexist, but also contribute to the partnership's ability to accommodate the complexities that characterize the nature of the social missions they are engaged in.

UCP's can be seen as a field in which different agencies negotiate identity and hierarchy as part of the search for a common meaning. Thus, partnership is defined as an area in which academics and community converge in discourse and redefine power relations and the distribution of social, cultural, economic and symbolic capital. This theoretical approach can help researchers, professionals and community members alike to overcome the attitude that views conflict as dysfunction. Paradox perspective helps integrate features that may create a great deal of internal stress such as ambiguity, inequality and insecurity, considering that they are an integral part of institutional success.

In the context of promoting social solidarity and fighting exclusion, the connection between academy and community creates a new and exciting space - a third space that is not subject to perceptions of organizational culture and power relations that currently exist between communities who face exclusion and the academy. Bhabha's work, a critical discourse anchored in post-colonialism, refers to the third space as an area of resistance to oppression that develops in the margins of a new cultural politics (Bhabha 1994). The third space exists as a meeting place between social groups of different cultural traditions and power potentials, which enter into a process of dialogue and negotiation. This process should mix the cultures to create a new joint identity, one that is therefore not the identity of either of the separate sides (Ikas and Wagner 2009). In this way, it is the very act of creating an equitable alliance between academy and excluded communities that defines a new space. One that may contribute to liberation from oppression and promote authentic dialogue between different voices. In a time when society is extremely challenged by social exclusion, growing disparities and rising national, racial and class conflicts, academic institutions have the privilege and obligation to embrace UCP's and the paradoxes that they entail. By acknowledging their capacities to manage such complex paradoxes, they may act as facilitators of hope, encouraging dialogue and developing shared spaces to promote positive change.

9.6   Conclusions

Although UCP's tend to be highly complex initiatives, it is imperative that academic institutions strive to expand their ties with communities. The case study of the University of Haifa Flagship program, suggests that paradox theory is useful in implementing such projects, as this perspective gives room for the many contradictions, tensions and dichotomies that characterize the complex relationship between academy and community. While we present four areas of paradox, it is important to note that, each partnership might have its own specific fields of paradox depending on the nature of the partnership, the stakeholders and their shared goals. It is therefore suggested that partners devote adequate time and resources towards mutual identification of the partnership's fields of paradox in initial stages of project planning and through all partnership stages. Such practice requires openness and honesty necessary for such a reflexive process from all stakeholders, which "play" on these fields of paradox. In order to overcome these paradoxical states, UCP's must have a strong and committed leadership. UCP's leaders must be able and willing to support faculty, students and community engaging in the implementation of academy-community projects. Lastly, partners should acknowledge the shifting nature of paradox management that privileges emotions in relation to rationality and favors the unpredictable, volatile and sinuous dialectic between order and disorder at the expenses of calculable, calm, and linear planning (Putnam et al. 2016).

9.6.1 Limitations

As this study is based on case study methodology, it also has many limitations such as difficulties to generalize results and conclusions to a wider population and to replicate it in different institutional contexts. This is particularly true in this case, which represents a very singular type of UCP based on a long-term, comprehensive and transformative partnership, strongly anchored on a critical, egalitarian and emancipatory ideology. Nevertheless, we still believe that the paradox paradigm engenders a promising theoretical contribution to the understanding and advancement of UCP's.

References

Altman, D. (2005). Communities, governments and AIDS: Making partnerships work. In P. Aggleton, P. Davies, & G. Hart (Eds.), *Aids: Safety, sexuality and risk* (pp. 109–117). London: Taylor & Francis.

Amey, M. J., & Brown, D. F. (2005). Interdisciplinary collaboration and academic work: A case study of a university–community partnership. *New Directions for Teaching and Learning, 102*, 23–35.

Andriopoulos, C., & Lewis, M. W. (2009). Exploitation-exploration tensions and organizational ambidexterity: Managing paradoxes of innovation. *Organization Science, 20*(4), 696–717.

Arches, J., & Apontes-Pares, L. (2005). Dilemmas for university–community partnerships and service learning. *Humanity & Society, 29*, 209–227.

Barnes, J. V., Altimare, E. L., Farrell, P. A., Brown, R. E., Burnett, C. R, I. I. I., Gamble, L., et al. (2009). Creating and sustaining authentic partnerships with community in a systemic model. *Journal of Higher Education Outreach and Engagement, 13*, 15–29.

Baum, H. S. (2000). Fantasies and realities in university–community partnerships. *Journal of Planning Education and Research, 20,* 234–246.

Bhabha, H. K. (1994). *The location of culture.* London: Routledge.

Boyer, E. L. (1990). *Scholarship reconsidered: Priorities of the professorate.* New Jersey: The Carnegie Foundation for the Advancement of Teaching.

Boyer, E. L. (1996). The scholarship of engagement. *Bulletin of the American Academy of Arts and Sciences, 49,* 18–33.

Brown-Luthango, M. (2013). Community-university engagement: The Philippi CityLab in Cape Town and the challenge of collaboration across boundaries. *Higher Education, 6,* 309–324.

Butcher, J., Bezzina, M., & Moran, W. (2011). Transformational partnerships: A new agenda for higher education. *Innovative Higher Education, 36,* 29–40.

Buys, N., & Bursnall, S. (2007). Establishing university–community partnerships: Processes and benefits. *Journal of Higher Education Policy and Management, 29,* 73–86.

Carlton, E. L., Whiting, J. B., Bradford, K., Dyk, P. H., & Vail, A. (2009). Defining factors of successful university–community collaborations: An exploration of one healthy marriage project. *Family Relations: An Interdisciplinary Journal of Applied Family Studies, 58,* 28–40.

Cherry, D. J., & Shefner, J. (2004). Addressing barriers to university–community collaboration: Organizing by experts or organizing the experts? *Journal of Community Practice, 12,* 219–233.

Cobb, P. D., & Rubin, B. A. (2006). Contradictory interests, tangled power and disorganized organization. *Administration and Society, 38,* 79–112.

Cox, D. N. (2000). Developing a framework for understanding university community partnerships. *Cityscape: A Journal of Policy Development and Research, 5,* 9–26.

D'Augelli, A. R. (2006). Coming out, visibility, and creating change: Empowering lesbian, gay, and bisexual people in a rural university community. *American Journal of Community Psychology, 37,* 203–210.

Dantnow, A. (1998). *The gender politics of educational change.* London: Falmer.

Davies, B., Edwards, J., Gannon, S., & Laws, C. (2007). Neo-liberal subjectivities and the limits of social change in university–community partnerships. *Asia-Pacific Journal of Teacher Education, 35,* 27–40.

Dayan, Y. (2003). Methodology of qualitative research. Case Study. *Bamichlala, 11,* 79–96. (In Hebrew).

Desivilla, H., & Palgi, M. (2011). *The paradox in partnership: The role of conflict in partnership building.* Miami, FL: Bentham Books.

Dulmus, C. N., & Cristalli, M. E. (2012). A university–community partnership to advance research in practice settings: The HUB research model. *Research on Social Work Practice, 22,* 195–202.

Farquhar, S. A., & Dobson, N. (2004). Community and university participation in disaster-relief policy and practices: An example from eastern North Carolina. *Journal of Community Practice, 12,* 203–217.

Feagan, R., & Rossiter, K. (2011). University–community engagement: A case study using popular theatre. *Education and Training, 53,* 140–154.

Feagin, J. R., Orum, A. M., & Sjoberg, G. (Eds.). (1991). *A case for the case study.* Chapel Hill, NC: The University of North Carolina Press.

Fisher, R., Fabricant, M., & Simmons, L. (2005). Understanding contemporary university–community connections. *Journal of Community Practice, 12,* 13–34.

Flyvbjerg, B. (2006). Five misunderstandings about case-study research. *Qualitative Inquiry, 12,* 219–245.

Gray, B. (2003). Framing of environmental disputes. In R. Lewicki, B. Gray, & M. Elliott (Eds.), *Making sense of intractable environmental conflicts: Concepts and cases* (pp. 11–34). Washington, DC: Island Press.

Gray, B. (2004). Strong opposition: Frame-based resistance to collaboration. *Journal of Community & Applied Psychology, 14,* 166–176.

Gronski, R., & Pigg, K. (2000). University and community collaboration. *American Behavioral Scientist, 43*, 781–793.

Huxham, C., & Vangen, S. (2000). What makes partnerships work? In S. P. Osborne (Ed.), *Public-private partnerships: Theory and practice in international perspective* (pp. 293–310). London: Routledge.

Ikas, K., & Wagner, G. (2009). *Communicating in the third space*. London: Taylor & Frances.

Jarvis-Selinger, S., Ho, K., Novak Lauscher, H., Liman, Y., Stacy, E., Woollard, R., et al. (2008). Social accountability in action: University-community collaboration in the development of an inter-professional aboriginal health elective. *Journal of Interprofessional Care, 22*, 61–72.

Johnson Butterfield, A. K., & Soska, T. (Eds.). (2005). *University–community partnerships: Universities in civic engagement*. New York: Routledge.

Jules, C., & Good, D. (2014). Introduction to special issue on paradox in context: Advances in theory and practice. *Journal of Applied Behavioral Science, 50*(2), 123–126.

Kaufman, R. (2004). A university–community partnership to change public policy: Pre-conditions and processes. *Journal of Community Practice, 12*, 163–180.

Lewis, M. W. (2000). Exploring paradox: Toward a more comprehensive guide. *The Academy of Management Review, 25*, 760–776.

Luscher, L., & Lewis, M. W. (2008). Organizational change and managerial sense making: Working through paradox. *Academy of Management Journal, 51*, 221–240.

Luscher, L., Lewis, M. W., & Ingram, A. (2006). The social construction of organizational change paradoxes. *Journal of Organizational Change Management, 19*, 491–502.

Maginn, P. J. (2007). Towards more effective community participation in urban regeneration: The potential of collaborative planning and applied ethnography. *Qualitative Research, 7*, 25–43.

Maurrasse, D. J. (2002). Higher education-community partnerships: Assessing progress in the field. *Nonprofit & Volunteer Quarterly, 31*, 131–139.

Mulroy, E. A. (2004). University civic engagement with community-based organizations: Dispersed or coordinated models? *Journal of Community Practice, 12*, 35–52.

Mulroy, E. A. (2008). University community partnerships that promote evidence-based macro practice. *Journal of Evidence-Based Social Work, 5*, 497–517.

Nation, M., Bess, K., Voight, A., Perkins, D. D., & Juarez, P. (2011). Levels of community engagement in youth violence prevention: The role of power in sustaining successful university–community partnerships. *American Journal of Community Psychology, 48*, 89–96.

Nocon, H., Nilsson, M., & Cole, M. (2004). Spiders, fire souls, and little fingers: Necessary magic in university–community collaboration. *Anthropology & Education Quarterly, 35*, 368–385.

Ostrander, N., & Chapin-Hogue, S. (2011). Learning from our mistakes: An autopsy of an unsuccessful university–community collaboration. *Social Work Education, 30*, 454–464.

Perkins, D. D., Crim, B., Silberman, P., & Brown, B. B. (2004). Community adversity and community development: Ecological and strengths-based theory, research and policies. In K. Maton, B. Ledbeater, C. Schellenberg, & A. Solarz (Eds.), *Investing in children, youth, families and communities: Strengths based research and policy* (pp. 321–340). Washington, DC: American Psychological Association.

Putnam, L., Fairhurst, G., & Banghart, S. (2016). Contradictions, dialectics, and paradoxes in organizations: A constitutive approach. *The Academy of Management Annals, 10*(1), 65–171.

Richardson, V. (1994). Conducting research on practice. *Educational Researcher, 23*(5), 5–10.

Rogge, M. E., & Rocha, C. J. (2004). University–community partnership centers: An important link for social work education. *Journal of Community Practice, 12*, 103–121.

Russell, J. F., & Flynn, R. B. (2001). Setting the stage for collaboration. *Peabody Journal of Education, 75*, 1–5.

Sabar, N. (Ed). (2001). *Qualitative research: Genres and traditions in qualitative research* Tel Aviv: Zmora Bitan. (in Hebrew).

Sandy, M., & Holland, B. A. (2006). Different worlds and common ground: Community partner perspectives on campus-community partnerships. *Michigan Journal of Community Service Learning, 13*, 30–43.

Smith, W. K., & Lewis, M. W. (2011). Toward a theory of paradox: A dynamic equilibrium model of organizing. *Academy of Management Review, 36,* 381–403.

Stake, R. E., & Savolainen, R. (1995). *The art of case study research.* Thousand Oaks, CA: Sage publications.

Stewart, T., & Alrutz, M. (2012). Meaningful relationships: Cruxes of university-community partnerships for sustainable and happy engagement. *Journal of Community Engagement and Scholarship, 5,* 44–55.

Strand, K., Marullo, S., Cutforth, N., Stoecker, R., & Donohue, P. (2003). Principles of best practice for community-based research. *Michigan Journal of Community Service Learning, 9,* 5–15.

Strier, R. (2011). The construction of university-community partnerships: Entangled perspectives. *Higher Education, 62,* 81–97.

Strier, R. (2013). Responding to the global economic crisis: Inclusive social work practice. *Social Work, 58*(4), 344–353.

Strier, R. (2014). University-community partnerships: Fields of paradox. *Higher Education, 68,* 155–165.

Suarez-Balcazar, Y., & Kinney, L. (2006). Realities and myths of safety issues for community researchers working in a marginalized African American community. *American Journal of Community Psychology, 37,* 303–309.

Taylor, R. R., Braveman, B., & Hammel, J. (2004). Developing and evaluating community services through participatory action research: Two case examples. *American Journal of Occupational Therapy, 58,* 73–82.

Werkmeister Rozas, L., & Negroni, L. (2008). University/community partnership: Promoting anti-oppressive action on behalf of Latino youth. *Journal of Community Practice, 16,* 441–458.

Wiewel, W., & Lieber, M. (1998). Goal achievement, relationship building, and incrementalism: The challenges of university–community partnerships. *Journal of Planning Education and Research, 17,* 291–301.

Yin, R. K. (2013). *Case study research: Design and methods* (5th ed.). Thousand Oaks, CA: Sage Publications.

Chapter 10
Evaluating Service Leadership Programs with Multiple Strategies

Cheryl de la Rey, Wendy Kilfoil and Gernia van Niekerk

Abstract The University of Pretoria (UP) functions within the context of a highly unequal society emerging from decades of politically entrenched racism that has left many of its communities impoverished in educational, social, cultural and economic terms, with little access to development opportunities or knowledge that is the stock in trade of universities. Through its Strategic Plan 2025, the University deliberately seeks to exercise its social responsibility through integrating community engagement in its academic programmes and research, as well as in its operations, practices and partnerships. The approach and scope of social responsibility activities encompassing credit-bearing curricular engagement as well as volunteerism, which forms the focus of the chapter, is unique in its scale and scope in South Africa. In terms of the University's Policy on Community Engagement, each programme should include at least one community engagement component. The practical outcome of this policy is that approximately one third of the University's 30,000 undergraduate students annually undertake community engagement as part of their curriculum at hundreds of community sites and their work is supported by thousands of students who volunteer beyond the requirements of the curriculum. The activities contribute millions in financial terms to the communities around the University each year through student service. The paradigm has moved from treating communities as beneficiaries of charity and objects of research to more equal partnership for mutual benefit: to use university knowledge to solve problems identified by communities while simultaneously enabling students to gain knowledge and skills as well as apply knowledge.

C. de la Rey (✉) · W. Kilfoil · G. van Niekerk
University of Pretoria, Pretoria, South Africa
e-mail: rector@up.ac.za

W. Kilfoil
e-mail: wendy.kilfoil@up.ac.za

G. van Niekerk
e-mail: gernia.vanniekerk@up.ac.za

© Springer Nature Singapore Pte Ltd. 2017
D.T.L. Shek and R.M. Hollister (eds.), *University Social Responsibility and Quality of Life*, Quality of Life in Asia 8,
DOI 10.1007/978-981-10-3877-8_10

Keywords The University of Pretoria · Community engagement · Partnerships · Case study · South Africa

10.1 Introduction

It is often said that the most significant contribution a university makes to society is through its graduates and indeed there is ample evidence that educational attainment is an effective lever for a society to increase social capital and social cohesion. From a financial perspective, there is no doubt that the investment in higher education—the private investment in the form of fees and other living costs and the public investment in the form of government subsidies and grants to our higher education institutions—pays dividends in the form of benefits for both the individual and for society as a whole. Research comparing several countries has shown a positive and statistically significant correlation between tertiary education enrolment rates and indices such as health outcomes, absence of corruption, rule of law and public administration quality.

Is this sufficient, however, especially for developing countries? In highly unequal societies, especially those with a long history of social oppression and discrimination, governments, communities and other stakeholders have multiple expectations of universities extending far beyond the traditional expectation of producing quality graduates. When a university takes its social responsibility seriously, it can contribute much more to society. The first national education policy framework in post-apartheid South Africa called on institutions to "demonstrate social responsibility" by showing a commitment and "making available expertise and infrastructure" and to "promote and develop social responsibility and awareness amongst students of the role of higher education in social and economic development through community service programmes" (Department of Education 1997: 11). In response, South African universities have sought to enhance student access, increase the relevance of teaching and research and give focussed attention to community engagement. However, little consideration is sometimes given to what students could offer in regard to both the type and nature of services through community engagement activities from which communities could benefit. Furthermore, little attention is given to what impact community engagement could have on students and the communities they work in, and what role communities play and have to offer in this overall process (Bezuidenhout and Van Niekerk 2015).

This chapter then focuses on the University of Pretoria as a case study to illustrate new ventures, successes, challenges, complexities and dynamics that this University is experiencing in regard to the implementation of large-scale university social responsibility activities in a society that is grappling to transform itself from a long history of inequality and oppression.

10.2   University of Pretoria

10.2.1   Profile

The University of Pretoria (UP) is one of 26 universities in South Africa and one of the top five universities in terms of research impact and international stature. In 2015 the University registered 59,514 students in total, distributed across seven campuses. Compared to other South Africa universities, UP has the widest range of academic programmes offered by the Faculties of Veterinary Science; Health Sciences; Engineering, Built Environment and IT; Law; Humanities; Natural and Agricultural Sciences; Economic and Management Sciences; Education and Theology. It also has a business school, the Gordon School of Business Science (GIBS), which is located in Johannesburg.

The University makes a significant contribution to South Africa's professional workforce:

- 1 in every 10 degrees awarded in South Africa is a UP degree.
- More than 17% of all Master's degrees in South Africa annually are granted by UP.
- 15% of all doctoral degrees are awarded by this University.
- 27% of all engineering degrees in South Africa have been obtained at UP.

Measured in graduate output alone, UP makes a significant contribution to high-level skills development in a national and regional context where there is a dire shortage of such skills.

In a resource-constrained world where vast disparities remain, particularly in Africa, UP positions itself as a public university that has a distinct role to fulfil in relation to national and regional development. The University sees its social responsibility as integral to its identity and it has the largest commitment in the country as measured in terms of the number of academic programmes and modules that include community engagement, the number of students who are doing community engagement every year either as compulsory, credit-bearing, curricular community engagement or voluntary community engagement and the number of activities undertaken in the process of carrying out its social responsibility. In 2016, there were

- 152 credit-bearing curricular community engagement modules across nine faculties;
- 4000 projects, many well-established and longitudinal;
- 1339 sites of learning, many of which support activities by more than one faculty; and
- five streams of voluntary community engagement by student societies and student residences.

Basically it comes down to the fact that almost all students are in some way or the other involved in activities related to the social responsibility of the University during their years of studies at the University. The vision of UP is tied to its commitment to local needs and development challenges and, at the same time, the University strives to remain a hub of knowledge production recognised within the global scientific community.

10.2.2 Brief Historical Overview

There has been a clear progression over the past three decades in the paradigms adopted at UP in relation to community engagement. During the 1980s and 1990s, academics realised that, through the practice of needs-based projects, they could benefit in terms of research in gaining experience and knowledge of issues about which they were ignorant and to which they had had no exposure in the past (Council on Higher Education 2010). Unfortunately, this was also the beginning of the (problematic) project era when it became common practice to try to address community "needs". In most instances this was done through charity-like projects and services, which resulted in communities becoming increasingly dependent on hand-outs. These projects were mostly financed on a once-off basis by donors and proved unsustainable. UP no longer works within this paradigm and has not done so since the beginning of the 21st century.

In the period from 2003 onwards UP changed its community engagement approach from 'community service' to 'community development'. Communities increasingly began to speak out against service-oriented approaches that disempowered them and sustained a dependency cycle rather than bringing about sustainable change and empowerment. After the University adopted a development approach, communities began to benefit profoundly in a much more sustainable way (Van Niekerk and Kilfoil 2014). Establishing this 'new' approach to community engagement took hard work over a number of years by a small but dedicated team working with practitioners in faculties, students and student societies, communities and other partners. Programmes became multi-disciplinary and included

- the assessment of nutritional needs and education for vulnerable groups;
- life skills and employment of people with disabilities, which covered issues related to the inclusion of people with disabilities into the community and workplace;
- sustainable use of renewable natural resources in communal rural communities and the incorporation of nature conservation in development programmes;
- all aspects within the field of education with specific reference to: adult education, learning facilitation, curriculum development, policy and politics, health education and sustainable development; and
- child and family care: the child in his or her family system, children in substitute care, childhood disability, facilitation of family problems and the enhancement of healthy social family life, the establishment and development of theoretical

and practical knowledge on family therapy and changes in the South African society, especially with regard to family life.

More importantly for the changing paradigm, there was a concerted attempt to promote the involvement and empowerment of people in communities in determining their own priority needs as well as in planning, implementing and evaluating development programmes. To enhance sustainability, in 2003 the University established the Unit for Development Support and it became responsible for the administration, integration and coordination of all the community engagement processes at UP. During 2011, the community engagement unit was incorporated into the Department for Education Innovation as a result of the University's adopting the approach of integrating community engagement into its core activities of teaching and research rather than having it as a stand-alone function.

As one of its first tasks in 2003 the Unit assessed UP as a community itself and its potential for following a holistic approach towards community engagement in applying the knowledge, technologies, theories, practices and methodologies developed/researched/owned/used at the University to establish and/or sustain community development programmes in society. At the time components of community engagement were fragmented and distributed in many different academic fields and departments. The coordination and integration of community engagement at UP became essential. A working model for the process of community engagement at UP was developed. Typically, different disciplines define problems in their own language. However, most single discipline solutions are not that effective. In order for community engagement to be effective, each discipline must realise that it has only part of the solution and that success lies in integrating and synthesizing the contributions of single disciplines into a functional mesh of ideas necessary for the transformation of community life. That is why the new paradigm led to the creation of platforms or community sites of learning where students from different disciplines could make a contribution to sustainable and holistic community development. New intellectual challenges were thus created through community engagement and new interdisciplinary insights were developed. Service learning was stimulated and impacted on academic programmes, created new teaching ideas and opened up new fields for research.

In 2004 one of the tasks of the Unit for Development Support was to implement the beginning of an analytical process to categorize and bring up to date available information about community engagement. Various programmes were established, aimed at attending to issues with which communities experienced difficulties for a variety of reasons and for which the expertise existed at the University. These programmes dealt with social development and empowerment and included interventions such as employment and income generation; early childhood education and therapy to children with impairments; teacher development; science and technology awareness; legal aid; child law and a host of other pressing societal needs, where students and lecturers offered their expertise in their subjects to communities. The University's initiatives began to empower and develop people and their communities and enabled greater responsibility for their own future development.

By 2005 community engagement had become a multi-disciplinary activity incorporating collaborative application of diverse intellectual resources. An example of such a venture would be the Basa Magogo project, which brought together theology and engineering. This project was aimed at reducing air pollution through the use of coal with an alternative ignition and combustion process. Such collaborative partnerships offered new opportunities for learning and research and enhanced multi-cultural understanding, both within the campus community as well as between the University and its environment. Another example is the Clinic for High Risk Babies (CHRIB) that rendered early communication intervention services to families with infants and toddlers at risk for communication disorders. The aim of CHRIB was to provide specialized assessment services conducted by a team of early interventionists to families who were concerned about the early stages of communication development in their infants and toddlers. Intervention services were also provided in the form of parent and/or caregiver training and support. Additional functions of CHRIB included under- and postgraduate student training from various disciplines, a strong research component, the management of a research database, and continuous education in the developing field of early communication in South Africa.

More than ever before, the University was taking up the challenge to educate the leaders of tomorrow by connecting future leaders with the demands and realities of the present. From its experimental beginnings the University continued to consolidate its gains so that by 2013 the model was well managed and showing impact.

10.2.3 Changing Paradigms Through Practice

In adopting community engagement as a vehicle to realise their social responsibility, tertiary institutions follow numerous approaches. After many trial-and-error initiatives, over more than a decade, UP has managed to streamline and coordinate its community engagement efforts, which have included embedding community engagement into the curriculum and integrating voluntary and curricular-related community engagement with a specific development focus in relation to communities with whom there is a relationship. When replacing "community service" with community development in this way, UP also integrated its resources and expertise into a holistic development approach from which both the individual and the group (community) can benefit.

Partnerships are key to this approach and the University has formed partnerships across a spectrum of sectors. Partnerships range from government departments such as the prison services, small and medium street enterprises and residence groups in informal housing settlements. While there is a small financial cost to the students who typically have to cover the transport costs needed to get to the community and back to their respective campuses, supplies and materials are paid for or are sponsored by businesses who partner with UP. This sponsorship provides businesses with opportunities to fulfil their corporate social responsibility role without feeding further into the dependency cycle by doing charity work. Community engagement is a dynamic process and society changes all the time. As more experience is gained, student initiatives are continuously reorganized and streamlined. A tertiary institution that is taking on large-scale community engagement has to be flexible enough to be responsive to whatever direction society is taking and has to stay in tune with local dynamics. If a university optimises the potential that community engagement as a practice has to offer, what is learned and experienced through community engagement should feed back into teaching, learning and research.

The governance of community engagement is through the Senate which focuses on decisions regarding curricular community engagement that require institutional adoption and policy changes. There is also the Community Engagement Forum that is representative of groups involved in community engagement. The Forum has a particular role to play in providing a platform for reflective critique and the sharing of good practices.

All opportunities offered by communities are listed on the Community Engagement Management System (CEMS) operated by the Community Engagement Unit and academics and students can identify projects in which they wish to participate. CEMS includes headings for bookings (for volunteers and modules); opportunities (e.g. teaching mathematics and science); opportunity types (e.g. after-school Maths literacy in high school); sites (e.g. the name of a high school); site types (e.g. school or community centre); area (e.g. Mamelodi) and security (maps of safe routes). Various types of reports can be generated on the system. Student timetables form part of the booking system so they can be tracked fairly easily for quality assurance and related purposes. Too many unnecessary expenses owing to bad planning and management may cause financial problems to both the university and the students involved. Curriculum overload brings about many problems and confusion among students and happens when one academic programme has many modules with community engagement components, while another programme may only have one structured component. At UP community engagement components that are added to academic programmes and modules go through academic processes and quality standards. Central to the University's strategy is that community engagement can and must have a positive impact on its immediate and broader communities and environments, and that it will remain a hub of knowledge production that speaks to the global academic community.

The Community Engagement Unit carries out many tasks. It:

- liaises with communities on behalf of the University to identify and quality-assure community sites of learning for students;
- loads new sites of learning and opportunities on the Community Engagement Management System (CEMS—developed in-house from specs provided by the

Manager: Community Engagement and now in its second iteration) and registers students to the sites where they are working;

- consults frequently with academic faculty and deans;
- provides orientation to students and briefs students and academic faculty who are about to become active in the community on various community dynamics worthy of and important to note;
- integrates voluntary community work with curricular community work for the purpose of sustainable development;
- develops and sustains relationships with community partners; i.e. schools, orphanages, old age homes, companies, etc.;
- resolves problems or conflict that might affect the relationship between the University and the community partners;
- works out transport logistics for the students/departments based on the budget and students' needs and adjustments are made as needed continuously;
- conducts follow-up courtesy visits to:
  - monitor community engagement at the sites;
  - identify new opportunities;
  - assess community engagement as a practice; and
  - assess and follow up on any problems encountered during the year.

10.3 Case Studies

It is not possible to do justice to thousands of community development activities by reference to a few but we have included here five examples of community engagement across the University.

10.3.1 Case Study 1: UP Multi-disciplinary Platform at Viva Village

At least 400 students from ten departments across six faculties are involved in a programme initiated in February 2009 to find new ways to deal with very difficult social problems that develop as a result of the ways people solve problems in the Alaska community in Mamelodi. The programme is run by the Viva Foundation (http://www.viva-sa.co.za/index.php) in collaboration with the staff and students of UP and various partners such as the Department of Health, Social Work statutory bodies, schools, etc. The main role-players at the University are the Manager: Community Engagement, community engagement coordinators in faculties, programmes or departments, students earning credit for their programmes and students and staff volunteering for community service.

There have been positive benefits for the community:

- An after-school centre was established and is run by students and the community (Faculty of Education).
- A hospice was built by students and the community, housing destitute mothers and their children who have AIDS (Faculty of the Engineering, Built Environment and IT and Faculty of Health Sciences).
- Social support and counselling are provided to mothers and children (Faculty of Humanities).
- A crèche was built and is run by education students together with the community (Faculty of the Engineering, Built Environment and IT and Faculty of Education).
- Various preventative health care workshops and services are presented to the community by medical students, student nurses, etc. (Faculty of Health Sciences).
- A general shop and a fast food outlet were established and they are run by the community and students from nutritional science (Faculty of Natural and Agricultural Sciences).
- Workshops are run on waste management by students and a community project on using waste in the area was launched (Faculty of Natural and Agricultural Sciences).
- A library was established by students and is run by the community (Faculty of the Engineering, Built Environment and IT).
- A computer centre was set up by students and community members and computer literacy classes are provided by students and a community member (Faculty of the Engineering, Built Environment and IT).
- A health post was established from which medical students do house visits (Faculty of Health Sciences).
- Small and medium manufacturing enterprises have been established (Faculty of Economics and Management Sciences).

10.3.2 Case Study 2: Faculty of Law, Law Clinic

In 1980, during the dark days of apartheid, 13 idealistic and enthusiastic students from the segregated all white University of Pretoria reached out to the disenfranchised, marginalized, indigent black and coloured communities, living in townships east of Pretoria. From a classroom at a local school, they rendered legal advice on a limited scale (one evening per week). They did so without receiving any fee, reward or academic credit. Supervision and involvement by the Faculty was on a limited and ad hoc basis. From this humble but brave beginning, the Clinic evolved over 30 years to be the largest law clinic in the country, employing 32 staff members (attorneys, candidate attorneys and support personnel). The Clinic forms part of the Faculty of Law and is accredited as a legal aid clinic by the Law Society of South

Africa. Between 40 and 60 final-year law students receive experiential training through the medium of community service. The Clinic operates as a law practice from three sites in urban (Hatfield—since 2008), semi-urban (Mamelodi—since 2008) and rural (Hammanskraal—since 2001) communities. Legal advice and representation in litigious and non-litigious matters are provided free of charge to persons who meet the criteria set out in a means test (currently approximate monthly income below R7,000 and a determined asset value). Students enrolled for this elective module in Procedural Law work personally with indigent clients and are supported and supervised by admitted and practicing attorneys who guide the students' development of skills and knowledge. The University supports the programme as a credit-bearing module in the curriculum and provides infrastructural assistance. In 2015, 4137 clients were served.

10.3.3 Case Study 3: Faculty of Engineering, Built Environment and Information Technology

In 2005, the Faculty of Engineering, Built Environment and Information Technology at the University of Pretoria implemented a compulsory undergraduate module, Community-based Project (JCP). The decision to create a free-standing module was motivated by the need to accommodate community service projects within the curricula of all undergraduate programmes in the faculty. In 2015 approximately 1700 students registered for the module and worked on more than 550 projects with around 350 community partners. The module requires students to work in the community for at least 40 h (50% of the total credits for the module), during which time they address a specific need in the community and transfer knowledge or a skill in the process. The module uses a blended learning approach to coordinate the projects and manage the logistics of such a large group of students. Students have to complete various online assignments where they reflect on their experiences. Popular student projects include teaching Mathematics and Physical Sciences at secondary schools, doing renovation projects, repairing old computers for schools and non-profit organisations, and teaching basic computer skills to community members. Some exceptional projects were laying pipes to bring water to a rural community and building a composting machine for a community of people with AIDS who wanted to start a business to support themselves. This module gives students the opportunity to render a service to a community of their choice. The aim of the module is to develop an awareness of personal, social and cultural values, as well as to inculcate multidisciplinary and life skills in the students, such as communication, interpersonal and leadership skills, while providing a service to the community. Students have the option of completing the eight-credit (80 h) module in any one of their undergraduate years of study. The module was accredited by the Engineering Council of South Africa and is the only one of its kind in higher education in South Africa. As part of the curriculum, a section is included on gender awareness, as well as HIV/Aids in the workplace. The module has had such a positive impact on students that former JCP students become mentors for the new group of students and assist in the administration of the module. These students also assist as drivers, as many of the projects are not accessible by public transport. Graduates also remain involved in the module. After attending a contact session that includes a briefing on the nature of communities and engagement as well as security issues, and discussing their projects with the lecturer, students may start with their minimum 40 h of fieldwork. Students receive limited funding and have to find sponsors for their projects. Many students are able to find sustainable funding. The students are partly assessed on various assignments on the University's learning management system, a presentation and a report in the form of a YouTube video. A representative in the community takes responsibility for overseeing the students' project, assessing it, verifying the hours that the students have worked and approving the final YouTube video on the project. If the community does not pass the students, they fail the module. The module has a number of sustainable community partners. Students may also identify their own community partners. An advisory committee, comprising members of the communities involved in the modules, assists with planning and identifying possible projects.

10.3.4 Case Study 4: Voluntary Community Engagement

One example of voluntary community engagement by a student society, Enactus, serves to demonstrate how this type of community engagement works. Enactus is an international organization that connects students, communities and business leaders through sustainable projects that empower people to transform their communities. It was established on the UP campus in 2009 and involves about 150 students annually. The main goal of Enactus UP is to enable progress through entrepreneurial action. Enactus provides a platform for university students to collaborate with business, communities and academic leaders in the development of entrepreneurial-based projects that empower people and communities. The programme is run by students in conjunction with university staff, mainly from the Department of Student Affairs, and a Business Advisory Board, consisting of university staff and Enactus UP alumni. The Executive Committee is made up of seven students, diverse in race, culture, religion and academic fields. Each Executive Member independently supervises a team of students to enhance their professional skills in specific portfolios. Community projects are headed by Project Leaders (both senior and junior members) and an Executive supervisor. The issues addressed by Enactus UP are those identified by the government as needs of the country: poverty, unemployment, skills shortages, lack of resources, lack of funding, as well as an increase in crime, obesity and waste (food and recyclables). These are significant to communities and to the country as they affect the quality of life and standard of living of South Africans, which further affects the country's overall growth and development. These issues are more precisely identified through engaging with communities. Enactus UP members undertake extensive research, review statistics and conduct surveys and needs-analyses for every project. Some examples of successful interventions are the following:

- AgriUP, in Rustenburg, addresses the challenge of sustainable sourcing of agricultural raw materials and effective use of farming land. AgriUP has implemented a vertical farming structure, partnered with professionals in the agricultural sector and ensured positive environmental approaches with the help of the Water Research Commission. In 2014, thirteen lives were directly impacted through employment, financial training, and agricultural skills. R13,000 was saved in opportunity costs through sponsored training and free subscriptions to online apps.
- In 2014, Project Dimpho assisted a woman in an underprivileged community of Pretoria to establish a bakery that now supports a feeding foundation and aftercare centre for children in the area. Within five months the project directly impacted four lives through employment and baking skills. 250 children at the feeding foundation were indirectly impacted. R43,000 was generated, with a profit of R11,500.
- Project Kickbax, in Mphumalanga, allows members of the community to explore their creative side while generating an income. The business employs people to custom-paint sneakers in unique designs for sale. In 2013, seven lives were directly impacted through employment and skills development, such as financial training, design and painting skills. R44,650 was generated, with a profit of R18,500.
- Project Learn.ED assisted Donald Ramatsetse to turn his library into a community centre in 2011. Books, computers, printers and desks were sourced by partnering with charity organizations, textbook distributors and UP. Regular courses on computer literacy are held at the centre for students and senior citizens. Furthermore, Enactus UP partnered with Pledge-a-Pad, a non-profit university organization, to create health awareness and assist women. Owing to the growth of the centre, employees have been hired. This project has been self-sustaining for several years.

10.3.5   Case Study 5: Health Sciences

The Department of Family Medicine and its Head of Department, Professor Jannie Hugo, won a national teaching award for their re-imagining of medical training. The awards committee considered that their approach had the potential to revolutionize medical teaching in South Africa. The Family Medicine team comprises University appointees and doctors as well as clinical associates, registrars and support staff at various hospitals. The team's practice is always informed by a clear philosophy to serve the needs of 21st century South Africa: "The practice is your curriculum and the outcome is your test", which means that learning is authentic engagement where practice informs theory. The team's impact on UP students, communities around Pretoria, communities in Mpumalanga and nationally is impressive and they also work in SADC and the rest of Africa. They have extensive community and municipal partnerships. In their words, the "story of the team ... is different every time you tell it". Their story shows how they have progressively moved their practice outwards and downwards to people in their communities. They have integrated their approach from doctoral level to their three-year Bachelor's in Clinical Medical Practice (BCMP). University students traditionally work in tertiary hospitals. At UP they also work in clinics in communities. However, Family Medicine uses community oriented primary care to give students experience of working in areas where problems are experienced. The Department collaborates with the city, which has mapped all areas on a grid. Accompanied by community health workers, students walk to people's homes and do assessments or follow up on treatments or new borns, etc. or visit house-bound people who are ill. Related to their success in primary health care, an agreement was reached with the city in early 2016 to do large-scale harm reduction interventions with the addict programme. Professor Hugo has already spoken to Social Work but there are opportunities for other Faculties to join the initiative as there is an expectation of skills development being available for the addicts. In another related project, Health Sciences has received CDC funding to work with Stellenbosch University on community-based health education and home visits using cell phone technology developed at UP. Besides capturing data, the location feature could be used for SOS purposes. Data captured on the phones can be integrated with other data bases. They currently have data on over 300,000 people. The national Department of Health is thinking of using the system for NHI sites which means that it will be useful to practitioners as well as students. Other Faculties could make use of the system as well.

10.4 Contextual Interpretations of Social Responsibility

Ever since the democratic government's call to demonstrate social responsibility, there has been an on-going debate about the question of how to translate this into the mission of universities. While the contribution to national human capital development is core to the institutional mission of universities, the South African university sector has sought to do more to demonstrate social responsibility.

One interpretation of social responsibility is that it is about the quality of graduates. Industry representatives and professional societies have sometimes expressed criticism that universities are not producing graduates who demonstrate work readiness. Another interpretation relates to an expectation that higher education should be producing graduates who are not only skilled but also feel a sense of responsibility towards society and have acquired skills in cultural tolerance and good citizenship. In initial post-apartheid period the notion of "service" as the third responsibility of universities became pivotal in defining social responsiveness and a great variety of practices manifested themselves, ranging from student volunteerism, service learning, engagement with policy-makers, and community-based action research, to offering specialist skills to communities and other consulting work.

In the initial phase of embracing its social responsibility mission UP, like many other South African universities, focussed its efforts on community engagement as a vehicle to carry out and meet its social responsibility. One of the lessons from the initial community engagement projects is that the conceptualisation of the relationship between the university and communities is a critical success factor. In the early years of implementation, the benefit was often one-way and in many ways the community was treated as an object with no agency or power: the community benefitted from outreach/service, although with little or no say in the matter. This issue was a focal point in the proceedings of a conference held in Cape Town in September 2006 that drew more than 200 delegates from around South Africa as well as from Ghana, India, Mexico, the United Kingdom, and the United States of America. What was learned from this conference was the importance of developing partnerships instead of venturing on one's own and to form or establish a holistic, integrated plan that serves as a road map to do community engagement as a university in such a way that both the individual and the group (community) can benefit and that at the same time is mutually beneficial for all stakeholders. From 2003, the University has changed its approach using as its point of departure the explicit recognition that universities are organically part of the communities in which they are located. Engagement was conceptualized as mutually beneficial, based on respect and trust. Furthermore, it was decided to move away from a situation where there was a plethora of well-intended ad hoc projects.

Today UP has a large, wide-ranging community engagement programme supported by an online Community Engagement Management System (CEMS). Without the latter, managing large-scale community engagement would not be possible. Little more than six years ago, community engagement was still practiced as the third but separate pillar of the University's core business; now it is conceptualized as a key aspect of an institutional strategy that views social responsibility as integral to the identity and purpose of the University. However, it has taken as many as fifteen years of hard work, creativity and innovation and lessons learned along the way to get to this point.

The role and position of the community in a community engagement programme is extremely important. The University deliberately reaches out to its local communities to encourage them to meet UP halfway, to speak face-to-face and on the same level, and to work with us as equal partners.

10.5   A Sustainable Model

In 2000, the University of Pretoria had 1000 projects all over the country—only two proved sustainable in the long-run. Ownership of projects was with the University and not with the communities. Academics did not have time to manage projects in addition to teaching and research. Beginning in 2003, several communities made it clear they did not like the "service" approach (what we do for the community), which created dependency along with charity work. We had to change from a needs-based approach to a solution-orientated approach (what we can do together with the community).

By building trust relationships with communities and partnering with them as equals, the University is able to negotiate opportunities for students to apply their knowledge and skills while reaching desirable learning outcomes. The community has knowledge as well and students learn from community members; thus, there is mutual learning. The model at the University is in the first instance based on credit-bearing curricular community engagement while volunteers (students and personnel) are also welcomed. The latter makes up 20% of the overall community engagement activities undertaken by the University. Voluntary community engagement is integrated with curricular related community engagement activities to form a continuum of engagement in the communities in a purposeful way. This approach and practice help to make community engagement more sustainable. We also integrate multiple disciplines on one platform to contribute to sustainable community development.

The model for community engagement at UP at this stage is four-fold:

(i)   to achieve the three common objectives within the University's main focus areas of:

  – creation of knowledge (research);
  – translation of knowledge (teaching/learning); and
  – application of knowledge (community engagement).

(ii)   to establish partnerships which support and strengthen community agencies relevant to local priorities in order to impact on community development (and to treasure and maintain these partnerships);
(iii)   to integrate teaching and learning, and research with current realities in society; and
(iv)   most importantly, to embed community engagement into the curriculum.

There are different types of community partners. In a country with stark gaps between wealth and poverty, there are also many formal and informal communities, the latter typically with shack housing without infrastructure such as water and electricity. Besides the partnerships with the formal institutions, community partnerships may involve building relationships with community leaders who do not hold any formal position within a clear structure. Then there are often meta-partnerships to be negotiated with government departments such as the Department of Education or the Department of Correctional Services.

As complex as it may be, community engagement produces a number of educational benefits and improves graduate outcomes. Students learn how to work in teams; treat people vastly different from themselves with respect; make decisions together with all stakeholders; manage projects and budgets; plan and set realistic goals and evaluate the success of an activity relative to the intended outcomes. We find that many students work far beyond the required number of hours on particular projects and many continue with community engagement as volunteers once their curricular obligations have passed. The Community Engagement unit does the overall quality assurance of all new and existing sites of learning and draws up maps for safe routes to take to particular sites. These are available on CEMS, our sophisticated, customised, home-grown system.

The impact on communities is visible compared to the situation in past years. The contribution of student engagement to the local economies runs into millions every year as students devote their knowledge freely and often source funds and materials needed to implement projects and activities from the business sector as mentioned. While funding is necessary, throwing money at problems is not the solution. Innovation, creativity and relationship building are the critical success factors.

University policy requires each academic programme to offer one community engagement opportunity to students, although some offer more. Currently more than 90% of our programmes offer at least one module. We have found that it is better not to have students with more than one module per programme as timetables become too loaded, which may undermine students' academic success. A logistical factor is time as students are required to travel to sites, often relying on the underdeveloped public transport system.

The assessment of impact remains a complex and not fully resolved issue. University performance indicators tend to be quantitative such as student numbers in community projects; number of sites of learning in communities; contribution to local socio-economic development—to the neglect of qualitative factors. Measuring impact needs to be participatory as well, so that communities evaluate the impact of an activity. In some modules, communities are asked to provide their evaluation of the students' work. For example, Engineering students make YouTube videos for assessment purposes as evidence of their projects and reaching module outcomes and the community has to agree that the video is an accurate representation of their joint work before it is evaluated. Van Niekerk and Kilfoil (2014) argue that impact assessment should include an analysis of the community's problem, as identified by the community, capacity built in the community and how engagement is practised taking ethical issues into account.

It has taken years of authentic engagement to develop a set of partnerships where the power differential between the University and the community is less asymmetrical and perceived as more equal and where the aim of community engagement is developmental for both the community and the students. Community engagement, among other experiences at the University, helps students to achieve a number of graduate attributes but, most importantly, a sense of social responsibility and civic, cultural and environmental awareness. The core values that drive engagement are human dignity, respect, human rights, social justice and environmental sustainability.

In 2012 the university adopted a long-term strategy, UP2025, which positioned impact on national social and economic development as one of five priorities. In this strategy the University further endeavours to ensure that community engagement frames and becomes integral to the teaching and research nexus. Therefore, although traditionally in South African higher education reference is made to three pillars, namely teaching and learning, research and community engagement, UP intentionally took the approach that community engagement is not separate from the other two pillars and must therefore be integral to them.

10.6 A Research Perspective

Social responsibility in research has multiple dimensions. The scholarship of application, to use one of Boyer's categories of scholarship (1997), is evident in the many publications emerging from the University's practice of community engagement. UPSpace shows that we have 15,725 publications on community engagement in our Open Educational Resources. While some of these are popular publications, most are scientific publications on community engagement over the years. In the social sciences, humanities and law, social responsibility is frequently evident in the topics of research and in the methodologies. Qualitative methodologies such as participatory research and narrative analysis are some examples.

In 2012 when the University began implementation of UP2025, a decision was taken to use identified areas of existing research strength as catalysts to develop cross-cutting research themes of national, regional and/or international relevance. Consequently, in allocating research funding, resources have been concentrated in a selected number of areas or institutional research themes as it was recognised that in a society like South Africa the University must address issues such as establishing effective and just legal systems, sustainable rural development, water and food security, sanitation, energy use, and improving the efficacy of school and college education. Today this commitment is manifested in institutional flagship institutes and centres such as the Institute for Malaria Control, the Centre for Human Rights and the Centre for Food, Nutrition and Well-being, among others.

The Albert Luthuli Centre for Responsible Leadership (ALCRL) is a research centre created five years ago. Almost 3000 first-year students in the Faculty of Economic and Management Sciences are annually exposed to the concept of responsible leadership as part of their formal curriculum. They are challenged on what it means to be socially responsible, the factors that lead to ethical behaviour and, as business management students, they should be well versed in their role as future managers on their responsibility to encourage ethical business behaviour. They study ethics and environmental sustainability (green management) and get to understand the difference between the light green approach (meeting legal and social obligations) and the dark green (activist) approach when considering the impact of organisations on the natural environment. In 2014, in addition to a number of commissioned reports, ALCRL staff produced several scholarly publications.

10.7 Corporate Social Responsibility

Besides consideration of social responsibility in how it conducts its academic mission, UP has given concerted attention to its corporate social responsibility, assessing how, through its business operations, it may better contribute to the transformation of South African society. A major component of this commitment is reflected in its procurement and employment policies, for example. In order to facilitate social change from a system where the majority of people were racially excluded from access to opportunities, in the post-apartheid era South Africa has implemented a policy framework that promotes access for black South Africans in particular. The University actively monitors and ensures its compliance with the spirit of redress, equity and social justice in all its operations and it seeks to go beyond this by making commitments to environmental sustainability especially with respect to energy and water.

The University describes itself as a public research-intensive university that is engaged with the broader society and operates on the basis of the public good; a university that fosters mutually-beneficial interaction with its communities and contributes to the advancement of these communities, that impacts meaningfully on society, is socially responsive and contributes to South Africa's socio-economic development. In alignment with this identity, the University has a partnership with the city government via the office of the executive mayor. The goal of this partnership is to work together to achieve the long-term vision of the city. Pretoria is situated in one of South Africa's three large metropolitan areas, Tshwane, which is the administrative capital of the country. Rapid urbanisation and migration from rural areas and from the rest of Africa has placed enormous pressure on city planning and the provision of services such as health, housing and education. As a public institution, through the partnership, UP provides expertise to the city to support its planning and service delivery. One component of the partnership is the Capital Cities Programme which is an inter-faculty project involving academics and postgraduate students from Humanities; Law; Health Sciences; Natural and Agricultural Sciences; Engineering, Built Environment and Information Technology; Theology and Economic and Management Sciences. This is a programme that works on new questions about Pretoria/Tshwane as a city, capital and metropolis. The uniqueness of capital cities in general, and our capital city in particular, is investigated from the viewpoint of a variety of disciplines, including the arts and language, architecture and urban planning, social work, criminology, law, history, drama, psychology, anthropology, political science and economics.

There are mutual benefits in this relationship as no institution can be a centre of excellence as an island apart from its context. UP is not a closed system, an "ivory tower"; but an institution that is interconnected with society, and is alive to its critical role of contributing to the advancement of South Africa, Africa and the world. This institutional identity is not only aligned with the University's vision but also the dominant understanding of the role of the modern university in the 21st century.

10.8 Conclusion

Through social responsiveness in our operations, academic programmes, research and community engagement we have, as a University, an opportunity to take co-responsibility for the future of South Africa and the planet. We share the vision of a peaceful, democratic, prosperous and just world and we show our commitment towards social responsibility through our large-scale community engagement.

University social responsibility can be interpreted in many different ways. At the centre of these debates is the extent to which social responsibility or community engagement should be identified as a third responsibility for higher education, separate from teaching and learning, and research. Some have argued that while this is intended to give such imperatives priority, the inadvertent effect is to remove it from the well-understood core processes of the university. Rather, it has been suggested that teaching and research should take cognizance of the public good and contribute to learning through rendering service, community participation in engaged and responsive research, and social entrepreneurship.

This brief chapter has given a perspective from UP as we grapple with what it means to be a research-intensive university in a context of societal transition and significant challenges related to inequality. The University is committed unequiv-ocally to the ethos and values of engaging with communities, forming partnerships, applying our knowledge to solve social problems and working towards develop-ment, but as we do so we continue to reflect on the complex meaning of social responsibility in action. To enhance social responsiveness, efforts have been made to integrate the three pillars of university education, namely teaching and learning, research and community engagement within an overall strategic framework that positions UP as an engaged institution. In the broader national context, the more recent focus has been on the role and identity of universities in South African society with specific attention to the role of universities as agents of change. To date engagement at the University in its various forms has created opportunities for UP to confront the relevance of knowledge; stimulated the learning process, opened up new fields for research and enabled students to participate in community devel-opment. It has also enabled students and staff to change perceptions and to become change agents.

While there is still no national consensus on what form it should take, social responsibility is receiving serious attention at all public institutions. The lack of a uniform definition should not be seen as an obstacle or problem but rather as indicative of a dynamic higher education sector where diversity and the freedom to experiment with different approaches allows for the emergence of robust programmes. Continued debate and research are required to analyse what has been learned, to give voice to new ideas and new interventions. In the process, the role of higher education in addressing social and economic development will be strengthened. In the current context, the university is a central institutional actor of scientific and technological change, but also of other dimensions—of capacity to educate and train skills responsive to changing economic and social conditions and a significant contributor to equalisation of chances and democratisation of society.

References

Bezuidenhout, C., & Van Niekerk, G. (2015). Community engagement in correctional facilities: Changing perceptions to make correctional centres sites of preferences. Special issue: Change in African corrections: From incarceration to reincarnation. *Acta Criminologica. South African Journal for Criminology, 2*, 38–51.

Boyer, E. L. (1997). *Scholarship reconsidered: Priorities of the professoriate*. San Francisco: Jossey-Bass.

Council on Higher Education. (2010). Community Engagement in South African Higher Education. Council on Higher Education. *Kagisano* No. 6. Durban: Fishwicks.

Department of Education, Republic of South Africa. (1997). Education White Paper 3: A programme for higher education transformation. *Government Gazette, 18207*, August 15, 1997. Pretoria:Government Printers.

Van Niekerk, G. & Kilfoil, W. (2014). Managing large-scale compulsory curricular community engagement and the partnerships required to make it work. Presented at *TLNC 2014, Talloires conference*, Cape Town.

Chapter 11
Culture, Extension and Social Inclusion in the University of São Paulo

Marcelo de Andrade Roméro, José Nicolau Gregorin Filho and Gerson Yukio Tomanari

Abstract Social responsibility is a fundamental principle to the University of São Paulo (USP). The University aims at providing higher education of excellence status to the most underserved communities. Social-Inclusion Programs are carried out in order to increase the number of students coming from public schools. Concerned about inequality stemming from the ethnic relations in the country, the University of São Paulo has developed more egalitarian University enrollment means. The promotion of culture and university extension is one of the University missions. The Pro-Rectory of Culture and University Extension seeks, through the multiple actions pointed out in this chapter, to establish programs and agencies to give visibility to art and culture, as well as to promote changes in the field of social equality, always with the objective of contributing to the development of the country.

Keywords University of São Paulo · Social responsibility · Social and ethnic equality · Social-inclusion programs · Culture and university extension

11.1 Introduction

The identity of the Pro-Rectory of Culture and University Extension at the University of São Paulo is constructed through different institutional spaces. Thus, at the University of Sao Paulo (hereafter USP), each field of action counts with the

M. de Andrade Roméro
Faculty of Architecture and Urbanism, University of São Paulo, São Paulo, Brazil
e-mail: marcelo_romero@icloud.com

J.N.G. Filho
Philosophy, Letters and Human Sciences, University of São Paulo, São Paulo, Brazil
e-mail: jngf@usp.br

G.Y. Tomanari (✉)
Institute of Psychology, University of São Paulo, São Paulo, Brazil
e-mail: tomanari@usp.br

© Springer Nature Singapore Pte Ltd. 2017
D.T.L. Shek and R.M. Hollister (eds.), *University Social Responsibility and Quality of Life*, Quality of Life in Asia 8,
DOI 10.1007/978-981-10-3877-8_11

work of different Pro-Rectories, whose works are aimed directly for graduate studies, post graduate studies and research.

The area of culture and university extension has the ability to add value and dialogue with the University, as well as with the wider social adjacencies, thus implementing many projects that begin primarily with teaching and research. Therefore, it may be complex to clearly measure the products and actions of these activities, because they are comprehensive and unify actions, thus interconnecting all areas of university life.

As such, the fundamental goal of the Pro-Rectory of Culture and University Extension is to develop and promote social responsibility at the University of São Paulo. The goal is to provide a higher education of excellence status to the most underserved communities, as well as to look for ways to better serve students whose primary education was carried out in public schools. Public schools in São Paulo face numerous hardships related to low budget, lack of resources, location, as well as unprepared staff.

As an example of this social-responsibility and social inclusion at USP, the chart below (Fig. 11.1) shows the percentage of students that completed high school in public institutions and enrolled the University of São Paulo since the year 2012.

The percentage of students coming from public schools has increased 10% in the last 10 years. In order to have around 35% today, USP has implemented and adjusted a series of actions in the selection process of its students along the past years:

- One of them is called INCLUSP, a Social-Inclusion Program that consists of up to 15% as "bonus" for those candidates from public schools.
- PASUSP is a program that also gives bonus points to candidates from public schools; however, this program aims to stimulate students that are still attending high school to know the application process to USP.
- Free application fees for students from public schools depending upon a social assessment.

In addition to these social responsibility activities with students from public schools, there is a concern of the University of São Paulo with inequality stemming from the ethnic relations in the country and, therefore, the institution has sought to develop more egalitarian University enrollment means. During the application process to enroll to USP, the candidates that declare themselves as African or Native-Indian descendants have 5% bonus in their grades, which can sum up to 20% bonus, if this candidate has studied in public schools.

This chart below (Fig. 11.2) shows the access of African-Brazilian descents, Native-Indian communities and their descendants in the last 10 years. The percentage has been from 13% (2006) to 29% (2016), what represents an increase of 16% in the last 10 years.

For many students that achieve their goals and enroll at USP, having enough resources to keep the studies going is a barrier to overcome. For support those

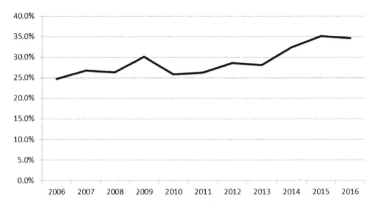

Fig. 11.1 Percentage of students that completed high school in public institutions and enrolled the University of São Paulo from 2012 to 2016 (*Source* Inclusão Social da USP)

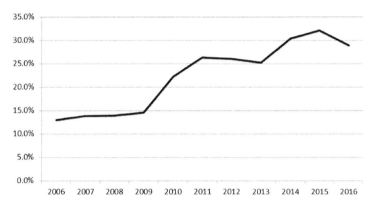

Fig. 11.2 Percentage of students that declare themselves to be African or Native-Indian descendant at the University of São Paulo from 2006 to 2016 (*Source* Inclusão Social da USP)

students, USP has provided, in 2016, 6000 scholarships for students to develop projects in one of these three concerns: teaching, research, culture and extension.

Such actions seek to offer more equality in terms of teaching and research developed at the University of São Paulo. Thus, the Pro-Rectory of Culture and University Extension and the Pro-Rectory of Undergraduate Education seek, through multiple actions, to establish programs and agencies to give visibility to art and culture, as well as to promote changes in the field of social equality, always with the objective of contributing to the development of the country.

As previously mentioned, we aim to better translate the plurality of actions that the University of São Paulo performs in the realms of culture and extension, always bearing in mind our inherent social responsibility as a large institution.

11.2 The Pro-rectory of Culture and Extension at USP (PRCEU)[1]

The Pro-Rectory of Culture and University Extension (hereafter PRCEU) has the mission of making students and academia to be both aware of the fact that culture and extension has the power to reconcile research and teaching with topics and issues of social relevance. Moreover, the Pro-Rectory coordinates and executes cultural and extension-related events within the University of São Paulo, through action teams. For activities in teaching units, specialized museums and institutes, the Pro-Rectory acts as an inducer authority, focusing on regulation and development. The mission of PRCEU is also to spread its scope, the core values of academic life, among which highlights the constant zeal for excellence in relations with society. Cultural and extension activities require, by its very nature, a full tune with these values and also with community expectations. From this concept, goals are set such as:

- Mobilize community students to new forms of artistic and cultural events;
- Encourage foreign participation through advisory councils, in all organs of the PRCEU;
- Develop joint activities with teaching and research units, specialized museums and institutes from the understanding that are dynamic specialized research centers that help people analyze the past, understand the contemporary thinking about the future;
- Have a critical attitude towards mass media given its importance as to its former role of culture in the Brazilian and Latin-American society.

The university extension is a credential of excellence, because only universities with history and high quality levels within the research and teaching can pass on to society in the form of services or teaching, and the knowledge gained in all areas. It is the trait that best characterizes the public university profile in Brazil, understood as **an institution in the service of the community**.

Another growing area of mission and outreach in the country is to seek the recognition of their importance to the research and teaching, as the academic approach also favors research work and graduate teaching.

The management of PRCEU is made by the Council of Culture and University Extension (CoCEx), whose main competencies are to:

- Outline the guidelines leading the University's action in the fields of culture and university extension, which are subject to the general rules set by the University Council;
- Ensure, through ongoing assessments, the quality of work and the appropriateness of the means to the purpose of each activity performed;
- Monitor the functioning of the cultural activities and university extension;

---

[1]*The PRCEU*. Retrieved from http://www.prceu.usp.br.

- Decide on the general guidelines for the use of the budgetary allocation for PRCEU, as well as other resources that will be allocated;
- Deliberate on the creation, transformation and dissolution of centres and services in the area of Culture and University Extension;
- Analyze the cultural and university extension activities, indicating the fields that should be given priority for aid;
- Decide on matters submitted by the Rectory, by the University Council or by the Pro-Rectory of Culture and University Extension.

11.2.1 Centres of Culture Maintained by PRCEU

11.2.1.1 Cultural Preservation Center (Hereafter CPC)

It aims to promote actions and reflections on the preservation of the cultural heritage of the University, including its monuments, collections and memories. It is our responsibility to formulate guidelines for the preservation of university heritage inventory related to the cultural property of USP, thus promoting and developing recovery programs focused on documentation and assisting restoration processes, intervention, development as well as the commercialization of items.

Located in a historic building in the neighborhood of Bixiga in São Paulo, the Cultural Preservation Center increases cultural and university extension activities, museum communication activities, heritage education, dissemination of expertise and cultural socialization through research, workshops, courses, lectures, symposia, exhibitions, guided tours as well as artistic presentations. These activities have contributed to the strengthening and diversification of the links between the university and the society.

11.2.1.2 Brasiliana Guita and José Mindlin Library

The Brasiliana Guita and José Mindlin Library (hereafter BBM) houses the *Brasiliana acquis*, which was gathered for over 80 years by the bibliophile José Mindlin, whose donation to the University of São Paulo was held by him and his wife Guita and consolidated by their offspring.

With its massive set of books and manuscripts, the contents of the BBM Library are considered to be a result of one of the most important private collections in the country. There are approximately 30,000 titles including works of Brazilian literature, traveler's accounts, historical manuscripts and literary (original and galleys), journals, scientific books and textbooks, iconography (prints and illustrated albums), art books as well as artist's books (prints). Part of the donated collections belonged to the bibliophile Rubens Borba de Moraes, and was incorporated into the collection upon his will. This is a library whose notorious contents became known in country, as well as abroad, as a single collection including the work of a lifetime dedication to the Brazilian culture and its manifestations.

11.2.1.3 Ruins of "Engenho São Jorge dos Erasmos"

The National Monument Ruins "Engenho São Jorge dos Erasmos", located in Santos, is an Advanced Research Base, Culture and Extension of the PRCEU, with archaeological site and nature park, open to visitations and scientific research, comprehensive educational program with free guided tours aimed at different audiences and calendar free educational and cultural events for all ages.

The open-air museum is a legacy of a period still little known in the history of Brazil. Maintenance witnessed the essence of a settlement and forged the chains of slavery and acculturation of the natives. His scientific activities include extensive research on societies and economies sugar, preparation of teaching materials of history, archeology and biology.

It receives approximately eight thousand visitors annually. The visitation policy aims at the monument of the relationship with the community seeking the identification and valuation of assets by visitors.

11.2.1.4 The "Maria Antonia University Center"

The Maria Antonia University Center (hereafter CEUMA) is housed in historic buildings that housed the old Faculty of Philosophy, Sciences and Letters of USP - FFCL. Having had over two decades of multidisciplinary approach, CEUMA is a place among the cultural institutions of the city, guided by a comprehensive training concept. Strategically located in the central region of São Paulo, an area of high concentration of institutions of culture and education, it serves a diverse audience.

This center has a program of art exhibitions with the general policy of bringing together contemporary artists from different generations, giving way to the most different technical and production areas, and architecture exhibitions and retrospectives that aimed at discussion of the recent past of Brazilian art.

The Maria Antonia University Center offers monthly short courses linked to the area of the humanities and the arts in general and promotes lectures, debates and workshops with experts from various parts of Brazil and abroad, as well as other events that result from the various units of research at USP and partner institutions.

CEUMA also houses the Mello Gilda Library and Souza, with a collection mainly dedicated to contemporary arts and related areas, whose core generator is the collection of books on art, aesthetics and history of art that belonged to Professor Gilda, first professor of Aesthetics at the Faculty of Philosophy, Sciences and Letters of USP.

11.2.1.5 Cinema USP (CINUSP)

Cinema USP "Paulo Emílio" (hereafter CINUSP) is a movie theater that organizes film screenings, debates, previews and other activities for both the academic community and society.

CINUSP presents, with free admission, movies both in the University City area as well as in the previously mentioned University Center Maria Antonia. The trusteeship is performed by the team of teachers and students of the University, and in partnership with major festivals and other cultural institutions.

11.2.1.6 Theater of the University of São Paulo (SUDs)

The Theatre of the University of São Paulo (hereafter TUSP) aims to disseminate the performing arts in its various manifestations and forms of expression, stimulating discussion and reflection about doing theater in Brazil. It encourages the development of university theater groups, especially in USP *campuses,* and provides the integration of internal and external community of the University in its own projects and in partnership with other units.

Located in Maria Antonia University Center, it offers the public a rich program of theater performances, meetings, lectures, seminars, exhibitions and festivals, defined by invitations, occupation edicts and curatorship. In order to give visibility to the research and production of theatrical university environment, this program seeks to address both training schools, newly graduates work, companies and established collectives.

In addition to its headquarters, the TUSP also seeks to stimulate cultural production in the state, working in various campuses of USP. The actions promoted within the escope of TUSP are enhanced by the presence of cultural agents, building on dialogue between different audiences inside the campus.

11.2.1.7 USP Choir

The Choir of the University of São Paulo (hereafter CORALUSP) is open to the participation of the whole community, consisting of 12 groups and 03 choir workshops. It aims at improving the performance of the singers, offering all of them a proper didactic orientation program, vocal technique and musical structure. The varied collection of choir works mainly composed of Brazilian popular music arrangements which is available for consultation.

11.2.1.8 USP Symphony Orchestra (Hereafter OSUSP)

The Symphony Orchestra of the University of São Paulo, founded in 1975, had its first conductor the composer Camargo Guarnieri (1907–1993). In 1996, he released a CD with works of his own. In 2000, OSUSP toured Germany, being warmly applauded. In 2003, he released a new CD with compositions specially chosen for their core strings. In the same year, it was created the National Composition Competition Camargo Guarnieri. In 2005, it was released a CD to commemorate the 30th anniversary of the OSUSP and in 2006 the Orchestra received the Carlos Gomes Award for "Best Orchestra of the Year". The Orchestra promotes Academy Project aimed at postgraduate students and professional musicians.

11.2.1.9   Science and Technology Park (CienTec)

The Science and Technology Park (hereafter CienTec Park) is a space that invites to discover how science and technology are present in your life, with the mission to promote recognition, appreciation and preservation of scientific cultural heritage of the University of São Paulo, through the relationship between society, culture, science and technology, ensuring accessibility and environmental sustainability.

The CienTec Park opens its doors to schools, general visitors and researchers who want to conduct field work in various areas, such as astronomy, meteorology, education, ecology, among others.

The CienTec Park is located in the State Park Ipiranga Sources in the southern part of the Greater São Paulo, and it features a rich mix of historical and natural heritage. Among the activities offered to the public, a few include: the planetarium, sky observation in historical scope, forest trails and experiments in the fields of physics, geophysics, soil, microbiology, among others.

11.3   The Actions of Culture and Extension PRCEU/USP

11.3.1   The PRCEU Programs

The PRCEU defines program as a set of organizational and institutional character of actions of medium to long term, with clear guidelines, aiming at a common goal, linking the extension actions with projects, courses, events, service delivery and publications, in addition to research and teaching activities. Our most prominent programs are:

11.3.1.1   Nascente Program

The Nascente Program aims at encouraging artistic creation to stimulate reflection on art and culture, bringing together the whole of the university community.

It is an initiative that is intended to reveal new talents through a competition opened to undergraduate and USP graduate, including students from the School of Dramatic Arts of the School of Communications and Arts.

Each year the Spring Program awards actors, poets, musicians, photographers, painters, directors, performers, writers, composers, designers, sculptors, filmmakers, among others, all belonging to the universe of young people daily by various institutes and colleges of the University.

11.3.1.2 Giro Cultural Program

The Giro Cultural program aims at disseminating the architectural, artistic and scientific heritage of the University of São Paulo. This is done by a bus tour, departing and arriving at the USP Sports Center. A team of mediators, formed by the students of the University, guides the tour and interacts with participants. The scripts are: "USP and modernist São Paulo", with visits to modernist monuments of the São Paulo city; "Scientific Collection"; "Cultural Assets" and "Panoramic View: A tour of the *campus*". The last three routes seek to show visitors the achievements of science, culture and the architecture of the University of São Paulo.

11.3.1.3 Rights Center

This program aims at encouraging and supporting actions of the university community, which are: (1) the interface between culture and extension measures, (2) teaching and research, (3) contributing towards an ever greater engagement of USP in cultural construction, (4) science, technology, and policy in a just, free and democratic manner. In this sense, it brings together initiatives that are in congruence with human rights, in their individual, social and political expressions.

Basis of the relationship between universally defensible values of mutual recognition and human emancipation and the construction of answers to particularized needs—concerning social identities (class, gender, race/ethnicity, religion, sexual orientation), the life cycle (children, youth, elderly) and physical and mental disabilities—the horizon of rights shows up as a powerful perspective for solidarity and plural construction of the various programs and projects that constitute this core with the following programs:

Approaching Action Program

The Approaching Action Program's goal is to become a privileged space for dialogue between actions and projects of the University of São Paulo (USP), on *campus* of Butantã in São Paulo, and community social demands, inventorying, coordinating and supporting the training activities and social inclusion through actions within the various areas of knowledge. Their activities developed aim at:

- Disseminating a culture of respect for diversity and recognized rights of children and adolescents on the *campi* of USP;
- Performing diagnosis of social demands and the actions carried out at the University;
- Remoting educational activities that encourage social development of the neighboring communities to the *campi* of USP

Using methodologies of community education, and in an open environment, it seeks to create links between the children and adolescents, their families and the institutions that serve, through socio-educational monitoring. Additionally, it aims at systematizing the experiences accumulated by the University in the field of social education, to assist in the training and Integral Protection Network strengthening and spread them on the campus of USP, as well as providing the knowledge generated to other universities to experience similar issues.

Facilitators provide means for conducting research on issues related to their field, and contribute to educate and train university's staff and students of this university in the area covered by the program, its methodologies and experiences.

Open University for the Third Age (UATI)

The purpose of this project is to enable the elderly to deepen their knowledge in areas of interest. Given the UN and UNESCO criteria, it prioritizes the age from 60 years. With this program, seniors enroll in courses offered at USP, allowing the continuity of learning and updating the individual.

USP Diversity

Program has been created in order to develop actions that encourage solidarity and the promotion and respect for human rights. Initially, the program dealt with sexual diversity. Gradually, other segments and groups are included. The USP Diversity articulates with projects, programs, activities and groups existing in the university. This program's actions are based on a continuous assessment of the local context conditions that hinder or exclude the exercise of rights and a consultation with the university community to create diversity policies. At the same time, create specific working groups to address themes and issues identified through consultation with the university community and ratified by the Academic Committee of the program. It also develops training and mobilization work of multipliers in different units, training and sensitization of teachers and non-teaching servers, including outsourced. It promotes a broad discussion on the formation, in order to incorporate the related topics in research, teaching and extension and stimulate the creation of courses on diversity. Thus, a fundamental part of the work is done with the support of organized groups within the institution itself.

USP Legal

In Brazil, there is a significant portion of the population involved, directly or indirectly, to the issue of disability. This program has the mission to coordinate joint actions of different areas of the University (undergraduate, graduate, research, culture and extension) to ensure the full inclusion of students with disabilities, faculty members and staff. The program operates with a socio-technical approach to dismantle the exclusionary processes within the University, removing attitudinal, architectural, educational and communication barriers, putting up as a repository of experiences of inclusion and reference point for the units, agencies and community USP.

The USP Legal program also conducts external partnerships, providing communication channels for dissemination of information on the subject. Thus, the program encourages social inclusion, improving the quality of life and citizenship of people with disabilities, with a space for reflection and interaction between the University and the society.

Technological Incubator of Popular Cooperatives

The Technological Incubator of Popular Cooperatives is a University Extension Program that operates in fostering solidarity economy. Founded in 1998 from a study group led by Professor Paul Singer and the initiative of the Executive Coordination of University Cooperation and Special Activities (CECAE), the Technological Incubator of Popular Cooperatives-USP encourages and supports the establishment of enterprises in communities in the outskirts of São Paulo, forming groups to practice the self and its place in the market in various economic activities, such as food, clothing and sewing, urban agriculture, producing cleaning and hygiene products, services and technical assistance in information technology. Workers seek alternative income generation against the inequality and unemployment are organized in labor unions, whose basic principles are the collective ownership of production and distribution means, democratic management and enhancement of the worker.

Such projects are created through a process of continuing education aimed at autonomy and emancipation of managed groups, as well as the development of new relations of production and labor. The inseparability of teaching, research and extension is another important assumption. Training and production research are practices that are part of the intervention carried out by ITCP. Since 1999, the ITCP-USP set up the National ITCPs Network. Scattered throughout the country, currently about 40 institutions of higher education have similar programs.

11.3.2 Main Events of PRCEU/USP[2]

11.3.2.1 Week of Art and Culture

Held annually, it is consolidated in the academic calendar of the University. This achievement is due not only to Resolution 4366 of the Council of Culture and

---

[2]The PRCEU. Retrieved from http://www.prceu.usp.br.

Extension, which established the Week of Art and Culture in 1997, but also to spontaneously unifying character of its artistic and cultural actions implemented in all the *campi* of USP.

It fulfills its role as integration with society, carrying out activities planned by teaching units, agencies and coordinators of the *campuses* of USP. It shows the cultural potential of our teachers, students and staff in such a way that essentially technical units exhibit artistic and photographic exhibitions, choirs, theater groups, orchestras, concerts and dance. In this rich environment, it is not uncommon vocations and talents are revealed in the midst of units and agencies dedicated essentially to culture. Society, to honor these events, it is also fully benefited—not only for the diversity and quality of activities, but also for their free admission.

11.3.2.2   USP and the Careers Fair (FEPUSP)[3]

The shows "USP and the Careers" are big events lasting three days are held twice a year. Arranged stands format is free and targets mainly students of high school and preparatory courses for college entrance. Groups of visiting students receive University teacher teams, monitors (undergraduates and graduate) and clarifications employees about the Teaching Units and their infrastructure, the courses offered, the college entrance examination, the academic, the bars disciplines the syllabus and specializations. There is one in São Paulo and other organized annually in each of the other campuses of USP (Bauru, Lorena, Piracicaba, Pirassununga, Ribeirão Preto and São Carlos). The purpose of roaming is to give visiting students a general knowledge of the infrastructure offered in these campuses. The FEPUSP discloses only the courses offered in the countryside campuses, receiving an average audience of seven to eight thousand visitors including students, teachers, parents, other stakeholders and companions.

11.3.2.3   Scientific Journey

Its goal is to make the world of science and technology closer to society from the state. They carried out hundreds of activities, including workshops, experiments, shows, games, lectures, film and planetarium sessions. There are activities for all ages and admission is free.

In the state capital, the activities are held in various units of the USP campus, as well as in its centers and institutes in the countryside campuses.

---

[3]*A USP e as profissões* (2016).

11.3.3 Publications

11.3.3.1 Journal of Culture and Extension[4]

Biannual publication that aims to disseminate extension projects in language accessible to the general public. Its printed version is distributed free to public and private educational institutions, libraries and cultural centers of diffusion. There is an online version of the journal.

11.3.3.2 Paths of Culture

Monthly guide brings highlights of the cultural program and science communication at the University of São Paulo. The brochure is distributed for free in USP Teaching Units, public libraries and cultural centers and the full version, permanently updated, it is on the website of the Culture and University Extension.

11.3.3.3 Extension Course Catalog and Training Activities

Biannual publication that aims at disseminating the courses of the following ways: improvement, dissemination, updating, specialization and the activities of professional practice, residence and upgrade programs.

11.3.3.4 Catalog "USP and the Careers"

Annual publication that disseminates information about careers and courses at USP, labor market and infrastructure provided by the teaching units. The catalog is available for consultation on the website of the Pro-Rectory of Culture and University Extension and is also distributed in public schools.

11.4 Fostering Culture and Extension

Given the characteristics of the activities developed at the University of São Paulo, PRCEU supports the holding of symposia, meetings, forums, national and international meetings related to the area of Culture and Extension, and seeks to support new initiatives of culture and originating extension of the Units, Institutes, Museums and Halls.

---

[4]*Revista de Cultura e Extensão da USP*. (2016) Retrieved from http://www.revistas.usp.br/rce.

These initiatives should aim at university extension through the application, dissemination of knowledge and cultural initiatives produced at the University, in actions aimed at interaction with the society in general, giving priority to reach a wide audience to explain the combination of these actions with research activities and teaching,—even if the project does not contemplate the simultaneous and immediate realization of these three spheres of activity.

The PRCEU has an annual budget of approximately US $3,000,000.00, part of which is applied to foster culture and extension programs described above, such as: support for events, scholarships for undergraduates and graduate students, scientific and cultural information, as well as assistance to teaching and student mobility.

All funds for conducting activities are requested by a corporate online system known as "Apolo", system that also provides for accountability and consolidation impact, indicators of the shares of PRCEU, indicators these updated by DataUSP system and available to all internal and external community.

11.5 Future Possibilities

In this short text, actions were shown the Pro-Rectory of Culture and USP University Extension and by themselves, they can already show the diversity of actions and the size of its operations, or within the activities of its agencies and programs, either in promoting the extension of undergraduate and graduate and research developed at the University of São Paulo.

There are thus two main tasks regarding the role of culture and extension at the University of São Paulo: the first points to the culture and extension as disclosed agent of the research carried out; the other one, points to actions that, through debate, promote the reduction of inequalities of all sorts still very present in our society and, in this sense, the actions already undertaken to human rights and the so called minorities are also required.

So, to think of these two tasks as a priority for the community, it is clear, on the one hand, the need for continuity of outreach activities, leading to society teaching and research activities developed here, and on the other hand, culture as priority in the constant quest to trim the edges through the promotion of dialogue, a dialogue built through science and art in all its expressions.

Steps for the future can be enlarging:

- continue collaborating with USP in promoting social responsibility;
- foster culture and extension programs at the University of São Paulo through partnerships with public and private institutions;

- promote actions related to human rights through actions of the PRCEU Rights Center;
- edit *on-line* publications for scientific and cultural dissemination;
- exchange actions with Brazilian and foreign institutions to enlarge experiences in the field of culture and extension.

Finally, we must rethink the culture area in our universities, with new studies, reflections and debates, always with the objective of carrying pathways that may change, since the University is an integral part a society that recreates itself.

Chapter 12
Cultivating Competent Individuals Thinking Globally in a Local Setting: Service Learning at Kyoto University

Naoki Egami and Takami Shigeru

Abstract COCOLO-IKI project is a nickname of Kyoto University's Center of Community (COC) project. COC project is an important new subsidized project that was set up by the Ministry of Education, Culture, Sports, Science and Technology (MEXT). A proposal by Kyoto University titled "KYOTO Future Creation Project for Establishing the Center of Community" has been selected for FY 2013 COC project by MEXT. COCOLO-IKI project aims at promoting community-oriented education, research and social activities with local community and contributing to the development of global human resources with a broad education. To achieve the aim, we developed "Kyotology Education Program." The program consists of lecture-based learning (MANABI-YOSHI classes) and project-based learning (IKI-YOSHI classes), offering a greater number of learning opportunities that take advantage of Kyoto's rich historical heritage and other unique features. In addition, we established Education and Research Unit for Regional Alliances as a one-stop service center to promote collaborations between students, researchers, and the local community. The unit also supports students contributing to revitalization of local communities.

Keywords Kyoto University · Community-oriented education · Center of community · Japan

12.1 Fundamental Policy and Local Commitment of Kyoto University

12.1.1 Fundamental Policy of Kyoto University

Kyoto University has defined its fundamental policy based on freedom and harmony in four areas: (1) research, (2) education, (3) relation with society and

N. Egami (✉) · T. Shigeru
Kyoto University, Kyoto, Japan
e-mail: info@coc.kyoto-u.ac.jp

© Springer Nature Singapore Pte Ltd. 2017 191
D.T.L. Shek and R.M. Hollister (eds.), *University Social Responsibility and Quality of Life*, Quality of Life in Asia 8,
DOI 10.1007/978-981-10-3877-8_12

(4) management, and set it as the goal of the entire university. The university thus intends to solve multifaceted problems and contribute to harmonious coexistence in the global community, while preserving and developing its liberal atmosphere nurtured in the university since its foundation.

1. Research

   - Creation of globally distinguished intelligence (knowledge and wisdom) based on freedom and autonomy through research activities conforming to highly ethical standards
   - Diverse developments and integration of basic and applied researches, humanities and science studies, etc. attainable as a university

2. Education

   - Facilitation of dialog-based self-learning, succession of distinguished intelligence, and cultivation of creative minds under the diverse and harmonious educational systems
   - Nurturing excellent researchers and individuals with excellent expertise who are equipped with superior education, rich humanity and a strong sense of responsibility, and capable of contributing to harmonious coexistence in the global society

3. Relation with society

   - Reinforcement of cooperative relations with the Japanese and local societies; transmission to the society of the intelligence based on freedom and harmony as a university open to the public
   - Contribution to deepening international exchange and realization of harmonious coexistence in the global society as a university open to the world

4. Management

   - Promotion of respect for autonomy of education and research institutions as well as harmony in the entire university with the view to help facilitate unfettered advancement of academic studies
   - University management that respects environmental considerations and human rights; reliable response to social accountability

12.1.2   Kyoto University's Commitment to "Community-Oriented Initiatives"

Kyoto University has a tradition as a so-called "research university", pursuing the creation of intelligence (knowledge and wisdom) that is distinguished not only in Japan but also in the world. Meanwhile, in light of its history, the university is destined to play another important role. The historical fact is that Kyoto Prefectural

Government contributed as much as a little more than 60% of the university's founding cost at the time of its foundation and also offered land and other support when the new faculties were later established. Thus, the support from local governments and communities brought birth to this school, and it can be said that the university virtually started as a "state university". This strong bond with the local communities in the early days has rather tended to be forgotten as the university became renowned as a "research university". In recent years, however, Kyoto University has repeatedly referred to its historical origin, attached greater importance to its "relation with society" and placed "cooperation with regional society" as another important pillar of the university management strategies.

As part of this movement, in April 2010, we initiated a "meeting for discussing the future of Kyoto", to take the initiative in opinion exchange from different angles about the "vision of what Kyoto wants to be in 30 years." This meeting was made up of the representatives of the local governments, academic circles, financial community, tourism, culture, and mass media, among whom are the governor of Kyoto Prefecture, the mayor of Kyoto City, the president of Kyoto University, the president of the Kyoto Chamber of Commerce and Industry, the chairpersons of Kyoto Prefecture Tourism Federation and Kyoto City Tourism Association, the succeeding head of the flower arrangement school Ikenobo, and the owner of the Kyoto Shimbun, a newspaper publishing company. At the meeting, the members have had a lively discussion on a broad range of subjects, e.g., population issues in the local communities, environmental and energy issues, town planning and local transportation, regional development, protection of cultural assets, creation of new cultures, tourism promotion, industrial development, university town and so forth. They have also agreed that they do not just create an "ideological vision", but share the "vision of how Kyoto wants to be in 30 years' time" and take a step forward to make an all-out effort for its realization.

In addition, the meeting's final recommendations included the following statement: "The role of the university is to create knowledge and wisdom and to transmit them to the world. The university is also considered to assume the duty as the Center of Community (COC). While the university communicates with the regional communities and strives to solve urgent regional issues, learning also has to contribute to the society by making innovations." In April 2010 when the meeting started, the university also instituted the Comprehensive Practical Research Unit for Regional Sustainability Science with a view to respond to the regional challenges of Kyoto and play its role as the decision-making and promotion center for town planning. Since then, under the leadership of the university president, we have implemented projects for solving various regional problems as the driving force for realizing the future Kyoto vision in cooperation with Kyoto Prefecture and Kyoto City. The Mayor of Kyoto's remark that "Kyoto University has changed" as recorded in the minutes of the meeting truly shows the high expectations from the regional society toward our "community-oriented" initiatives. The university arranges regular meetings for opinion exchange among the local governments, academic circles, and financial community, and works on promoting town planning, solving regional problems and developing the regional communities through close communication. All these "community-orientated initiatives" are reinforcing the functions of the university as a so-called COC.

12.1.3 Details of "Community-Orientated" Initiatives of Kyoto University and Related Programs

Our "community-oriented initiatives" are stipulated in details as the second stage mid-term program and the annual program of the university. The objectives are: (1) enlarging the opportunities for the young generation and local residents to experience the most advanced part of academic fields; (2) promoting cooperation with society to help develop the cultures, arts, and industries of Kyoto, in which the tradition and state-of-the art are woven, by making the most of the academic resources available within the university; (3) sorting out the research results obtained within the university, acquiring intellectual property rights, and promoting their practical use; (4) working out a teacher assessment system that incorporates social contribution assessment items in light of the university's fundamental policy and goals. The following are the specific details of the community-orientated initiatives.

1. Enlarging the opportunities for the young generation and local residents to experience the most advanced part of academic fields and for working adults to resume learning

   - Opening the lectures of Kyoto University to university students studying in the Kyoto region through "The Consortium of Universities in Kyoto"
   - Enlarging the opportunities of lifelong education for local residents by holding Kyoto University forums, Future forums, Kyoto University Public Lectures "Sunju Kogi", exhibitions at the Kyoto University Museum, etc., and utilizing them as the bases for cooperation with the local communities
   - Organizing Junior Campus events, working on projects in cooperation with Super Science High schools; further promoting cooperation with secondary schools through visiting lectures; supporting teachers' training; providing support for correcting the educational gap between the regions

2. Promoting cooperation with society to help develop the cultures, arts, and industries of Kyoto by making the most of the academic resources available within the university

   - Making recommendations on recycling society by developing energy-conserving and energy creation technologies; conducting studies on the lifestyle that is symbiotic with forest, villages and sea
   - Conducting studies and making recommendations on effective and efficient operation of the bus system in the regions facing transportation problems as well as aging and declining population

- Coordinating preservation and exhibition of local cultural assets; studying the relations between cultural assets as tourist attractions and regional development
- Developing, spreading and providing instructions on cultivation of new Kyo-yasai or Kyoto vegetables; conducting pluralistic research on local agricultural promotion measures; facilitating communication with local growers
- Studying and disseminating measures against damage caused by animals, i.e., deer, boars and especially monkeys
- Experimental promotion of depopulated regions by enhancing the opportunities for lifelong learning; arranging scientific communication in science cities; examining the items to be deregulated in line with the application for the designated university utopia zone
- Promoting the local marketing for creating the Kyoto brand and disseminating its effects
- Working out a technical and management support system for declining local industries, e.g., Nishijin brocade

3. Sorting out the research results obtained within the university, acquiring intellectual property rights, and promoting their practical use

- Creating a database of industrial property rights and open patent information at the Office of Society-Academia Collaboration for Innovation (SACI)
- Creating a market for carbon emission trading and its dissemination in the Kyoto region

4. Working out a teacher assessment system that incorporates social contribution assessment items in light of the university's fundamental policy and goals

- Gradual shift from the conventional teacher assessment system based primarily on research achievement to a well-balanced comprehensive system incorporating educational outcomes and the extent of social contribution

12.1.4 Kyoto University's "Community-Oriented" Initiatives and Education

In recent years, cultivation of global leaders has been a pressing need, in which Kyoto University plays an important part. The global competence, however, needs to be bolstered by deep understanding and knowledge of our national history, culture and tradition. To attain this, enlargement of opportunities for their acquisition is indispensable, and fortunately, the Kyoto region offers an abundance of such opportunities.

Young people gathering from all over Japan to Kyoto University are able to acquire the basic skills to become globally active experts by taking up the challenges facing the Kyoto region. Thus, the Kyoto region provides the optimal field for carrying out the university's mission to cultivate such competent individuals.

In 2013, as part of the project for cultivating global leaders through hands-on experience with problems in the local community, Kyoto University newly started "Kyoto University Design School" and "Shishu-Kan Graduate School of Advanced Leadership Studies Program" as well as other graduate school educational programs (Kawai n.d.).

Kyoto University Design School aims to develop experts with doctoral degree who are capable of designing the "social systems and architecture" in collaboration with the experts in informatics, mechanical engineering, architecture, management and psychology. The school incorporated a "field internship" as a feature of the curriculum for attaining this objective. This is a new attempt to exploit the "power of field education" (Design School of Kyoto University n.d.). Students from different specialties make up a team, and while they stay together for several weeks at the universities and the fields both in Japan and abroad for problem solutions, they experience problem detection through solution. This field internship aims to develop leadership skills through group activities, unlike traditional internships that are individually served.

Shishu-Kan aims to develop knowledge through the integration of humanities and sciences as well as interdisciplinary studies and the abilities to think and practically implement the acquired expertise in society. The curriculum incorporates a "project-based research", in which the students are required to draw up a plan for their own project and implement it with the involvement of Japanese enterprises and government agencies.

This kind of educational activities at the graduate school are deeply related to service learning in that students undergo practical education by understanding the regional needs and working toward the solution of the regional issues. Thus, the university places the prime importance on these programs in educating global leaders in a local community. However, the nature of these programs that requires an extremely high quality of education limits the number of students to be admitted.

Accordingly, the university newly launched in the academic year 2014 a community-oriented project titled "COCOLO-IKI" for undergraduate students. The details of this project are described in the following section.

12.2 COCOLO-IKI Project

12.2.1 COCOLO-IKI as Part of the MEXT's University COC Project

Kyoto University's COCOLO-IKI project has been implemented as part of the Ministry of Education, Culture, Sports, Science and Technology (MEXT)'s supplementary project called "The University COC Project". The University COC Project is explained in the MEXT's website as follows:

> In collaboration with the local governments and communities, the university implements reforms of university-wide curricula and educational organizations to become a "university for the local community" which implements community-oriented education, research and social contribution. In the meantime, the university strives to solve regional problems by effectively matching the regional problems (needs) and the resources of the university (seeds). The university also shares the understanding of the regional challenges with the local governments and communities, and collaboratively launch projects based on the shared understanding, considering the planning and implementation of regional development measures. Through these efforts, the university cultivates individuals who deepen their understanding of the regional challenges and other issues by learning at the university and responsibly work on the solutions. At the same time, the university promotes governance reform and differentiation by mission by capitalizing on its strength to become a center of regional revival and revitalization (MEXT n.d.).

In summary, the objective of the University COC Project is to promote the reform of educational curricula in collaboration with the local communities. In the academic year 2013, MEXT started inviting the applications for participants in this project. In the academic year 2013, 52 proposals were selected from 319 applications, whereas 25 proposals were selected from 237 applications in the academic year 2014. The selected universities are to implement educational curriculum reform in cooperation with the local communities, while receiving the subsidies from MEXT for five years starting from the time of adoption. Kyoto University is one of the 52 universities adopted in the academic year 2013. The university started its activities as part of the University COC Project in September, 2013, and publicly launched the full-fledged COCOLO-IKI project in April, 2014.

12.2.2 COCOLO-IKI Project—Its Objectives and Outline

The COCOLO-IKI project has the following three major objectives:

1. University organization reform to promote cooperation with the local communities
2. Cultivation of global leaders who have learned history, culture and tradition from the local communities and are bolstered by such knowledge and deep understanding
3. Regional revitalization through educational activities performed in collaboration with the local communities

As part of the university organization reform to promote cooperation with the local communities, the university renamed the "Education and Research Unit for Regional Alliances" in the Center for Promotion of Interdisciplinary Education and Research (C-PIER) as the "Unit for Promotion of Education and Research in Cooperation with Local Communities", and inaugurated it an organization responsible for the COCOLO-IKI Project operation. This unit also functions as a one-stop liaison office for regional cooperation that receives a broad range of inquiries from local groups and companies.

As a matter of course, Kyoto University has already had the Office of SACI and other organizations that handle collaborative research with outside institutions. However, these organizations have mainly dealt with relatively large-scale collaborations mostly in natural science fields; local bodies, therefore, had been rather hesitant to bring their immediate problems in to the university. Since its inauguration, the unit has been receiving inquiries even from the local governmental bodies in the neighbourhood, and some of them actually remarked, "we did not know before which organization of the university we should send our inquiries to, but now we can as we know that this unit works as a liaison office". This exemplifies the fact that the university has not been open to the local communities not only due to its institutional problems but also in terms of the image the local people have of the university. The COCOLO-IKI project sets the organizational reform for promoting cooperation with local communities as one of its major objectives partly because the university strives to improve its image.

The second objective is (2) cultivation of global leaders who have learned history, culture and tradition from the local communities and are bolstered by such knowledge and deep understanding. One of the features of the COCOLO-IKI educational program is that the group of related subjects is included in the common subjects for all students so that students from all faculties can attend the lectures regardless of their majors. The details of this educational program is explained in the following section, but in short, the so-called "*Kyotology* Educational Program" provides a multiple of subjects for learning about the history, culture and the current problems of Kyoto as the common subjects for all students. Students who have completed six subjects are awarded the "Elementary Public Policy Consultant" qualification by Consortium for Local Public Human Resources Development (COLPU) (COLPU n.d.).

The main objective of the COCOLO-IKI Project is to attain (3) regional revitalization through educational activities performed in collaboration with the local communities, specifically by establishing the one-stop liaison office for regional cooperation and providing the *Kyotology* Educational Program. However, in responding to the inquiries from local communities, the unit may find some proposals that cannot fit well into the university's conventional organization or regular curricula. In order to respond to such proposals to the greatest extent possible, the unit also works as a coordinator to organize a student team (or ask an existing student circle for cooperation) so that the student team and a local body can work on a joint project that would lead to "regional revitalization". These activities are extra-curricular but practical in that students are directly involved in regional problems. Thus, they have a strong aspect of service learning, providing students with opportunities to lean various things. The specific details are described in the following section.

12.2.3 Qualities to Be Cultivated in Kyotology Educational Program

The "University Reform Action Plan—developing universities that will work as the engines for societal changes" submitted by MEXT in 2012 says that Japan is now required to meet the needs of the times and grapple with drastic societal changes.

The plan underlines that nurturing of future leaders capable of meeting this calling of time is a pressing need; it calls for cultivation of individuals who are equipped not only with highly advanced expertise but also with qualities of a whole person, e.g., the ability to utilize the acquired expertise, deep insight, ability to take a macroscopic view, high creativity, good judgment, ability to take quick action, ability to communicate actively ad constructively, ability to collaborate synergistically, strong sense of responsibility, and high morality.

In view of this MEXT plan, the *Kyotology* Education Program of the COCOLO-IKI Project aims to nurture the following five qualities:

1. **Strong Sense of Responsibility** To be aware that the student himself/herself is the person to take the initiative in creating the future image of Kyoto and realize it.
2. **Ability to Take a Macroscopic View** Ability to understand the current problems of Kyoto or the community-oriented efforts made to date from a long-range, global, and macroscopic viewpoint.
3. **Creativity** Power to work out a future image of Kyoto and solutions anew to the problems observed macroscopically, utilizing the advanced "intelligence" of Kyoto University.
4. **Frontline Capabilities** Practical skills to ensure realization of the newly created future image and solutions to the problems in a feasible way with a limited resources.
5. **Ability to Collaborate** Ability to discuss with other students, instructors and members of local communities to work out a new future image and solutions to problems and collaborate with them in implementing the worked out solutions.

12.2.4 Outline of Kyotology Educational Program

Kyotology Educational Program aims to cultivate the qualities as listed above through lecture-based learning "Manabi-yoshi" and fieldwork project-based learning "Iki-yoshi", in which students take the initiative in solving the real problems of the local communities. Figure 12.1 shows the system of this program, and the tables show the list of subjects included in the common subjects for all students as part of *Kyotology* Educational Program in the academic year 2015.

In *Kyotology* Educational Program, students who have completed five subjects (10 credits equivalent) selected from among those listed in Table 12.1

| 10 credits are needed to award the qualification. | 2credits are needed to award the qualification. | COLPU (Consortium for Local Public Human Resources Developmen) awards the qualification. |

Fig. 12.1 The system of Kyotology Educational Program

Table 12.1 "Manabi-yoshi" subjects included in common subjects for all students in 2015

Theories for the Future Development of Kyoto Region
The Tradition and Potentialities of the Kyoto School
Japanese History
Politics and Culture in Ancient and Medieval Japan
Historical Society in Ancient and Medieval Japan
History of Kyoto University
The Creation and Suggestion of Travels in Kyoto by Utilizing Geography and Classical Literature
Active Local Engagement based on Kyoto University Museum
Issues of Kyoto as an Industrial City
Science for Kyoto Studies
Science-Communication Learning at Kwasan Observatory
Environmental Studies I [Fundamental Part]
Environmental Studies II [Application Part]
Nature and Culture: Perspectives from Agriculture
Utilization of Nature and Cultural Landscape in Kyoto
Practice-Oriented Area Studies by Learning from the local people and areas in Kyoto and Shiga Prefecture
Practice Cultivating Traditional Kyoto Vegetables
Medical and Health Issues & Policies in Super-aged Communities

"Manabi-yoshi" and one subject (2 credits equivalent) from among those listed in Table 12.2 "Iki-yoshi" are awarded the "Elementary Public Policy Consultant" qualification by Consortium for Local Public Human Resources Development (COLPU). To obtain this qualification, one of the five Manabi-yoshi subjects shall be "Theories for the Future Development of Kyoto Region". Three of these subjects are briefly described below.

Table 12.2 "Iki-yoshi" subjects included in common subjects for all students in 2015

Community Development Policies in Kyoto Prefecture—Community Problem Solving
Utilizing Kanban for Beautification of Cityscapes—Studies and Proposals
An Alternative Development by Learning from Rural Bhutan
Ecotourism in Kyoto: Studying Emotional Dynamics in Forest
The Forest Supporting Kyoto [The study of sustainable forest management based on ecological knowledge]

1. **Theories for the Future Development of Kyoto Region** This is designated as the core subject and required for obtaining the "Elementary Public Policy Consultant" qualification. In about half of the 15 lectures, guest speakers who play an active part in the local communities are invited from outside the university to lecture on the problems of the Kyoto region and how they currently grapple with them. The rest of the lectures are given by university faculty members on the theories related to town planning and solutions to regional issues in reference to the guest speakers' lectures. The guest speakers invited to date include the mayor of Kyoto City, the governor of Kyoto Prefecture, representatives of newspaper and other local media, representatives of local companies and Nonprofit Organization (NPO)'s, a flower arrangement master, a cook and other cultural figures.

2. **Practice Cultivating Traditional Kyoto Vegetables** Students attend an elementary course on agriculture in Kyoto, which includes such topics as the soil, vegetable production and distribution in Kyoto. Students also practice cultivating traditional Kyoto vegetables in the cultivated field located on campus. Local Kyoto vegetable growers are invited to give instructions on their fieldwork. Thus, students learn about the history of food culture in Kyoto not only through lectures but also through practical training in fieldwork.

3. **Utilizing Kanban (Signboards) for Beautification of Cityscapes** Currently, in Kyoto City, signboards are regulated by Cityscape Preservation Ordinance, and the way signboards should be set up in the streets is one of the major points at issue in town planning as they significantly affect the cityscape. In view of such circumstances, this course aims to look at the signboards in cities, towns and villages in Kyoto as well as those within and outside Japan as cultural assets and find ways to pass their merits on to the next generation instead of backward-looking town planning heavily dependent on regulations. In this course, students conduct field survey on the cityscape of Kyoto and other regions and do a comparative analysis of signboards in Kyoto and those of other regions. Then, at the end of the course, students propose to Kyoto City Government officials constructive ways to promote signboard culture that would help create a cityscape of a new era.

12.2.5 Extracurricular Activities

In addition to *Kyotology* Educational Project and other regular curricula, COCOLO-IKI works on various extracurricular activities that are also contributive to local communities. Some of these activities were started by student teams organized by the "Education and Research Unit for Regional Alliances" in response to local needs, while others were based on proposals submitted to the unit by existing student circles within the campus. Recently, the number of the latter cases has been increasing because students can gain trust if they work on activities as part of a university project, not just private ones and the budget for the unit's activities may be appropriated depending on the degree of contribution to the communities. Four specific activities are briefly described below.

1. **COCOLO-JUKU** COCOLO-JUKU is a workshop in which students have discussion with the representatives of local companies and NPO's invited as guest speakers. First, the guest speakers give a lecture on the activities run by their organizations and the problems they currently. Then they have discussion with the students about the solutions to those problems. At the end of the discussion, if the students can propose a feasible solution and the guest wants to fund it, they launch a project for that solution. The COCOLO-JUKU workshops are planned, proposed, launched and operated by students. Currently, the workshop is held once a month on average.

2. *Kyotology* **Internship Program** This is a joint project of Kyoto University and Ashinaga Scholarship Society (supporting children who lost parents). The faculty members of Kyoto University give lectures on the distinctive features of Kyoto to the students from major universities around the world who have applied for the internship offered by Ashinaga Scholarship Society. Kyoto University students also participate in this program as guides for the foreign student interns, attend the lectures and experience global exchange in the local setting.

3. **Genius Table in Kyoto** This is a luncheon meeting for exchange between foreign guests and residents in Kyoto. In addition to a multitude of historical cultural heritage, Kyoto has many universities as education and research institutions. Accordingly, many of the foreign visitors to Kyoto are highly cultivated and learned. Kyoto is also ranked the No. 1 tourist spot of the world in TRAVEL +LEISURE website, thus attracting global attention as a tourist spot and actually experiencing an upsurge of tourists (Lieberman 2016). The university launched this project in view of this situation, considering that providing opportunities for intellectual exchange of people would add more value to the city of Kyoto than merely devising measures to increase the number of foreign visitors. The program is also planned, proposed, launched and operated by students (Genius Table n.d.).

4. **Tera School** This is a project to provide learning support to children and opportunities of lifelong learning to adults, using the local temples and shrine as the space for learning. It borrows motifs from "terakoya" or "tera school", a private educational facility in the Edo Period for which tera or a temple was often used. Students operate this project in collaboration with the local NPO's.

12.3   Kyoto University's Future Vision and Challenges

Kyoto University's future vision has been framed as the "WINDOW Concept". In this context, "enhancement of educational contents considering connection with society" is regarded as an important strategy of its educational policy. We also intend to enrich educational contents incorporating service learning. In furthering these objectives, however, the university is currently facing two problems, i.e., educational assessment and the actual costs to be incurred in terms of both time and money.

The COCOLO-IKI project is implemented as part of the MEXT's supplementary project for promoting the university's cooperation with local communities. Accordingly, the project achievement is evaluated in most part in terms of more easily measurable numerical figures such as the number of cooperative projects actually worked on than construction of a basic theory. For this reason, Our *Kyotology* Educational Program focuses mainly on the course contents and development of operation methods, while the assessment methods are not sufficiently reviewed. Students' academic performance is assessed by conventional exams and reporting assignments, but the abilities nurtured through this program cannot be sufficiently measured against the conventional courses. Thus, we need to develop evaluation indices that can measure the abilities actually nurtured in this program.

Another problem is pecuniary and time costs. In particular, courses provided with fieldwork or other practical training would require more cost and longer time to be spent by the students than conventional ones. Enhanced educational activities incorporating service learning may also result in reduced budgets and hours spent on other subjects. We have not duly examined how we could adjust the balance between these subjects with the conventional ones. The pecuniary cost in particular is a huge problem in the severe fiscal conditions in recent years. In view of the aspect of service learning that it helps solve regional problems, we may well have to create a mechanism for collecting funds for its provision from the local communities.

As explained earlier, our university's fundamental policy sets its educational goal to "facilitate dialog-based self-learning, succeed distinguished intelligence, and cultivate creative minds under the diverse and harmonious educational systems". Particularly, in facilitating dialog-based self-learning, service learning plays an important role in that it requires face-to-face communication. Nevertheless, in the present situation, we have not been able to measure objectively to what extent service learning supports students' growth, nor have we duly examined how we could carry on this system. It is an urgent challenge for us to create the assessment method and consider which activities we should enhance and carry on, taking the cost into account.

References

Consortium for Local Public Human Resources Development (COLPU). (n.d.). *Organization profile "elementary public policy consultant"*. Retrieved from http://www.colpu.org/colpu-biz3.html

Design School of Kyoto University. (n.d.). *Our "design"*. Retrieved from http://www.design.kyoto-u.ac.jp/about/our-design

Genius Table. (n.d.). *About: Genius table in Kyoto*. Retrieved from http://geniustable.com/about/

Kawai, S. (n.d.). *About: Message from Dean*. Graduate School of Advanced Integrated Studies in Human Survivability, Kyoto University. Retrieved from http://www.gsais.kyoto-u.ac.jp/en-top/about-message-from-dean

Lieberman, M. (2016). *World's Top 10 Cities 2015. TRAVEL+LEISURE*. Retrieved from http://www.travelandleisure.com/slideshows/worlds-best-cities/10

Ministry of Education, Culture, Sports, Science and Technology (MEXT). (n.d.). *About the Pamphlet on "Center of Community (and Intelligence)" (COC) Project in Academic 2016*. Retrieved from http://www.mext.go.jp/a_menu/koutou/kaikaku/coc/1358201.htm

Chapter 13
Reflections on and Practices of Peking University Fulfilling Social Responsibility

Jingyi Ye

Abstract This paper attempts to explain the meaning and connotation of Social Responsibility of Chinese Universities from the functional perspectives of university education, scientific research, social service and cultural inheritance. It presents a combination of three different ways through which a university can achieve social responsibility in modern times, in order to present information regarding Peking University's performance of social duties. Examples used include the cultivation of students' sense of social responsibility, localized poverty alleviation in Midu County in Yunnan Province, and advancing cooperation between school and enterprise.

Keywords Chinese students · Implementation model · Peking University · University education · University social responsibility (USR)

As a member of the community, and a bastion of social knowledge, thought and culture, universities are expected to commit to the fulfillment of social responsibility. Tracing back through a history of hundreds of years of university development, it can be concluded that a university, be it in medieval or modern times, has been assuming social responsibility. What kinds of social responsibilities should Chinese universities take, and how should they fulfill and achieve these responsibilities? Different answers may be given by different universities at different times. This paper aims to investigate models for achieving social responsibilities of universities in the new era.

J. Ye (✉)
Peking University Council, Beijing, China
e-mail: yezipku@pku.edu.cn

© Springer Nature Singapore Pte Ltd. 2017
D.T.L. Shek and R.M. Hollister (eds.), *University Social Responsibility and Quality of Life*, Quality of Life in Asia 8,
DOI 10.1007/978-981-10-3877-8_13

13.1   Definition of Social Responsibility of the University

University Social Responsibility (USR) is a multidisciplinary and interdisciplinary research field, originating from in-depth reflection on the organizational characteristics and functions of universities, and the relationship between society and universities. Researchers in various fields such as management, economics, philosophy, ethics, sociology and pedagogy, have forwarded different concepts of it based on their professional knowledge and specialized perspective. In general, the exploratory research findings on the concept of USR domestically and abroad suggest that USR can be viewed from the following perspectives: Principle-Based, Action-Based, Function-Based, Stakeholder-Related, Citizenship-Based, Ability-Based, and Holistic Synthesis-Based (Zhang 2015a). There is no consensus on the definition of USR domestically or overseas, and the reason for this phenomenon is that different researchers understand USR from their own perspectives, and that their respective implementations and expectations of USR differ as well.

University Function (UF) and University Social Responsibility are two closely-related concepts. The traditional UF includes cultivation of talent, scientific research and social services. As society and the economy develop at a rapid rate, universities are given new requirements and missions. President Hu Jintao's speech at Tsinghua University's centennial anniversary celebration, April 24, 2011, emphasized improvement in the quality of tertiary education, scientific research, social services and cultural innovation. Thereafter, personnel education, science research, social services and cultural innovation have become officially acknowledged functions of universities in domestic academic circles. Based on this consensus, the author of this paper aims to explain the meaning and connotation of USR from the perspective of the University Function. In modern Chinese semantics, function means the roles and uses that are required of an entity or institution, while responsibility means duty. Function refers to the performance of a duty, with a focus on the regulations and requirements within an organization, without emphasis on whether the results of actions are negative or positive. In contrast, responsibility suggests being accountable for one's behavior, usually used with a positive connotation. UF represents the channels through which a university bears social responsibility, and through which it fulfills social responsibility. Some researchers believe that the UF and the USR are two sides of one topic: the functions developed by a university implicitly determine what responsibilities it should undertake and fulfill (Yu and Zhang 2011).

Societal demands and the university's own pursuit of excellence combine to jointly promote the updating and expansion of the UF, as well as the continued development of the meaning of USR. Every new establishment of social responsibility clearly reflects the close connection between universities and social development. The birth of the university in the Middle Ages signifies the establishment of a specialized mechanism and institution for the education and cultivation of talent, and it is since then that the university has played a role in bearing social responsibility. Università degli Studi di Salerno and Université de Paris are two of the most renowned medieval universities, which, like the earliest guild universities, pursued academic freedom, autonomy, religiousness and practicability with the four main curricula of literature, laws, religious study and medicine. "The major duty of universities is vocational training, and to educate professional applied talents." (Jiang 2013, p. 22) When Universität zu Berlin was founded in 1810, Wilhelm von Humboldt stressed the principle of academic freedom, and the principle of the unity of teaching and scientific research. These two principles remain influential to this day, and scientific research has gradually become an important function of universities (Zhang 2015b). Responsibility to knowledge became a mission of pride for universities, and the university broadened its function and created its own special values as well as promoted comprehensive societal development beginning with the foundations of society. From the 1860s to the beginning of the 20th century, with the development of state universities and land-grant colleges in the United States, the concept of service with its core function of serving society took form, informing the way in which modern universities undertake social responsibility (Kang 2012). After the middle of the 20th century, especially after the 1980s, social, political, economic, and cultural revolutions advanced the meaning and connotation of USR. To promote the well-being of human society, modern universities have expanded the traditional functional activities to global education and cross-border cooperation, providing the educated around the world with the means to pursue truth and wisdom, and promoting the development of cutting-edge knowledge and innovation worldwide; modern universities not only adapt to and promote the development of regional politics, economy, technology, culture and other aspects, but also undertake the crucial forward-looking, criticism and leadership social functions, which carry an important social responsibility of solving global problems, creating a better way of life for the world through cooperation and promoting the diversification of civilization and progress of mankind.

In terms of its function of cultivating talents, USR is reflected in whether universities can train people to be able to meet the needs of current and future development, whether universities can adapt to and promote the comprehensive development of individuals, and whether they can ensure the equity, quality and social relevance of higher education. The ultimate achievement of social responsibility depends on whether the trained personnel make a contribution to promoting social progress and development in the future. In terms of its scientific research function, USR lies in the university's perseverance in the pursuit of knowledge and innovation, its insistence on social responsibility with academic responsibility at the core, its comprehensive application of various disciplines of knowledge for the public interest and the development of society, and its attention to the promotion of human development. In terms of its social service function, USR is reflected in the university's positive and supportive view towards the healthy, stable and sustainable development of society, and its role in adapting to and promoting national and social development using its uniquely powerful public influence. In terms of its function of cultural inheritance and innovation, USR is reflected in the university's role in influencing and guiding society with advanced thoughts and ideas through a profound cultural consciousness, and its important role in inheriting, promoting and developing culture, and continuously advancing human civilization.

13.2 Implementation of Modern University Social Responsibility

The meaning of USR is abstract, but its implementation is specific. In modern society, in what ways can a university implement its social responsibility strategy? Based on the history of university development since the latter half of the 20th century, a university is able to achieve its social responsibility goals through the following approaches.

13.2.1 Core Actions

Initially, the basic driving forces for modern universities to fulfil social responsibility are the perceived societal pressures and the spirit of volunteerism of teachers and students. Universities' teachers and students, as the driving force of modern society, take initiative and voluntarily shoulder university social responsibility in and out of their organization. They analyze in depth the major issues existing in social progress, illuminate objective contradictions, disadvantages or dangers in society, advise or even criticize the government and society, and serve vulnerable groups, etc. (Kang 2014). The realization of university social responsibility depends on the academic community's every individual's clear acknowledgement and conscientious fulfillment of social responsibility. In particular, the organization's ability to meet social needs through holding various activities and providing social services is largely determined by teachers' and students' awareness of their mission. The attitudes, beliefs and abilities held by teachers and scholars in their professional conduct of teaching, research, service, etc. are the keys to fulfilling the university's social responsibility goal, so the university cannot afford any claim of functions or missions without teachers' observance of social responsibility. College students are the major undertakers of modern university social responsibility, and they will become the major undertakers of social responsibility once they enter society, therefore they are the most progressive and dynamic force to fulfill university social responsibility.

13.2.2 Integrated Organization

Since the 1980s, with the modern university taking center stage in society, society's needs and expectations of the university have been ever increasing. Derek Bok believed that in this period the goal of the modern university was no longer simply the pursuit of knowledge, but also the undertaking of a more substantial social responsibility to "improve China's core competitiveness" and "seek well-being for all mankind" (quoted in Qu 2014, p. 45). When the power of a single individual teacher and the system cannot effectively achieve these ideals systematically, the university organization begins to act as the guide, fulfilling USR at the organizational level, and thus making the behavior of the overall organization socially responsible. Thus, the implementation of USR by an integrated organizational USR appeared and has continued to this day. At this stage, modern universities have gradually clarified their own important role in society and their social responsibility, with extensive attention and discussion paid to the types of talents universities should cultivate, the kinds of scientific research these talents should engage in, and the kinds of social service these talents should provide to meet national, social and university needs. The modern university also integrates social responsibility into the organization's culture and values, gradually building a vision of institutionalized social responsibility (Kang 2014). As the "Peking University Constitution" proposed, the school shall "through teaching, research and service, create, preserve and disseminate knowledge, inherit and innovate culture, promote the progress of the Chinese nation and the development of human civilization" (Peking University 2015). In recent years, some universities have begun to publish social responsibility reports, systematically describing and disclosing the social responsibility concept and practices of the organizations, the deployment of a series of time-bound social responsibility projects, their focused attention to a series of specific social problems, in order to ensure that universities work together to fulfill their social responsibility on these issues and make a difference (Shanghai Jiao Tong University 2016).

13.2.3 Sharing Social Responsibility

In a responsibility-oriented society, universities, the government and enterprises, which represent academic, political and economic organizations respectively all have their specific roles and specific social responsibilities. The social system that is made up of the three has a shared social responsibility (Kang 2012). USR is a part of the "shared responsibility" and every party should shoulder its share of responsibility that comes with its position and sphere of influence. Universities are the core and the dominant force to shoulder USR. The government must ensure that universities are able to undertake their social responsibility, and society (including enterprises, non-profit organizations and the public, etc.) should provide motivation for universities to shoulder their social responsibility. Media institutions help universities to undertake their social responsibility through supervision of the university's practices, and through gathering supporting public opinion. From the social level, the key for the fulfillment of the USR is to improve and perfect the "shared social responsibility mechanism" of the university, the government and the enterprise, which is a process of competition and cooperation, coexistence and harmonious development and will eventually form a situation of self-adaptation, effective interaction and dynamic equilibrium.

13.3 Practices of Peking University Fulfilling Social Responsibility Based on Implementation of Modern University Social Responsibility

13.3.1 Cultivate Students' Sense of Social Responsibility— Cases of Undertaking Social Responsibility Through Individual Action

Based on the aforementioned Core Actions approach to achieving a university's social responsibility strategy, it is necessary to strengthen teachers and students' ability to undertake independent social responsibility, to decide how to shoulder their responsibility and to answer to the consequences of their actions. Responsibility awareness should be instilled throughout one's education. Teachers and students' awareness as well as capability to shoulder their responsibility should be enhanced and improved through different ways (Zhou 2014).

Since its establishment, Peking University's fundamental mission has always been to cultivate students of a high caliber, who have a strong sense of social responsibility and who are able to assume the responsibility of national rejuvenation. Peking University and its students have always been closely invested in three grand causes: China's development, social progress and national rejuvenation. It has become a common consensus for colleges and universities at home and abroad to teach students to be citizens with social responsibility. In general, the cultivation of social responsibility has to do with awareness and practice. It is through study that students develop their sense of responsibility and it is through practice that they shoulder their responsibility.

13.3.1.1 Value Standard—Helping Students to Develop Their Sense of Social Responsibility

Social responsibility is an important part of one's values and also a key indicator of one's standard of values. Peking University (PKU) has always attached great importance to the cultivation of students' values. Cai Yuanpei promoted worldview education and moral education when he served as President of PKU. In his "The

Young China Association" speech, PKU President Hu Shi emphasized the importance of educating young students on outlook on life. Such educational ideas have been upheld by PKU in its education. In recent years, PKU has attached great importance to the cultivation of students' dreams, faith, moral character and wishes to make contributions to society with special emphasis on the "Chinese dream" education. The university instilled its education ideas into students' study and life, educating the student to pay close attention to national and social development and to shoulder the responsibility that falls upon today's young people.

The cultivation of a sense of social responsibility is carried out from the beginning to the end of student's study in PKU in all of their activities. Forming a correct judgment about one's social responsibility can only be achieved given that one's self perception is in line with one's role and position in society (Xia 2013). PKU uses systematic thinking to strengthen education regarding one's role and position in society. Teachers formulate targeted social positioning education methods by analyzing carefully students' understanding capability and physical and mental characteristics at different grades. For example, freshmen listen to speeches on PKU's history and visit the university's history museum at the beginning of their study to understand that PKU's development has been closely connected with the fate of China ever since its establishment. These activities motivate them to inherit PKU's spiritual tradition to "take society's responsibility as their own responsibility". Since 2014, PKU has been carrying out the "Professors' Tea Hour" project. In this project, professors chat with students over tea. The conversation is not about study but about life. The professors share their experiences and thinking with students and the students are always be influenced by their sense of social responsibility. As for graduates, PKU implements "Home and Country Strategy" and teaches students to "contribute to the development of one's hometown" and to "go wherever the motherland needs most". Nearly 1100 PKU graduates chose to work in west China and remote areas or villages from 2012 to 2014.

PKU instills social responsibility education into students' study and life and students are influenced by the rich and colorful PKU culture. The essence of social responsibility is a person's social values, the formation of which is under the influence of the macro environment including politics, the economy and culture (Xia 2013). The concept of "holistic education" is formed in the interaction of the macro-environment and one's sense of social responsibility. In 2013, the opera "Just For You: Song of Wang Xuan", which was written by PKU teachers and students, presented the story of the renowned scientist Wang Xuan, who devoted his life to furthering the development of scientific technology for the benefit of the nation. His story greatly impressed the students. Departments in charge of students' affairs and almost all colleges for various disciplines have opened WeChat public accounts and created columns that cover the performance of outstanding students. Reports on "Stories That Touch the Heart of Yan Yuan" and "Stars of Wei Ming" introduce students and teachers in PKU who care about others and charitably serve society. The positive energy of their actions promotes the moral growth of other students. It can be said that the multi-centric influence of new media platforms creates a culture that promotes "loving society and being willing to help others."

13.3.1.2 Education in Practice—Teach Students to Take Actions to Shoulder Their Social Responsibility

Actions speak louder than words. The ancient Chinese saying goes, "knowledge and action should go hand in hand". The concept of "responsibility" should not only be "internalized in the heart" but also be "reflected through actions". Following education laws and answering to the call of the times, PKU regards "education through action" as its educational philosophy and writes this philosophy into its constitution, along with teaching students to take action to fulfill their social obligation and shoulder social responsibility.

To jointly foster awareness of shouldering social responsibility and cultivate students' talents, PKU carries out targeted guidance in light of students' growth and the characteristics of different grade levels. It creates various platforms that students can join, such as practical courses, academic research and innovation, social activities, volunteer service, voluntary teaching, employment and entrepreneurship, and overseas activities, etc. For example, PKU encourages sophomores who have adapted well to university life to take part in more social activities, so that they can learn more about society; guides juniors who are clear about the direction of their future study to participate in academic research and teaching; supports seniors who are deciding whether or not to further their study to find internships and entrepreneurial experience; helps graduate students who are mature and fully prepared for research activities to participate in research projects, policy study and voluntary teaching in less developed regions. Through these activities, the students put the theories they have learned into practice, not only serving the public but also broadening their horizons, improving their capabilities and building character.

Shouldering social responsibility must be combined with social development. Taking social activities as an example, PKU was the first university in the mainland that started students' practical, society-focused activities when it launched the "One Hundred Villages' Social Investigation" in 1982. For more than 30 years, every year nearly 4000 students on average would go to places across China to conduct surveys, teach in underdeveloped regions and carry out volunteer activities. PKU has been carrying out the "In-Depth Empirical Social Study—Social Investigation On the Health and Living Condition of Chinese Retirees" project since 2012. Each year hundreds of PKU students go to towns and villages across China. They visit the local residents to collect statistics on the health and living conditions of the retirees. By the summer of 2015, the project members had visited 450 villages and 150 counties in all provinces and municipalities except for Hong Kong, Macao and Taiwan. By visiting about 17,000 people in 10,000 households, they collected a large number of high quality statistics on people who are over 45, which has greatly contributed to the analysis and interdisciplinary research on China's aging population.

Shouldering social responsibility should be combined with meeting the demands of the disadvantaged groups. In 1918, under the advocacy of PKU President Cai Yuanpei, PKU established the "Evening Classes" which were taught by masters such as Fu Sinian and Luo Jialun. Later, supported by Mr Cai, students such as

Deng Zhongxia and Liao Shucang established "Civilian School" and "Civilian Education Speech Society" with the purpose to "increase the common people's knowledge and awaken their self-awareness." In 2006, in accordance with Mr. Cai's ideal, PKU resumed the "Civilian School". The School provides free training for workers to help improve their vocational skills and cultural literacy, in hopes of establishing a "University Educational Resources Plus Volunteers" model that helps with the continuing education and training of the more than 200 million migrant workers. The "Civilian School" makes full use of PKU's educational resources, asking experts and scholars in various fields including many well-known professors and senior or graduate students to be the teachers. The courses are divided into two groups: courses on vocational skills, which include English, computer literacy and so on; and courses on cultural literacy, which covers legal knowledge, art appreciation, traditional culture, interpersonal communication, finance and so on. The School has its own council that is presided by PKU's administrative personnel. The council has set up management and service mechanisms and has funds for special use. The School also organizes many extracurricular activities such as volunteer activities, visits, speech contests and talent contests to enrich students' lives and improve their comprehensive capabilities. More than 990 workers have graduated from the School over the last ten years. Thanks to the high quality of teaching resources, over 500 security guards were granted a college degree by the end of 2013. A student in the third session, a security guard Gan Xiangwei, who was admitted by PKU through the Adult College Entrance Exam, published a book, Attending Peking University on His Feet. Moreover, he was chosen as one of "2011's Top 10 Influential People in Education" and "2013's Top 10 Prominent Readers in China".

It is necessary to build long-term mechanisms for students to shoulder social responsibility. PKU designs activities that emphasize professionalism. Since the summer of 2011, PKU has been providing three advisors for social activity groups—activity advisor, academic advisor and research method advisor—in order to offer in-depth guidance throughout the activities, from which students can derive long-term benefits. PKU has also expanded the scope of activities and constructed internship and training centers. In the past, students themselves were required to look for internships. Now, the university reaches out to establish all kinds of internship centers and pays special attention to the system, structure and stability of those centers. PKU aims to guide students to self-education, self-management and to strengthen the establishment of volunteering societies. It shall develop relevant regulations and methods, borrow the operation modes and modern management concepts of NGOs and strengthen standardized and scientific construction of the system, funding, training, etc., to achieve long-term "responsibility to act" and the inheritance of this spirit. There are more than 18 student societies devoted to voluntary service, such as the Loving Heart Society and Legal Aid Society. Take the Loving Heart Society as an example, it developed from only 17 student members who gathered together for spontaneous snow clearing in 1993 to a society with nationwide influence with more than a thousand registered members, holding more than 30 regular volunteering activities per week and more than 30 large public welfare activities per year in the scope of voluntary teaching, nursing the elderly, helping the disabled, donations to support students, and cultural service. These achievements can be owed to standardized management.

13.3.2 Designated Poverty Alleviation—Cases of Social Responsibility Fulfillment Based on the Integrated Organization Mode

Fulfillment of its responsibility to society is a fundamental way for the academic community to realize its self-worth and social value. If every member of the academic community expresses their willingness to promote service to society, and lead the way for cultural progress, reflection and criticism, etc., yet fails to achieve this dream as an individual teacher or student, the university as an organization will naturally become the guide. Through the integrated organization mode, universities can participate in the building of a global knowledge system by focusing on the forefront of global science development, conducting prospective and strategic research on the pressing issues restricting economic and social development and enhancing knowledge and intelligence conversion to meet the needs of the state, the society, and the public; integrating the exploration of new knowledge and innovation to education and even the international system of higher education, cultivating innovative and academic talents in various fields for China and the world. Advocacy, guidance and organization at school level is the most important feature of integrated organization. Here, the author will take the case of poverty alleviation in Midu county in Yunnan province as an example to illustrate how PKU fulfills its social responsibility by integrated organization.

In November 2012, eight departments, including the Poverty Alleviation Office of the State Council, the Central Organization Department and the Ministry of Education, jointly issued the release "Notice on the Central, State Organs and Relevant Units Doing a New Round of Poverty Alleviation Works", and organized a total of 310 units designated to help 592 key counties with national poverty alleviation and development. PKU was arranged to assist and support Midu County, in the Bai Autonomous Prefecture of Dali in Yunnan province. In October 2013, PKU and Midu county officially signed a corresponding assistance agreement.

Midu County, located in the west of the Yunnan Plateau and southeast of Dali Prefecture, is one of the sources of the Red River and the heartland of the economic zone of Lancang River's middle reaches. With a backward economy, it belongs to the key counties of western Yunnan border area where the national focus is on contiguous poverty alleviation and development. Based on research and practice, PKU drafted "Opinions on further strengthening the Designated Poverty Alleviation Work", and designated "school mobilization, pooling resources, suitable faculty, intellectual assistance" as the principle with intellectual assistance as the main theme. PKU has planned to optimize the resource allocation of personnel, education, science, culture, health care, etc., to alleviate poverty, and has focused on technology knowledge and talented personnel as the core drivers to get rid of poverty and allow the region to become better off. PKU has incorporated the Midu county poverty alleviation work into its school version of the 13th Five-year Plan, providing a green channel of "staff, finances, and material resources" for the poverty alleviation work, and scheduled a special budget every year to support the overall poverty alleviation work.

PKU has implemented the corresponding assistance of 8 departments to 8 designated towns in Midu. Guanghua School of Management, School of Economics, National School of Development, School of Art, School of Law, School of Information Science and Technology, School of Technology, and School of International Relations are respectively designated to help Deju village, Juli town, Niujie village, Mizhi town, Micheng town, Yinjie town, Xinjie town and Hongyan town of Midu county. The presidents of these colleges assigned counterpart staff for poverty alleviation work, and took the initiative to provide funds and financial intelligence to start the project. Each unit involved in the poverty alleviation task worked out a detailed list of tasks and schedules, tracking, testing and assessing the progress and quality of poverty alleviation work, and strengthening the implementation of responsibility.

PKU also coordinated health resources to improve people's livelihood and health. 16 doctors from PKU's Affiliated Hospital were sent to Midu county to give free medical treatment, to provide group consultations and seminars, to instruct pediatrics to become an independent department and to enhance the works of orthopedics, neurology and other key departments, and to improve the primary health care system. The major project "Stroke Screening and Prevention Project" of the National Health and Family Planning Commission was set up in Midu county with more than 800 million RMB of funding. This project was able to not only effectively prevent and control high blood pressure on a large scale, but also significantly reduce the incidence of stroke at the same time, saving a lot of pharmaceutical expenses for the residents of the county and significantly reducing the "return to poverty due to illness" phenomenon. PKU also coordinated the health projects of the China Population Welfare Foundation and PKU's Maternity and Children Care Center to support women and children's health care in Midu county.

PKU took full advantage of its talented personnel and placed emphasis on intellectual aid. It mobilized teachers and students to participate in local poverty alleviation work, coordinated the university's rich educational resources, and created conditions to invite officials and teachers from Midu county to attend training, study and information exchange programs at PKU. In 2015, PKU trained more than 500 people, including local cadres, teachers and medical staff. Peking University played the role of "talent pool", mobilizing teachers and students to actively participate in local poverty alleviation services. Under the support of Dali and Midu, outstanding teachers, cadres, graduates were selected to take a temporary post in government agencies, hospitals, schools and other units to provide personnel support to poverty alleviation. In recent years, 3 cadres have been sent to take temporary posts in Midu.

PKU has also endeavored to attract social resources and improve social security and social safeguards. It has worked with the China Teacher Development Foundation to donate 300,000 Yuan to support teachers in difficulty and to reward teachers who are on special contracts, as well as supported the construction of the primary school in Deju town's Yilang village. It has mobilized social power and organized for benefactors in the community to donate 300,000 Yuan in poverty alleviation funds to improve the living conditions of villagers and support the economic and social development of Bashi village, Mizhi town. It also organized for China Soong Ching Ling Foundation to donate ambulances worth several thousands to Midu.

13.3.3 Promote University-Society Cooperation—Social Responsibility Fulfillment Cases Based on Sharing Means of Social Responsibility

In order to encourage universities to perform social responsibility by sharing their responsibilities, we could research and design various social responsibility projects led by the government, universities and communities, to perform and achieve social responsibility step by step.

Over the years, PKU has regarded University-Society cooperation as an important way to fulfill USR, and has taken advantage of its role as a font of knowledge, source of innovation and breeding ground for talent, to implement its strategies of servicing the country based on the overall situation of national development. In 1999, PKU established the Domestic Cooperation Committee, affiliated with the Domestic Cooperation Office, which is responsible for the cooperation, coordination and implementation of business between PKU and domestic provinces and cities. Since 1998, Peking University has signed province-university cooperation contracts with 24 provinces, including Yunnan, Inner Mongolia, Xinjiang, Henan, Shandong, Liaoning, Ningxia, Jiangxi, Gansu, Jiangsu, Zhejiang, Tianjin, Hunan, Beijing, Guangxi, Chongqing, Guangdong, Shanxi, Fujian, Guizhou, Hainan and other provinces, and Xinjiang Production and Construction Corps, to establish broad and deep working relationships.

PKU is currently working with more than two-thirds of the country's provinces and autonomous regions, covering all municipalities. The number of cooperative projects between PKU and large state-owned backbone enterprises grows at an average annual rate of over 20%. Every year, important cooperation projects registered in different departments and faculties in the fields of science, education, culture, training and others exceed 1200. PKU carries out University-Enterprise Society cooperation mainly through the following channels.

13.3.3.1 Strategic Planning and Policy Advice

At the national level, Peking University makes full use of think tanks and research agencies such as Peking University International Institute for Strategic Studies, National Institute of Development, Population Research Institute and other research institutions to serve the national strategy. Li Yining, Lin Yifu, Yu Tiejun, Zhou Qiren, Jiang Ming'an, Wang Puqu, Li Ling and many other PKU scholars have participated in the preliminary research and drafting of important medium and long-term national plans pertaining to national and local education, science and technology, human resources and other areas. In addition, they have researched international financial crises, changes in the Middle East and North Africa, national health care reform, and achieving the formidable vision of the "Chinese Dream", as well as other key issues.

At the local level, PKU actively organizes experts and scholars for the government to expand applied research on difficult issues in our society, undertake development planning, and participate in decision-making consultation. For example, PKU experts submitted consultation reports concerning major issues of the Basic Law of the Hong Kong Special Administrative Region, the population policy, the European debt crisis and other issues to provide decision-making advice to the central government. The "Shandong Peninsula City Clusters Plan" of 8 cities and 22 county-level cities undertaken by PKU Urban Planning Center has had a tremendous impact within China and overseas, and promoted local development (Zuo 2015).

13.3.3.2 Science and Technology Development and Transformation

Facing the overall situation of regional economic transformation, PKU supports the development of local industries. In cooperation with Beijing and Haidian District, PKU helped a number of major industrial projects to settle in Haidian, including projects involving PKU-CFD fluid dynamics numerical simulation software, intelligent assistive limb technology, carbon Nano-material research, industrialization of primates, etc. Thusly, PKU attracted a large number of well-known domestic and foreign high-tech enterprises and research institutions to congregate in the area, and promoted industrial upgrading and economic restructuring throughout the region. PKU focuses on meeting national strategic needs, and vigorously promotes the industrialization of scientific and technological achievements. For example, faced with our country's severe lack of high-resolution data, PKU cooperated with Guizhou Aviation Group to develop China's first high-end multi-purpose UAV remote sensing system. The success of this system marks China's UAV earth observation technology's entrance into the world's most advanced ranks. The technology has been widely used in the census of homeland environmental resources, scientific research of meteorology and natural disaster monitoring (Zuo 2015).

13.3.3.3 Education and Training

Education in the central and western regions of China poses the greatest challenge to national education. PKU actively commits to the strategy of development in the west, using PKU's rich resources to support the development of universities in western China, making its due contribution to local education. Since aiding the construction of Shihezi University and Tibet University, PKU has been striving to help the two universities to improve the quality of teachers, quality of personnel training, scientific research and service capabilities and the quality of school management, by designing support work in strategic planning, promoting the exchange of personnel training, conducting joint research, promoting the construction of discipline system and other means. Under the joint efforts of tertiary institutions and relevant government units, Shihezi University and Tibet University became part of the Project 211 group of universities, demonstrating the remarkable results achieved by the aid work. PKU has won "Advanced Group in the Development of West China", "Model Group of National Unity and Progress", "Advanced Group of Assistance Work" and other national collective honors; a total of 8 staff were recognized as "Advanced Individuals of Assistance Work", ranking first among the best colleges and universities.

13.4 Challenges Peking University Faces While Fulfilling Social Responsibility

13.4.1 How to Strike a Balance Between Fulfilling Social Responsibility and Sticking to the Core Mission of a University

To Derek Bok, academics are not only the core mission but also the social responsibility of a university. A university has academic social responsibilities as well as non-academic ones, and it should focus on the former and try to avoid too many of the latter (Bok 2001). In contemporary China, universities play various roles and shoulder many responsibilities in socio-economic development. This is especially true for research universities as they are acclaimed to be "vital bases for cultivating higher-level innovative talents and they lead the original innovation in basic researches and high-tech areas, solving major technological problems in national economy and making technology transfer and fruition of researches a reality" (Ministry of Science and Technology 2006). Universities need to actively participate in various national "projects" and "programs" in order to promote economic development and social stability, and also improve the livelihood of citizens. In doing so, a university may undertake some unnecessary responsibilities, some that it might not be skilled at dealing with and which may weaken a university's core social responsibilities, leaving its functions and responsibilities in a more material gain-oriented state. In this increasingly complex society, a university should try to strike a balance between fulfilling social responsibilities and sticking to its core missions to continuously strengthen its sense of social responsibility and its ability to choose responsibilities.

13.4.2 External Environment Changes Bring up New Challenges for Cultivating Social Responsibility Awareness Among College Students

On one hand, China is currently undergoing a social transition. Along with the comprehensive deepening of reforms in all areas, social trends are clashing with each other, and the independency, choices, changeability and variety of people's mental activities are becoming increasingly prominent. On the other hand, the Internet's prevalence and its wide application is undermining the authority and integrity of education while providing new means and methods for education, thus negative phenomena such as contempt for authority, loss of values and moral improprieties have begun to arise. In this type of external environment, college students' understandings of social responsibilities and sense of social responsibility have become diversified, some of them even have little sense of social responsibility and pay no heed to the greater good. Therefore, methods of cultivating sense of social responsibility among college students are relatively outdated and need to be augmented.

13.4.3 The Expertise College Students Need to Perform Social Responsibilities Is to Be Improved

The aforementioned social activities are important means of fostering college students' sense of social responsibility and channels of undertaking social responsibility. Currently, Chinese college students' social activities and classes are not well integrated, as social activities are primarily arranged by the student affairs administrative, while the education department's involvement is relatively limited. The activities are carried out by ways of surveying, visiting and volunteering, and the choice of activities and the student's major are not fully cohesive. Besides, college students' social activities usually focus on social services, which leads to the following situation: students experience real life scenarios to some extent after they participate in physical and mental labor, yet their growth in subject-related fields and the skills they acquire are very limited. In the long run, the lack of professionalism will inevitably affect the validity and endurance of social activities. Peking University has adopted several measures to counter this problem, for example, allocating academic supervisors and investigation methodology instructors for social activity groups, establishing activity bases etc. These measures proved to be effective to some extent, however the holistic professional level of social activities still falls behind Peking University's academic standing, which calls for the concerted efforts of the faculty and the students.

This paper gives explanation to the connotations of Social Responsibility of Chinese Universities from the functional perspectives of university education, scientific research, social service and cultural inheritance. It presents a combination of three different ways through which a university can fulfill its social responsibility in modern times: core actions, integrated organization, and sharing social responsibility, thereby presenting information regarding Peking University's performance of social duties. Examples used include the cultivation of students' sense of social responsibility, localized poverty alleviation in Midu County in Yunnan Province, and advancing cooperation between schools and enterprises. Peking University is currently facing new challenges in fulfilling its social responsibilities as the work is progressing and the social environment is changing. The connotations of USR are changing with socio-economic developments, so models for universities to achieve social responsibilities need to be progressively updated. Reflecting on the past and looking into the future, Peking University will always cherish the work of fulfilling social responsibility so as to provide rational judgement for the value of social responsibility in the new era, while also carrying out explorations that help universities in fulfilling their social responsibilities.

References

Bok, D. (2001). *Beyond the ivory tower: Social responsibilities of the modern university.* (Trans. into Chinese Xu Xiaozhou et al.)

Jiang, S. (2013). Modern university social responsibility and reflections on Chinese university development. *University Academic, 9,* 20–27.

Kang, L. (2012). *On principle and achievement model of university social responsibility.* Unpublished doctoral dissertation, Dalian University of Technology, Dalian.

Kang, L. (2014). On the achievement approaches of social responsibility of modern university. *China Higher Education Research, 8,* 25–28.

Ministry of Science and Technology. (2006). *Outline of the national medium- and long-term science and development program.* Available at: http://www.most.gov.cn/mostinfo/xinxifenlei/gjkjgh/200811/t20081129_65774.htm (in Chinese).

Peking University. (2015, April 28). News. *Peking University.* Retrieved from http://pkunews.pku.edu.cn/2015zt/2015-04/28/content_288465.htm.

Qu, M. (2014). Investigation into Derek Bok's ideas of social responsibilities of a university. *Tsinghua Journal of Education, 2,* 44–54.

Shanghai Jiao Tong University. (2016, January 29). 2015 Annual Social Responsibility Report. *Shanghai Education News.* Retrieved from http://www.shedunews.com/shzrbg2015/shzrbg2015_gaoxiao/2016/01/29/2042202.html.

Xia, Y. (2013). Study on the path of social responsibility sense education of college students based on systematic way of thinking. *China Youth Study, 11,* 77–80.

Yu, X., & Zhang, X. (2011). A brief review of the researches on social responsibilities of universities in China during the past 15 years. *Higher Education of Science, 1,* 149–155.

Zhang, W. (2015a). Exploring the components and main characteristics of university social responsibility. *Modern Education Science: Higher Education Research Edition, 5,* 1–13.

Zhang, W. (2015b). Exploring the concept of university social responsibility. *Modern Education Science: Higher Education Research Edition, 1,* 1–9.

Zhou, H. (2014). Historical changes, international experience and the case in China: Social responsibility of university education. *China Journal of Beijing Normal University (Social Science Edition), 1,* 12–17.

Zuo, J. (2015). Improve social services capability and create world-class universities—Peking University's practice experience. *China Leadership Science, 1,* 50–53.

Chapter 14
Three Approaches to Cultivating College Students' Sense of Social Responsibility

Chuansheng Liu and Xudong Zhu

Abstract Cultivating college students' sense of social responsibility is an important task of college education. This paper proposes three approaches to cultivating college students' sense of social responsibility and establishes a corresponding theoretical framework. Based on the framework, the paper analyzes the case of Beijing Normal University and presents the effects of the three approaches. It points out that only by participating in academic and professional practices as well as public services can college students translate their conception of sense of social responsibility into actions and prepare themselves for taking social responsibility in the future.

Keywords College students · Sense of social responsibility · Accountability · Three approaches · Case study

14.1 Background and Object

"Report to the 18th National Congress of the Communist Party of China" states that we should cultivate a sense of social responsibility in students, which shows that both the Party and the government attach great importance to cultivating students' sense of social responsibility. "Outline of China's National Plan for Medium and Long-term Education Reform and Development (2010–2020)" presents the strategic theme of "enhancing students' sense of social responsibility to serve the country and the people", highlighting the role of education in cultivating students' sense of social responsibility. Indeed, cultivating college students' sense of social responsibility is an imperative task of college education. By cultivating college students'

C. Liu (✉) · X. Zhu
University Council, Beijing Normal University,
No. 19, XinJieKouWai St., Haidian District, Beijing, China
e-mail: liucsh@bnu.edu.cn

X. Zhu
e-mail: xudongzhu99@sina.com

sense of social responsibility, we encourage them to not only fulfill themselves but also serve the society. They can be, therefore, equipped with cognitive competence, initiative and self-discipline to take social responsibility in the future.

Cultivating college students' sense of social responsibility is of great importance to both the country and society. College students will shape the future of our society. If we do not cultivate in them a sense of social responsibility, the regulations about social responsibility will not perform any function and social tasks will not be completed. As a result, state apparatus will not work properly and the social order will get broken, thus impairing people's social life. So it is imperative and relevant to identify the approaches to cultivating college students' sense of social responsibility.

Sense of social responsibility refers to communities' or individuals' self-discipline and other personal qualities formed under certain social and historical conditions. These qualities encourage them to take their responsibilities and fulfill their obligations for a better society (Peng 2003). College students' sense of social responsibility means their feelings about the satisfaction of their inner needs in taking responsibilities for human and social development. It is essential for college students to identify their responsibilities for social development and human survival, and to connect their own growth with human progress (Pei 2007). Quite a few of studies have been made on cultivating college students' sense of social responsibility. Some researchers reviewed all the studies in the last twenty years (Yu et al. 2014) and others sorted Chinese and foreign studies on cultivating college students' sense of social responsibility (Guo et al. 2015). But those studies have some shortcomings: in terms of object, most studies focus on the definition of "sense of responsibility" and "sense of social responsibility" while few studies pay attention to the definition of "college students"; in terms of value, most studies advocate college students taking the responsibility for themselves, their families, the country, the world and all mankind while few studies emphasize their responsibility for the development of the universities they are living in; in terms of methods, most studies apply induction and deduction based on literature review while few studies analyze cases; in addition, most studies reveal the problems about college students' sense of social responsibility, such as laying too much stress on personal interests and not enough on public interests, too much on personal needs and not enough on social needs, too much on interests and not enough on morality, too much on material needs and not enough on mental needs, and too much on demands and not enough on contribution (Peng 2003). Some studies analyze the reasons why college students lack sense of social responsibility, such as impacts of social reforms, insufficient education and their inaccurate identification of themselves (Cui 2010). But most of the studies stop at the surface while few explore deep reasons (Guo et al. 2015). Besides, few studies point out college students' unique problems such as unawareness of their academic responsibility. Sense of social responsibility, as an important quality college students should have, concerns the development of our country and nation. So we should not only study why college students lack sense of social responsibility but also look for ways to cultivate their sense of social responsibility. Despite heated discussions, studies on the approaches to cultivating college students' sense of social responsibility in this respect are limited. Most of them generally analyze universities, family and society, while few studies introduce pragmatic measures (Guo et al. 2015). To sum up, some achievements have been made in studying college students' sense of social responsibility, but in-depth explorations of approaches to cultivating college students' sense of social responsibility should be made in a practical manner.

This paper proposes the three approaches to cultivating college students' sense of social responsibility. It answers the following questions: What is college students' sense of social responsibility? What is embedded in the sense? How to cultivate the sense? Through establishing a theoretical framework of the three approaches to cultivating college students' sense of social responsibility and analyzing the case of Beijing Normal University, this paper makes some conclusions which may facilitate future studies.

14.2 Three Approaches to Cultivating College Students' Sense of Social Responsibility

College students' responsibility usually consists of individual responsibility and social responsibility. Responsibility suggests an individual's duties in line with his roles in society that has to be performed and completed (Zhang 2015). Likewise, college students' responsibility includes the duties they have to perform and the tasks they have to complete in college. College students should take both responsibility and accountability. Responsibility suggests that they should strive to build their learning files. Accountability suggests that they should accept responsibility, admit and remedy the mistakes they may make in order to minimize losses. So we should cultivate college students' sense of both responsibility and accountability.

"Social responsibility means the responsibility individuals have to take for the survival and development of others and society at large." "It also means the due contributions individuals have to make to public services and the cause concerning the future of society." (Zhang 2015) According to the definitions, each and every member of our society should take both responsibility and accountability. And college students' social responsibility includes academic responsibility, professional responsibility and responsibility for public services.

> "When people have a sense of social responsibility, they identify with their social responsibility. (They know what their responsibility is, why they have to take the responsibility, and what is the significance of taking the responsibility.) They have a deep understanding of their social responsibility, internalize the understanding and take their responsibility on their own initiative." (Zhang 2015)

So we can define college students' sense of social responsibility as a psychological activity in which students have a right understanding of both the responsibility and the accountability they have to take for their study and the future of society, internalize such understanding and translate it into actions. But different from other social groups, college students have to take academic training, learn professional knowledge and participate in social services. So we can divide college students' social responsibility into academic responsibility, professional responsibility and responsibility for public services. Similarly, we should cultivate college students' sense of academic responsibility, professional responsibility and responsibility for public services.

We should improve college students' competence in recognizing their social responsibility. In this way, college students are expected to analyze the prescription of social responsibility in line with one's social roles, identify the tasks of each member of our society and analyze their own social responsibility, thus deciding to take their responsibility. People's consciousness controls their actions and behaviors. People connect themselves with the outside world through cognitive activities such as primary cognition including attention, memory and feelings and advanced cognition including analysis, judgment, reasoning and decision. So cultivating college students' sense of social responsibility enables the students to have a deeper understanding and develop a rational awareness of social responsibility. Therefore, we should improve college students' competence in recognizing their academic and professional responsibility and responsibility for public services.

We should improve college students' initiative in taking social responsibility so that they can be voluntary and active in taking their social responsibility. Thought is the precursor of action. Only when college students get a sound and deep understanding of their social responsibility will they determine to take their responsibility and accountability. Otherwise, they will shrink from taking their responsibility and accountability once they encounter difficulties. So we should cultivate college students' strong sense of social responsibility and encourage them to take their responsibility voluntarily in their daily life. In doing so, college students will take social responsibility spontaneously without external pressure. Therefore, this paper holds that we should strengthen college students' self-discipline to take academic, professional responsibility and responsibility for public services.

We should strengthen college students' self-discipline to take social responsibility. As a result, college students can be aware that their social responsibility is known to whole society and must be taken. In other words, we should strengthen college students' self-discipline to take academic, professional responsibility and responsibility for public services.

College students' sense of social responsibility has its own characteristics: Firstly, it is learning-oriented. College students still need to learn about sense of social responsibility. Colleges are expected to create a wide variety of learning opportunities for cultivating students' sense of social responsibility. Secondly, college students' sense of social responsibility is reality-oriented. College students are supposed to make conscious efforts to fulfill his responsibility in certain student organizations and finish his job or tasks in college. Thirdly, college students' sense of social responsibility is future-oriented. It focuses on how college graduates assume and fulfill their social responsibility in the future. Finally, college students' sense of social responsibility is also characterized by uncertainty, which is closely related with the feature of future-oriented. In other words, students' professional career in their later life may be related to their majors and social practices in college. According to these characteristics, colleges have to adopt corresponding approaches to cultivating college students' sense of social responsibility.

College students' sense of social responsibility needs to be cultivated in different ways. There are many different approaches, and some scholars have made theoretical analysis on those approaches from different disciplinary perspectives. These approaches can be classified into four categories: firstly, providing opportunities for college students to analyze and reflect rationally on various social phenomena by taking related courses and participating in classroom discussions. College students thus can establish noble values and strong sense of social responsibility; secondly, by participating in various social activities organized by colleges, students can apply related theories into practices and have stronger sense of social responsibility through personal involvement; thirdly, creating favorable campus environment and integrating the cultivation of students' sense of social responsibility into that of campus culture; finally, enlarging the communication zone of students by applying internet. In other words, colleges should provide correct guidance of values by using short message and other social platforms like QQ and We-chat. It is an undeniable fact that these approaches promote the cultivation of college students' sense of social responsibility. However, these approaches are mainly designed based on the needs of colleges without considering students' outlook on sense of social responsibility.

So the cultivation of college students' sense of social responsibility should be based on their own conception, that is to say, the approaches to cultivating college students' sense of social responsibility should be designed on the basis of college and students' learning. Based on that, this paper proposes three different approaches to cultivating college students' sense of social responsibility, namely taking part in academic and professional practices as well as public services. To be specific, the academic approach covers academic study, presiding over or participating in research programs and academic conferences. By participating in these academic activities, college students will realize the importance of fulfilling their corresponding social responsibility and understand their strengths and weaknesses in this part. The academic approach could not only inspire college students to think how to assume their social responsibility but also guide them to set up correct sense of social responsibility. The professional approach involves major-related surveys as well as professional probation and internship. Take students majoring in education as example: by participating in professional investigation, probation and internship, these students can have face-to-face communication with outstanding teachers who have devoted themselves to the education cause. Under the influence of these outstanding teachers, the students will realize the significance of assuming their social responsibility and understand their own responsibility in society. The approach of public services mainly includes taking part in association activities, voluntary teaching and charitable activities. The college students will apply the related theories they have learned into social practices by participating in these public services. Or to say, the students will have preliminary sense of social responsibility by involving themselves in these activities. College students will

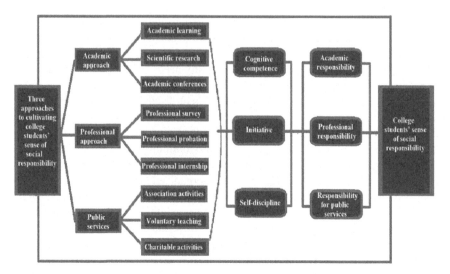

Fig. 14.1 Theoretical Framework for the three approaches to cultivating college students' sense of social responsibility

have the chance to experience some social problems personally by taking part in voluntary teaching and charitable activities. The students can engage themselves in solving these social problems, and thus acquire a more clear understanding of the necessity and importance of taking social responsibility. Meanwhile, students will feel proud and committed to shoulder their social responsibility and have a stronger initiative to do so.

In a word, the three approaches will be efficient in enhancing college students' sense of social responsibility. With these approaches, the initiative and cognitive competence of college students in academics, profession and public services would be improved. In addition, college students would become more self-disciplined. Therefore, the paper puts forward the theoretical framework (Fig. 14.1) for the three approaches to cultivating college students' sense of social responsibility.

14.3 Case Study on Three Approaches to Cultivating College Students' Sense of Social Responsibility: Beijing Normal University

Beijing Normal University has put the three approaches to cultivating college students' sense of social responsibility into practice, and some experience has been gathered in the process. Taking Beijing Normal University as the study object, this part analyzes how educational institutions can adopt the three approaches put forward in this paper to cultivate college students' sense of social responsibility.

14.3.1   Academic Approach to Cultivating College Students' Sense of Social Responsibility: Integrating Curriculum and Sponsoring Research Projects

Beijing Normal University attaches great importance to the role of the academic approach in cultivating college students' sense of social responsibility. In other words, Beijing Normal University makes the best of classes to cultivate students' sense of social responsibility. The university combines classroom teaching and extra-curricular activities and makes them two means of cultivating students' sense of social responsibility. In doing so, the university tries to integrate the cultivation of college students' sense of social responsibility into the whole teaching process. In terms of curriculum, Beijing Normal University implements general education and offers nearly 600 courses for undergraduates to select. The university runs the course of "social practice", which is worth two credits. In addition, it sets up a curriculum module called "Social Progress and Civic Responsibilities", which includes 132 courses.

On top of classes, Beijing Normal University also makes utmost of academic training to cultivate students' sense of social responsibility. The university establishes scientific research foundation and encourages students to apply for research projects at the levels of school, municipality and nation. From 2011 to 2015, Beijing Normal University invested a total of more than 16.7 million yuan in academic training, sponsoring 552 national research projects, 485 municipal research projects and 1504 school-level ones (Teaching Affairs Office of Beijing Normal University 2015). Such projects help the students have a right attitude towards scientific research. Beijing Normal University also cultivates students' sense of social responsibility by encouraging them to innovate, start up businesses and take an active part in social practice when they are in college.

14.3.2   Professional Approach to Cultivating College Students' Sense of Social Responsibility: Reforming Professional Practice Based Teaching and Innovating the Model of Education

Beijing Normal University attaches great importance to the role of the professional approach in cultivating college students' sense of social responsibility. Professional approach is about making professional practice a credit course in order to encourage students to apply what they have learned into practice. Beijing Normal University takes an array of measures to ensure that the credit course of professional practices plays a role in cultivating college students' sense of social responsibility. The university formulates dedicated documents such as "Guidance on the Implementation of 'Practice and Innovation' in 'Training Program for Undergraduates'" and "Procedures for Giving the Credit of 'Practice and Innovation'" and instructs schools and colleges to lay down corresponding rules. In 2015, the university established on its own five "Off-campus Practice Base" under the guidance of "National Training Program for Undergraduates". The university invested 1.9 million yuan in innovating the contents, forms and management of professional practice and establishing quality and stable practice bases (Teaching Affairs Office of Beijing Normal University 2015). To sum up, professional approach including professional survey, professional probation and professional internship makes a big difference in cultivating college students' sense of social responsibility.

14.3.3 Approach of Public Services to Cultivating College Students' Sense of Social Responsibility: Founding Baige Youth Volunteers Association and Other Public Service Organizations

Approach of public services is the most influential, effective and representative approach adopted by Beijing Normal University to cultivate college students' sense of social responsibility. Baige Youth Volunteers Association, which was founded in 1994, features prominently in the approach. The association takes "Responsibility, Dedication, Cooperation, Innovation" as its purpose and upholds the volunteer spirit of "Dedication, Fraternity, Mutual Aid, Progress". It remains committed to volunteerism and makes a significant contribution towards promoting social harmony and social progress. The association has set up more than 30 volunteer projects, which span assistance to publicity to elementary education and environmental protection. It has established itself as a brand public service organization and an important platform to cultivate college students' sense of social responsibility. The association organizes a number of brand activities including "Public Service Month in Beijing Normal University", the public service forum featuring "Youth, Public Service, Prospect" and "Supermarket of Public Service". What's more, Beijing Normal University adopts the approach of public services to cultivate college students' sense of responsibility for education, culture, welfare and environmental protection. It encourages students to teach in remote areas and ignite their expectations about future, to popularize scientific knowledge and spread positive energy, to offer help to the disadvantaged and bring them warm and care, to contribute to environmental protection and the building of "Beautiful China".

14.4 Conclusions

Based on the theoretical framework of the three approaches to cultivating college students' sense of social responsibility and the case study on Beijing Normal University, the paper draws the following conclusions:

The academic approach will not only improve the college students' sense of academic responsibility but also tap their cognition of social responsibility. The academic approach is the most basic and important way to cultivate students' sense of social responsibility. Practices like classroom learning, scientific research and participating in academic conferences are efficient in improving students' sense of social responsibility in academics.

The professional approach will improve college students' ability in professional practice and offer them chances to apply their professional knowledge into practice. What's more, the approach will mobilize student's initiative in taking professional responsibility. Practices like professional survey and investigation, probation and internship will improve students' initiative to be responsible in profession and make them well-prepared for their future professional career.

The approach of public services will enhance students' ability in providing public services. With the help of the approach, college students would become more self-disciplined and will take an active part in public services on their own initiative. Practices like taking part in association activities, voluntary teaching and charity would improve students' self-discipline and initiative of taking part in public services.

On the basis of the foregoing, the paper is going to analyze the importance and necessity of cultivating college students' sense of social responsibility. The cultivation of college students' sense of social responsibility must conform to the pattern of their growth as well as characteristics of their college learning and the law of college education. The characteristics of college students' learning can be classified into three categories, namely "the characteristic of learning content", "the characteristic of learning method" and "the cultivation of self-awareness". The learning content of college students is characterized by "clear career direction, more professional" and "controversial and high level of subject matter". The learning method of college students is featured with "improving one's capacity" and "combining classroom learning with social practice". The cultivation of self-awareness refers to promoting one's "self-discipline", "self-judgment" as well as "initiative" (Zheng 1999). By creating opportunities for students to participate in various learning activities including classroom teaching, research practice, professional probation and internship as well as public services, college should cultivate students' sense of social responsibility from different perspectives including learning contents, leaning method and self-awareness.

College students' primary social responsibility is to do a good job in learning and academic research. They would be aware of their academic responsibility by fulfilling their obligations in learning, including writing academic papers and being trained in accordance with academic criterion. College time is the best and primary period for every student to receive academic training, which involves fostering the sense of academic responsibility, identifying one's academic responsibility and taking corresponding responsibility. Academic training will improve students' understanding of the world from perceptual level to conceptual one. Through academic training, college students will become responsible in academic research with qualities of inquiring, criticizing, questioning and creating. These spirits constitute the basis for the country's development and social progress. In this sense, college students are supposed to preside over or participate in research programs. Thus, they will become socially responsible with qualities like strong teamwork, respecting others and inclusiveness. The sense of social responsibility will get college students prepared for their personal-social development, especially that at high level including assuming responsibility for leading social development.

Cultivating College students' sense of social responsibility should conform to their study in certain majors. College is vital for every student to learn knowledge, and the sense of social responsibility will make them ready for his future professional career. All the students, regardless of their majors in college, will have to enter the workplace and assume their social responsibility. It is an essential part of study for all college students to cultivate their sense of social responsibility. They have to improve their sense of social responsibility through taking part in professional surveys and investigations as well as professional probation and internship. College students are thus expected to assume their professional responsibility actively and finish their professional tasks in a highly responsible manner. If something goes wrong in carrying out their task, they should be brave in taking their responsibility. What's more, college students should respect others' achievements. They have to be open-minded in learning from professional experts and superiors and try their best to assist them. In a word, college students could learn a lot from cultivating their sense of social responsibility.

College students' sense of social responsibility would be cultivated through taking part in public services, which is the most common approach in college to cultivate one's sense of social responsibility. Taking part in public services also meets the aesthetic needs of personnel development. For college students, the aims of participating in public services are to be educated and get some practices. By doing so, the college students are expected to establish correct outlook on the world, on their life and values as well as to have stronger sense of social responsibility. By taking part in public services, students can have the chance to get an insight on the society, accumulate practical experiences, improve themselves and shape healthy personalities. By doing so, they would ultimately become outstanding constructors both for the country and the society they lived. Public services can be seen as a scale of social civilization. Participating in public services is significant in cultivating college students' sense of social responsibility, it will also propel the youth to carry on their historical responsibility and establish concepts of caring about the society, the community and others (Zhong 2012). Actually, in one's life, the highest level of personnel development lies in that of aesthetic. As the most important part of aesthetics, social aesthetics is achieved through human activities, especially through their participation in public services like charitable activities. By taking part in public services organized by various associations in college, college students would embrace the sense of social responsibility, and they will have the opportunity to enjoy personal development in aesthetics as well as a happy and perfect life.

14.5 Summary

The sense of social responsibility is a strong initiative and lofty will or attitude propels human to assume their social responsibility. It is highly integrated with one's ideas, ambitions and values. It can also function as a driving force for one to serve his country as well as the people. "Everyone is responsible for the fate of county" has been a common belief for the Chinese people. Nowadays, college students are going to be constructors and successors of China's socialist modernization cause. The question if they have the sense of social responsibility or the strength of this sense they have will have a direct influence on the success of modernization cause. It will also determine whether or to what scale they can fulfill their own historical responsibilities (Xie 2007). For those higher education institutions that prepare citizen for the society, they should attach great importance to the cultivation of students' sense of social responsibility. They also should explore and practice continuously new effective ways to cultivate students' sense of social responsibility. The paper establishes a theoretical framework for cultivating college students' sense of social responsibility. With the case study on Beijing Normal University, it draws some basic conclusions on cultivating college students' sense of social responsibility. These conclusions will have guiding effect on improving college students' sense of social responsibility in the form of both theories and practices. There is great possibility for us to further discuss the study on college students' sense of social responsibility. We will ensure the cultivation of college students' sense of social responsibility to be more efficient by making it conform to the growth pattern of college students and follow the law of college education. For learners or college students, the society is an interactive framework instead of an object when taking from the perspective of social psychology. According to Mead, the interaction in a society is based on "mind" and "self". Undoubtedly, the interaction in a society has internalized into individual self as well as social self. Based on that, we should take account of the learning content as well as learning methods in discussion of cultivating students' sense of social responsibility, but we still need to pay more attention to the characteristics of self-awareness of learning subject or the college students including self-discipline, initiative and self-judgment. What's more, cultivating college students' sense of social responsibility should be in line with the needs of contemporary society featuring internalization, informatization, Internet Plus and Big Data. The contemporary young students grow up in a world with highly developed communication technology. The world is open to various internet connections and channels to accumulate knowledge. Every one of us is linked in the huge social network. The interactionism comes into being as we are born into the world and it is also an indispensable part in out latter life. It is also an important power constantly interacted and delivered between different people and it becomes more powerful in the information age. In what ways would college cultivate citizens with sense of social responsibility for the society has become the topic of the era. By doing so, the interactionism between different people will be improved, which will lead to better social interactions. And social harmony would also be achieved as individual experience being enriched, enlarged and transcended. The core of social civilization lies in the interactionism between different people. And a strong sense of social responsibility is the source of comfortable, peaceful and orderly interactionism.

References

Cui, N. X. (2010). Factors in college students' lack of sense of social responsibility and dedicated measures. *Modern Education Management, 0*(5), 111–113.

Guo, K., Lu, L. N., & Kuang, Z. H. (2015). Progress and trends of Chinese and foreign studies on college students' sense of social responsibility. *Chinese Journal of Education, 0*(4), 161–163.

Pei, T. T. (2007). *Studies on cultivation of college students' sense of social responsibility (Unpublished master's thesis)*. China: Southwest University.

Peng, D. G. (2003). The cultivation of college students' sense of social responsibility. *Modern University Education, 0*(3), 41–44.

Teaching Affairs Office of Beijing Normal University. (2015). *Report on the undergraduate education in the 12th five-year plan period (2011–2015)*. Retrieved from http://jwcold.bnu.edu.cn/jxyj/jxcgj/122315.htm.

Xie, S. C. (2007). *Research on innovation of ideological and political education for college students*. Wuhan, Hubei: Yangtze River Publishing Group.

Yu, Y. J., Zhang, Q. Y., & Zhou, Y. G. (2014). A review of studies on Chinese college students' sense of social responsibility over past two decades. *Journal of Yangzhou College (Higher Education Research Edition), 18*(6), 48–51.

Zhang, Y. (2015). Nurturing virtues, educating people and cultivating college teachers' sense of social responsibility. *XinHua Digest, 17,* 125.

Zheng, R. C. (1999). *Psychological consultation of college students*. Jinan, Shandong: Shandong Education Press.

Zhong, Y. B. (2012). *Introduction to college students' participation in public services*. Guangzhou, Guangdong: Zhongshan University Press.

Chapter 15
Developing Qualified Citizenship

Dongtao Lin, Junbo Yin and Yongzheng Hou

Abstract With the world facing increasing challenges in economy, society, culture and environment, university social responsibility has become a central topic of discussion in higher education sector. As the highest-level educational institution, the university should respond actively to social changes and assume the responsibility of remolding and promoting social development (Alzyoud and Bani-Hani 2015). Located in West China, where socioeconomic development lags behind and natural disasters happen frequently as compared to other parts of the country, Sichuan University has a three-dimension social responsibility system that is aimed to address the special needs of the area: teaching humanity and morals as well as knowledge and skills, encouraging student associations and promoting disaster management. In this chapter, we summarize the experiences of Sichuan University in fulfilling its social responsibility by developing qualified citizenship. We use nine cases of the University's service learning programs that have been successful to illustrate our understanding of university social responsibility, hoping that our experience is one that can be shared and duplicated and contribute to the betterment of the world we live in.

Keywords University social responsibility · Citizenship · Service learning program · Disaster management · Program implementation · West China

D. Lin (✉)
College of Foreign Languages and Cultures, Sichuan University, Sichuan, China
e-mail: 498616608@qq.com

J. Yin
Office for International Projects, Sichuan University, Sichuan, China
e-mail: oip@scu.edu.cn

Y. Hou
IDMR, Sichuan University, Sichuan, China
e-mail: 473828718@qq.com

© Springer Nature Singapore Pte Ltd. 2017   235
D.T.L. Shek and R.M. Hollister (eds.), *University Social Responsibility and Quality of Life*, Quality of Life in Asia 8,
DOI 10.1007/978-981-10-3877-8_15

15.1 Introduction

When commenting on the mission of the university, American scholar Brubacher (1977), who is a major figure in the field of history and philosophy of education in the 20th century, says that people do not explore profound knowledge for the sake of knowledge only; but rather, for the profound impact on nations and the human society. With the world facing huge economic, social, cultural and environmental challenges, university social responsibility (USR) has become a central topic of discussion in higher education sector. Based on the belief that universities have obligations to address these challenges and solutions so as to make our world more just, inclusive, peaceful and sustainable, USR is also seen in the contributions of the university to social betterment through integration of social responsibility policies into institutional management, teaching, research, services and public activities. This means that the university should respond actively to social changes and assume the responsibility of remolding and promoting social development (Reed 2004).

Ever since its birth, the university has been the highest-level educational institution that develops knowledge creatively with its primary responsibility being promoting the innovation and growth of knowledge. And with the university moving from the edge to the centre of the society, such analogies as the "light house" of the society, "axial institution", "social service station" and "toolbox" of the modern society were used to demonstrate the importance of the university. In the modern society, the university has become the "heart" of the society, an unparalleled high ever, suggesting that the university social responsibility has extended from the mere dissemination of knowledge to a much larger spectrum (Dima et al. 2013). The university shoulders the responsibilities of inheriting and passing on human civilization, promoting socioeconomic development and cultivating talents for the future society.

15.2 Brief Introduction of Sichuan University' Efforts in Fulfilling University Social Responsibility

Sichuan University (SCU) is one of China's key universities under the direct supervision of the Ministry of Education. Located in West China, it is identified as a high-level, research-oriented comprehensive university under Project 985 and Project 211. SCU has long been striving to cultivate first-grade talents, conducting first-grade research and providing first-grade social services. SCU also encourages its faculty and students to walk out of the "ivory tower" and turn university classrooms and labs into platforms to serve enterprises and society. By doing so, the University assumes more responsibility in social development and takes the lead in social progress.

In recent years, SCU has been endeavoring to build up and improve its own three-dimension social responsibility system, exerting its social impact and creating a win-win situation among various stakeholders. This system consists of three dimensions: teaching humanity and morals as well as knowledge and skills, encouraging student associations and promoting disaster management. In fulfilling these responsibilities, SCU aims to set up a good example.

First, SCU strives to help students form their humanity morals when attaching importance to knowledge and skill learning as well. The University offers about 100 general courses that involve multi-level and multi-facet subjects including law, history, society, philosophy and ethics etc. These courses cover social responsibility, morals and self-cultivation, honesty and courtesy. Social elite, role models and other people of all walks of life are invited to hold discussions with faculty and students, hoping that social responsibility and service awareness can be cultivated (Hill 2004). In the meantime, virtues and ethics are given priority over a specific occupation. As a Chinese saying goes, a person who has virtues possesses a compassionate heart.

Second, SCU advocates the notion of mutual help and encourages student associations, internship and social practice. Supported by the University, more than 200 student associations have been set up and more than 500 social practice bases have been established. The associations and social practice bases provide students with opportunities to learn and experience the happiness and achievement when offering mutual help and working for communities, rural residents and disadvantaged groups. For example, 66.5 million RMB, including 28 million from the Ministry of Education, has been invested in the building-up of social practice bases. Among the 550 more bases at the national-, provincial-, university and college/school levels, 19 are national-level engineering practice centres, 9 are national-level out-of-university social practice bases and 18 are provincial-level out-of-university social practice bases. These bases are located at large- or medium-sized enterprises, research institutes and governmental departments. Another example would be the cooperation between The Hong Kong Polytechnic University (PolyU) and SCU since 2012. Supported by SCU and the "Ten Thousand People Scheme", PolyU initiated a student service learning program of educating farmers on healthier food production at Shifang County of Sichuan Province, where PolyU students serve local community with their expertise and with the help of their teachers. Such service learning has benefited both students and local communities and promoted academic exchange between teachers and students of Hong Kong and the inland.

Third, SCU builds a platform of disaster prevention and relief, fulfilling its responsibility to the society. The University advocates concerning, attending to, participating in and serving the prosperity and development of world peace, economy and culture. It deems as its own responsibility settling crises that challenge the mankind. Seen as a whole, the world today is undergoing major development, transformation and adjustment, and mankind is facing opportunities as well as crises and challenges. The world we are living in is a place where social conflicts are aggravated with the ever increasing gap between the rich and poor; where international wars are started for the contest of resources; where economic recession worldwide is triggered by major economic and financial problems; and where even the survival of the human race is threatened by major and particularly severe geological disasters, extreme climate and major and particularly severe crises (Fang 2008). Under such circumstances of world development, Sichuan University will make even greater efforts in disseminating knowledge, cultivating talents, stimulating innovation in knowledge and research, inheriting, passing on and carrying forward culture, and thus make more remarkable contribution to the resolution of major global issues, especially those concerning major disasters and crises.

Located in an area where natural disasters are not uncommon, Sichuan University also felt the pain of the devastating earthquake in Wenchuan in 2008. Understanding its responsibility and obligation to the society, Sichuan University took the initiative in researching on global disaster and crisis response based on its own experience in the earthquake. Its efforts in addressing global crises and fulfilling its social obligations are best embodied in "Sichuan University-Hong Kong Polytechnic University Institute for Disaster Management and Reconstruction" (IDMR), which is the first of its kind in the world. Established in 2013, the Institute has four major functions: talent cultivation, scientific research, data base construction and social service. It is the common vision of both universities that taking the post-disaster construction at the earthquake-stricken Wenchuan as a prime example, we can provide understanding, experience and achievements to the world for the purpose of systematic research on sociology, economics, law, medicine, science and technology and social work during post-disaster construction. The Institute initiated social services that were tailored to address the needs of earthquake-stricken areas including Lushan, Ludian and Pishan with regard to relief, restoration and reconstruction in the field of rehabilitation, psychological aid, community comfort, post-disaster planning, disaster social workers and capacity building of officials at disaster areas.

A service learning scheme has also been developed and a course named "Disaster-relief Service Learning and Volunteer Activity Leadership" was offered. Since 2014, the "International Forum on Post-disaster Reconstruction Efforts of Sichuan University Students" has been held on May 12 each year in commemoration of the devastating earthquake in Sichuan on May 12, 2008.

Facing the future, Sichuan University will fearlessly assume its obligation and fulfill its mission. Working together with all walks of life, Sichuan University will continue its endeavors in enhancing social obligations as a university and calling for its faculty and students to assume their own responsibilities. The University also encourages its faculty and students to go beyond the walls of the university, serve the society, help the general public to lead a healthy, secure and happy life, and contribute to the sustainable development and civilization progress of the entire human race (Vasilescu et al. 2010).

We would like to share our experiences in developing qualified citizenship which we deem as an integral part of university social responsibility. Nine cases of service learning will be provided here to exemplify how we externalize the concept to serve the society.

15.3 Cases of Service Learning at Sichuan University

15.3.1 Building Capacity for Women in Rural Areas

Recent economic reforms in China have brought massive social changes which generate severe problems for rural women. The dissolution of the social safety net in rural areas further marginalizes women. Rural-urban wealth discrepancies further increase with China's entry into the World Trade Organization and its effects. Women now make up as high as 80% of the agricultural labour force in some rural areas, as most men are migrating to cities for work. Women shoulder the double burden of having to farm the land while continuing to care for the family. Although women with absent husbands are de facto heads of households, their male partners are viewed as the appropriate authorities in any official business affecting the family. Prolonged absence of the husbands due to migration provides opportunities to men for extra-marital relationships. Family relationships may break down and conflicts arise, sometimes leading to violence or abuse of women. Family violence is an acknowledged problem in China, and laws have been passed to protect women. Nevertheless, due to traditional values and ineffective enforcement of laws, many rural women remain trapped in distressing situations. The suicide rate among rural women is the highest in China, with little professional help available.

The University School of Public Health cooperated with University of Manitoba to initiate this project, centring on applying social work methodology to help rural women. Women cadres employed by the China Women's Federation (CWF) have been providing significant social services to women in many parts of rural China, under challenging circumstances of limited support and resources. This project responds to the CWF's request for training which is informed by professional, Chinese and international social work knowledge and research, yet at the same time is relevant to Chinese rural women's needs, and makes good use of the cadre's existing capacity and available resources. Therefore, the project aims to help build on the CWF cadres' extensive experience and local knowledge gained from working closely with rural women, and strengthen their capacity to better serve rural women as they respond to effects related to the dramatic transition occurring in China's social and economic structures. Training and a more accessible, gender-sensitive social services network operating on democratic principles will contribute greatly to helping rural women as they endeavour to build better lives for themselves and their families (Gibbon et al. 2002). Men were invited to take part in some social work and gender awareness training at various levels so that they, too, can participate in activities that promote well-being in individuals, families and communities.

With the devoted assistance from University of Manitoba, we sent faculty and students to the rural areas of Luojiang County and Xichang City to carry out extensive investigation of women's social situation, health condition, economic status and family relation. The rural women in the areas face fundamental problems related to numerous development priorities, but we believe social work best addresses their urgent needs related to gender equality and good governance. Included in training and other activities, the men are better prepared to provide the necessary support for the benefit of women and entire families. Participatory methods are used and the involvement of village women in local political processes is promoted.

With the objective of building social work human resource capacity at institutional levels to improve social service delivery to rural women in the selected rural areas, an indigenous and gender-responsive social work practice model has been developed and employed. Sustainable results are achieved through:

1. *A co-ordinated training-of-trainers program* to build capacity in front-line women cadres who work locally with women at CWF. Crisis intervention, interpersonal communication skills, gender awareness, participatory methods and other components of training will help higher-level CWF cadres to make use of what they have learned and, with support, train other cadres at lower administrative levels, ensuring a sustained effort from cities to villages.

2. *Resource centres for rural women that are* established at the county, township and village levels. They serve as the bridge between micro practice and macro policy linkages and for network-building between policy makers, grassroots trainers, and service providers. Coordinated under a national centre in Beijing, expert groups are formed to produce training materials for the cadre trainers. Research has been conducted on indigenous knowledge and an integrated model for research, social work practice, and social policy analysis affecting rural women. Trained faculty and students provide consultation with different levels of policy makers for policy implementation related to the livelihood of rural women. Knowledge generation from the project has been disseminated through means of colloquia, seminars, workshops, and publications to policy makers, service providers and academic communities.

The major results achieved from this project are that rural women in the targeted areas have a better understanding of their legal rights, are able to identify their needs and participate more actively in decision making processes in their own families and communities. Other expected results include strengthened capacity of the University and the Women's Federation to provide training to cadres providing social services to rural women in Sichuan Province.

Effective and sustainable Chinese rural social work services (RSWS) models will be gradually conceptualized and implemented to enhance the operation of social work services for rural women and their families, building on the experience and knowledge of the University and the Sichuan Province Women's Federation in the project areas. The RSWS models represent unique sets of methods and skills applied by trained cadres to respond to local needs of rural women, families and the community. Through interdisciplinary collaboration between Sichuan University and University of Manitoba, we expect to advance social policy in China to reduce gender inequality and enhance women's basic human rights for safety and well-being. The University of Manitoba collaborated successfully with the National

Women University, the All China Women's Federation, Sichuan University, and the Chinese Academy of Social Sciences and non-governmental organizations to deliver the project results.

15.3.2 Developing a Model of Health Care Services for the Elderly in Sichuan Province in China

In the late 1990s, the University's West China School of Public Health started a project of developing a medical care service model for the elderly. This model is intended to improve both physical and mental health of the elderly.

This Project has set up one centre, two networks and two service models for the elderly, namely, "Health Promoting and Training Centre on Aging", "Healthcare Network for the Elderly" and "The Education Network for the Elderly", "The Model of Taking Care of the Elderly in Community" and "The Model of Family-based Service for the Elderly". Five books and 71 papers on gerontology have been published.

Palliative Care and Rehabilitation were introduced into our curriculum. Our faculty and students have been practicing the concepts and procedures to serve the aged at selected communities, and our hospitals where over 3780 poor aged with incurable diseases have received service from our faculty and students.

Gerontology and geriatrics have become an important part of our curriculum for students of health sciences. Epidemical researches have been carried out for the elderly. Local health resources centres have been set up in urban and rural areas in Sichuan. More than 90 papers have been published, which are important evidence references for the government to make policies for the elderly.

Our faculty and students provided critical assistance in improving the health education courses in Senior citizen's schools, where health education lessons were offered to more than 100,000 elderly people. About 1500 doctors, 400 nurses, 400 village health practitioners and 200 local health officers received training either in our university or on their working sites.

Our faculty and students visited over 1000 aged people while practicing community health service in rural areas. Free medical check and treatment were offered to the elderly in nine minority villages and more than 4000 elderly benefited.

15.3.3 Institute for Disaster Management and Reconstruction (IDMR) as an Example

15.3.3.1 Introduction

On May 12, 2008, a devastating earthquake on Richter 8.0 struck Wenchuan County, Sichuan Province, causing heavy human and economic losses. In the light of the principle of "serving our people and inspiring confidence in our country", Sichuan University (SCU) and The Hong Kong Polytechnic University (PolyU) immediately engaged in earthquake relief missions. In June, 2008, SCU and PolyU jointly established the "SCU-PolyU Sichuan Post-earthquake Reconstruction Support and Research Centre", integrating strength, expertise and academician excellence in the field of social network resources of both universities with the aim to enhance capacity and services in disaster management, personnel relocation, post-disaster reconstructions frontline personnel training, and professional psychological and social work services.

In response to the increasing concern and demand on good training and risk reduction in all kinds of natural disasters, SCU and PolyU actively started the initiative of setting up the "Institute for Disaster Management and Reconstruction" (IDMR), a high-standard multi-disciplinary and sustainable institution, which is intended to integrate world-wide resources to serve the society and the disaster-hit areas and people with its scientific research, education and services in the field of disaster prevention and reduction. With strong support from the Ministry of Education, Ministry of Civil Affairs and Sichuan Provincial People's Government, as well as the 0.2 billion RMB donation from The Hong Kong Jockey Club, the two universities initiated the construction of IDMR in August, 2010.

IDMR was officially launched in 2013 as the world's first comprehensive institute dedicated to scientific research on disaster prevention and disaster reduction, and was ready to respond to major crises, related education and training, social service, and disaster information service (Wright 2002). With regard to disciplinary development, the institute will focus on three main areas: disaster medical science, safety science and disaster reduction, and disaster-related applied social science. It endeavors to develop competitive, distinct disciplinary curriculum on disaster prevention, disaster reduction and disaster management. It strives to nurture an excellent teaching and research team and provide education to top-notch talents aiming to find solution to issues of great challenges in the area of post-disaster management.

15.3.3.2 Actively Responding to Major Natural Disasters

As for social services, besides holding a series of conferences and training courses on disaster reduction and emergency management, IDMR also actively responded to natural disasters such as follows.

1. *Lushan earthquake in Sichuan Province: actively offered professional support to help national policy-making*. After the outbreak of Lushan earthquake, we offered professional suggestions to the central government regarding the emergency relief in stricken areas and post-disaster reconstruction under the guidance and leadership of IDMR.

In April of 2013, experts from IDMR were interviewed by Xinhua News Agency, and a report was published mainly on the post-disaster reconstruction model of Lushan earthquake, its impact on Sichuan Province and possible helpful measures and suggestions which resulted in important policy suggestions to the central government.

2. *Ludian earthquake in Yunnan Province: establishment of a disaster emergency response mechanism in Sichuan University*. After Ludian earthquake on August 3rd, 2014, with the support of China Foundation for Poverty Alleviation, IDMR organized a group of experts to research on the demand of disaster-affected areas. During that period of time, our postgraduate students majoring in Disaster Nursing visited the disaster area and opened training courses of clinical rehabilitation and rehabilitation theories and practices for local nurses and doctors. Later on, IDMR also ran a training course for civil administrative officials from the earthquake affected area on post-disaster reconstruction and management.

3. *Nepal earthquake: participation in earthquake rescue and post-disaster reconstruction*. Upon the 8.1-magnitude Nepal earthquake in 2015, IDMR immediately set up an emergency rescue responding mechanism and an international rescue squad coordination office in Sichuan University. Together with Beijing Normal University, China Foundation for Poverty Alleviation, One Foundation and some other organizations, we have established a social organization emergency responding coordination centre for Nepal earthquake. We collected and collated disaster related information and assisted social organizations in China in international disaster relief. As a result, 15 issues of April 25 Nepal and Tibet Earthquake Report and April 25 Nepal and Tibet Earthquake Rescue Information Manual were compiled. The very detailed and sufficient content provided much convenience and was highly appreciated.

IDMR conducted disaster area investigation and promotion of social organizations' participation in disaster relief. From May 1st to May 4th, 2015, IDMR representatives visited the worst affected area to conduct post-disaster investigation and worked with international relief organizations on the post-disaster demands investigation. Sichuan University also donated emergency relief and medical supplies to Katmandu affiliated hospital and successfully solicited donation and support from its faculty and students to support reconstruction.

4. *SCU provided strong assistance to post-disaster reconstruction work after Pishan earthquake in Xinjiang Autonomous Region*. Sichuan University organized a four-member expert team from IDMR and Collaborative Innovation Centre for Security and Development of Western Frontier China to investigate the Pishan earthquake post-disaster relief, rehabilitation and reconstruction work in Urumchi Municipality, Hotan Prefecture and Kashi Prefecture, and they have submitted the investigation report to the Government.

IDMR conducted post-disaster reconstruction training sessions for the local officials. According to the research results and upon the requirements of the Pishan County government, IDMR dispatched 7 experts to organize Pishan County

Post-disaster Reconstruction and Management Training Session for local officials. Meanwhile IDMR and Pishan Government signed the Framework Agreement on SCU-Pishan Cooperation on Pishan Earthquake Post-Construction and Societal Development.

Local officials were invited to participate in a short-term disaster reconstruction training program at Sichuan University. From October 12 to 17, 2015, fourteen officials from Pishan County and townships visited IDMR, aiming at learning reconstruction experiences from Sichuan.

15.3.3.3   SCU and PolyU Collaborating in Service Learning Programs

IDMR of SCU cooperated with students and faculty from PolyU in carrying a series of service learning programs in the rural areas and communities of Sichuan Province. Detailed information is listed in Table 15.1.

Over 1000 students and faculty have been involved in all these projects and other social service learning programs.

Self-rescue training was included in the program to strengthen the participators' disaster response skills. Before the program, students and teachers from PolyU and students from SCU Volunteer Association and Yimeng Association took training courses on fire escape, self-rescue in road accidents, self-rescue in floods, self-rescue in mountain accidents, etc. The training courses, through which various practical skills were delivered, improved participators' disaster response awareness and impressed everyone with the valuable experiences.

Investigations and researches were conducted. During the implementation of these programs, the participants visited multiple local memorial relics and organizations such as Beichuan earthquake relics, Wenchuan Earthquake Memorial Museum, the New Beichuan County, Yingxiu Elementary School of Wenchuan, Yingxiu Youth Centre, Bayi Rehabilitation Centre, and the Central-level Disaster

Table 15.1 Service learning programs (2016) jointly carried out by IDMR of SCU and PolyU

Program name	Type	Date	No. of PolyU students	No. of PolyU faculty
Eye care service to local Deyang communities	Eye care service to local Deyang communities	6.2–11	27	4
Medical service in Deyang rehabilitation centre	Service learning programs	5.31–6.12	7	1
Biotechnology application in disaster-stricken areas	Ten Thousand Talent Program	5.26–6.1	39	4
Sichuan disaster resilience summer program	Ten Thousand Talent Program	6.2–12	48	3
New looks in ancient towns visiting program	Ten Thousand Talent Program	5.12–17	30	1
Total number			151	13

Relief Materials Storage of the Ministry of Civil Affairs. Through these visiting trips, the participators learned about the gallant spirit of local people when combating disasters, and about disaster reduction and prevention knowledge and skills, thus strengthening awareness in this regard. The trip also showcased the great achievements made in post-disaster reconstruction.

Special Handmade Natural Disaster Map of China has been a good result of the cooperation. During field studies, teachers and students worked together for three days in drawing a map that features natural disasters across China. The map not only showcases the categories, frequencies and intensities of different natural disasters in various localities around China, but also earmarks their unique tourism resources. With its gifted design, delicate touch and handmade accessories attached to it, the map has captured the vastness and abundance of China in students' mind and has therefore become a special piece of collection of IDMR.

Apart from these programs, SCU is going all out to expand its cooperation with universities and organizations from all over the world in service learning. Up to date, SCU has over 150 partners, and over 3000 students and faculty are coming to and going out of Sichuan University to share experience and knowledge in social responsibility.

IMDR is now offering a series of courses in service learning, including Introduction to Social Service Learning, Disaster Education and Response, Disaster Reduction Service and Charity Leadership Development, The Use of Drones in Disaster Prevention and Relief, Basic Managing Tactics in Disaster Prevention and Reduction, Post-disaster Plan, Management and Reconstruction etc. Courses opened for graduate students include Basics of Safety Science and Disaster Reduction, Comparison of International Disaster Management Practices, Technology of Disaster Reduction and Application etc.

15.3.4 Toward a Healthy and Lively Existence for Left-Behind Children in Rural Chinese Communities

It has been widely recognized in China that rural-urban labor migration has played significant roles in the economic development. At the same time, however, such migration has triggered increase of left-behind children in rural villages. A national survey in 2005 showed that the number of left-behind children was estimated at 22.9 million and that 86.5% of left-behind children lived in the rural area.

Although migrating population has had a major positive impact on Chinese economies of both the sending and receiving communities during the migration process, the vulnerable life of left-behind children has been drawing growing attention of the Chinese society and government. Most of these left-behind children live with their grandparents in rural areas, which has brought about consequent problems such as inadequate schooling achievement, less-nourished health condition represented by physical growth, and psychologically immature development. If these serious problems are neglected by our society, the growth of left-behind children will be affected, not only in their childhood, but even in their adulthood as well. Thus, our efforts are made to develop effective ways for improving the life of left-behind children, building harmonious rural communities under globalization and for contributing to its social significance.

Sichuan Province is known as the province of sending the largest number of rural-urban migrants and of housing the largest number of left-behind children in China. Although fieldwork-based surveys on these children have seldom been conducted, a limited number of reports in Sichuan Province indicated that 51.2% of students in 3756 rural schools were left-behind children and 67% of them lived with their grandmother or grandfather. Meanwhile, 30–40% of them had under-nutrition and 80% had mental problems. It is generally agreed that children should stay with their parents in their childhood; however, under the current social system in China, it is not feasible for most parents to bring their children along when they go to the city to earn a living. For one thing, the school entrance system in the city remains unfriendly to children of migrant workers; and for another, the living conditions of the rural-to-urban mobile population need to be improved. Both problems take time to resolve, though.

Thus, we designed this program to develop a school-community intervention model in the target rural areas, by which schoolteachers, children's peers and their caretakers were mobilized to be involved in this intervention model to jointly improve the life of the left children.

15.3.4.1 Methods

- *Target population and measurement*. The field work was done in two primary schools located in the villages in Southern Sichuan. The target population included students, teachers, village carders and child caretakers. About 200 subject students in grades 3–6 were divided into two groups, in which students in one primary school were the intervention group and students in another school were the control group. All target children in the two schools were analyzed using anthropometric measurements, dietary record and questionnaire survey in the baseline and follow-up studies. In addition, teachers and children caretakers were interviewed using quantitative questionnaires.
- *School-community intervention model* (Li and Wang 2009). In order to improve the life of left-behind children, a school-based intervention model was developed and implemented. The main events were (1) building a teacher support team, in which each teacher must pay close attention to the life and study of 5 left-behind children; (2) peer helping groups, in which children were divided by their social networks in a class and by which children could help each other; and (3) hygienic course series for 120 children, 85 caretakers and 24 teachers.

15.3.4.2 Results

The results showed that (1) 74.8% participants were left-behind children; (2) most of such children had delayed physical growth, insufficient nutrient intakes, bad health habits, inadequate health knowledge, unsatisfactory school achievement and insufficient social support; and (3) 81.1% caretakers were grand-mothers or grand-fathers, who were old, uneducated and in poor health. Both caretakers and village cadres thought that schoolteachers could play the most important role in improving existence of left-behind children.

On the basis of the baseline results, a school-based intervention model was developed with the help of local schoolteachers. After the intervention was implemented in the intervention school for 7 months, the evaluation survey was completed. The results showed that, compared with the left-behind children in the control school, children in the intervention school had significantly better knowledge on basic health and first aid. In addition, children in the intervention school had improved nutrient intakes, physical activities, school achievement and social support. Furthermore, both schoolteachers and caretakers thought daily health behavior, dietary intake and school achievement in left-behind children were improved.

15.3.4.3 Social Impacts

- An increasing number of people begin to learn the real situation of the left-behind children in Chinese rural communities and to concern about the left-behind children. They try to improve these children's situation through publicizing our findings in many ways that not only include publishing scientific papers/presentations but extend to communications with various groups of citizens, schoolteachers and others.
- More researches will be focused on the left-behind children to develop more strategies to improve the life of the left-behind children, by publishing papers or giving presentations and communicating with research foundations.
- Government will concern more about the left-behind children. With increasing numbers of rural-to-urban migrants, left-behind children will be a social phenomenon for a long time. Our results will suggest local government to strive for a healthy environment for the left-behind children.
- Not only the target communities will continue to apply the school-based intervention model, but also more Chinese rural communities with left-behind children will adopt such a sustainable and effective model to improve the life of the left-behind children.
- Status of local rural teachers will be improved so that they would be more willing to play an active role in improving the situation of the left-behind children.

15.3.5 Tele-Medical Education to Train Medical Professionals for Tibet

Since Tibet is located in the far west of China, professionals, especially medical workers, are severely inadequate. The statistics in 1998 showed that Tibet had a population of more than 2 million, occupying an area equal to 20% of China's total surface area. There were only 10,000 medical professionals, most of whom received only 2 years of training in medicine. Tibetan Medical College (TMC) was the only educational institution to provide higher medical education (only 3-year program in 1998) in the Tibet Autonomous Region (TAR). TMC provided only 3 training programs due to the severe shortage of qualified teachers. Information provided by TMC indicated that TMC was unable to provide qualified teachers for some of the most important medical courses, including Anatomy, Introduction To Clinical Medicine, Biology, Biochemistry, English, Internal Medicine, Surgery, Obstetrics/Genecology, Paediatrics, etc.

In 1998, West China University of Medical Sciences (WCUMS) (the later West China Centre of Medical Sciences) initiated the project of Tele-medical Education, aiming at training medical professionals and improving medical service in Tibet through strengthening medical education using the satellite tele-medical education system. This system enabled real time and interactive learning of medical courses between WCUMS and TMC.

During the project period (1998–2003), TMC enrolled 156 medical students of which 75 were in the 3-year program and 81 in the 5-year program. Lectures of 15 medical courses were given via the tele-medical education system, and the total class hours amounted to 1805, including after-class tutoring. Medical courses offered through the tele-medical system were: Physiology; Microbiology; Immunology; Biochemistry; Pharmacy; Pathology; Diagnosis; Preventive Medicine; Internal Medicine; Surgery; Obstetrics/Genecology; Paediatrics; Radiology & Imaging; Medical psychology; and Histology/Embryology. All the tele-medical courses and some laboratory practices have been made into 27 tapes and 550 discs, which are presently in use at TMC. A total of 230 WCUMS teachers have given lectures for this project, among whom 43 were professors, 84 were associate professors and 97 were assistant professors. On the one hand, WCUMS sent faculty to TMC every year assisting TMC education management, teaching, research and discipline development; on the other hand, WCUMS received 22 faculty members from TMC and 9 medical workers from its affiliated hospitals for further study: 12 of them for advanced training, 16 for bachelor's degree and 3 for postgraduate study.

This project is a good supplement to the government effort of developing Tibet, and its implementation has set up a new model of providing help and support to the development of the remote areas, where the local medical students and teachers received high-quality training first and then helped set up a medical education system. Most TMC medical graduates are now providing medical services for people in counties and small towns of the Tibet Autonomous Region. In such a way, the number of medical workers from the local people and for the local people will be increasing steadily. The Tibetan medical students and teachers will play increasingly important roles in the promotion of the medical services and the improvement of health for Tibetan people.

15.3.6 Training Medical Teachers for the Medical School of Tibet University

Before the year 2000, Tibetan Medical College was the only institute that provided higher education in medicine (only a 3-year program) in Tibet Autonomous Region (TAR). In 2000, the College was merged into Tibet University and became the present Medical School of Tibet University (MSTU). After the merger, the school started to enroll 5-year medical students. However, the teaching resources were inadequate: 22 courses out of the 40 courses in the curriculum for 5-year medical students needed qualified teachers that MSTU could not provide.

To help MSTU address this shortage in medical teachers, West China Centre of Medical Sciences (WCCMS) of Sichuan University initiated the project of Training Medical Teachers for the Medical School of Tibet University in 2002, which consisted of degree plans, advanced training plan and English language skills training plan. During the project period (2002–2008), 36 WCCMS faculty have been sent to MSTU to assist their teaching through giving lectures and provide training courses in the field of internal medicine, surgery, microbiology, biochemistry, psychology, pathology, Obstetrics/Genecology, computer science for medicine and diagnosis etc. Meanwhile, 21 MSTU young teachers registered postgraduate programs in WCCMS, most of whom have finished their degree program training and have obtained master's degree in medicine at WCCMS. WCCMS English teachers have provided all the above mentioned candidates with an intensive English language training either on WCCMS campus or MSTU campus, so that they could either pass the degree-required English tests or improve their English language skills and build up confidence on international linkage and cooperation. Furthermore, 8 MSTU 3-year medical graduates and 10 5-year medical students have finished their training at WCCMS and have been conferred bachelor's degree in medicine. Most of them are now working in MSTU teaching hospitals.

Through the degree seeking program and the advanced training program on WCCMS campus, the TUMC faculty have been exposed to WCCMS educational system. They have not only improved their personal academic competency but also learned more about modern medical education. In order for MSTU to improve medical education quickly, the Centre for Medical Education, Research and Development of WCCMS has brought MSTU into the GMER Network initiated by WCCMS, and much importance has been put on the successful training of MSTU teachers not only in medical educational management and reform, teaching techniques, clinical skills, CAI and communication, but also in medical educational research. WCCMS has provided MSTU with an access to the best resources and the latest achievements in medical education.

15.3.7 Problem Solving for Better Health

Health, in its broadest sense, is perhaps the most important human resource. Without it, the quality of life, whatever one's situation, is diminished, and one's capacity to provide for one's family and contribute to the making of a healthier community is limited. Health is essential to human potential, both individual and societal. However, there is a terrible burden of illness and lost human potential around the world today. Despite great efforts these problems have not been solved. One of the major reasons is that the people with the problem are left out of the equation. The people with the problem are not the problem–they are the solution. We need to unleash their potential, their talents, and their ability to create change. Problem Solving for Better Health (PSBH) is a kind of methodology for solving health and social problems, which is created out of the concern that the people most impacted by the world's health problems often wait for solutions from the outside instead of becoming part of the process to identify solutions. PSBH encourages active participation and commitment from all concerned, and places the responsibility for change upon the individual by enabling him or her to identify local solutions to local problems. The process begins with a training workshop that helps participants define a problem, identify a solution, create a good plan of action and take that action.

In 1996, West China Centre of Medical Sciences (WCCMS) initiated the project Problem Solving for Better Health supported by China Medical Board (CMB), aiming at building a national Problem Solving Network in order to achieve better health.

Cooperating with Xi'an Medical University, Zhejiang Medical University and Tibetan Medical College, WCUMS established the nationwide network involving 14 medical institutions scattered at 14 different provinces and regions. During the project period (1996–2000), a total of 27 workshops and 10 follow-up workshops were held, offering training in the basic methodology and skills of PSBH, helping the participants to identify the solvable problems and to design action plans. Benefiting from the workshops were 2388 physicians, nurses, teachers, postgraduates and presidents from 27 medical universities. Because most trainees were teachers of medical universities, it meant that this PSBH project also benefited thousands of medical students. Moreover, the project team provided seed money and guidance as well as evaluation to subprojects. Altogether 270 PSBH subprojects were accomplished.

The success of the project helped us see that with commitment and perseverance from those involved, irrespective of educational, occupational, economic or political status, the health problems can be solved more effectively. Statistics in 2015 show that more than 9000 health professionals in 21 cities have participated in the PSBH training and accomplished approximately 4000 better health projects.

15.3.8 Establishing Chinese Birth Defects Pedigree Database and DNA Bank

The surveillance on birth defects of China shows that more than 1 million deliveries had birth defects per year. This has become one of the leading causes of infant death and deformity. However, these valuable bio-medical resources, which may serve as a treasury for the study of human genetics and genome-based diseases, have not been well tapped, or even well collected and protected.

In order to make full use of the possible health resources, West China Centre of Medical Sciences (WCCMS) of Sichuan University initiated the Project of Establishing Chinese Birth Defects Pedigree Database and DNA Bank in the year 2003. During the project period (July 1, 2003–June 30, 2008), the project team has not only worked out and officially published the MNM monitoring guideline, but also successfully developed the MNM data online report system. Data on 813,940 MNM cases from 124 project hospitals were collected, cleaned and analyzed, and the prevalence rate of pregnancy complications and MNM were finally obtained, plus some other indicators. Actually this project was based on the existing platform of Chinese Centre for Birth Defect Monitoring (CCBDM) established at Sichuan University, covering more than 500 hospitals from 31 provinces and autonomous regions.

This project has successfully helped to establish a nation-wide birth defect pedigree data collecting system on the basis of the existing CCBDM network for birth defect monitoring, to set up a birth defects pedigree DNA sample database and establish the protocol for the management and application of DNA samples, to standardize the procedures for data collecting and blood sampling, and to set up a computer management system for the pedigree database of birth defects to facilitate data entry, storage, retrieval, and statistics and analysis. Prospectively, the Chinese birth defects pedigree database and DNA bank will lay a solid foundation for the study of gene diversity of world-wide Chinese and for the comparative study of contributing factors of birth defect.

15.3.9 Creating Non-smoking Hospitals and Campuses in Sichuan University Through Joint Efforts of Faculty and Students

One out of every three smokers in the world is Chinese. As the biggest producer and consumer of tobacco products in the world, China has 350 million smokers and

540 million second-hand smokers, causing about 1 million avoidable Chinese deaths annually; and the health impact of smoking causes not only human suffering and death but also major economic burdens on China's healthcare system. Advancing China's health is impossible without success in tobacco control. Recognizing the threat, the Chinese Government has signed the WHO Framework Convention on Tobacco Control and accelerated many anti-smoking actions. Tobacco, however, remains a huge challenge. China's medical professionals have great responsibility and opportunity to do much more and much better for protecting the health of the Chinese people.

As one of China's leading medical universities, West China Centre of Medical Sciences (WCCMS) of Sichuan University initiated the CMB project Creating Non-smoking Hospitals and Campuses in Sichuan University through joint efforts of faculty and students to create smoke-free campuses and hospitals associated with WCCMS and to assume a leadership role in the anti-smoking activities among the general public and local communities in southwest China.

During the project period (2010–2012), WCCMS promoted 10 different policy-oriented and intervention-relevant economics, epidemiologic and social-behavioral researches to contribute knowledge and evidence on tobacco public policies, taxation and economic, behavioral change and cessation services, encouraged 24 innovative student-based and student-led anti-tobacco activities, opened a smoke cessation clinic at West China Hospital, and developed smoke-free policies to prohibit smoking within all university-affiliated buildings (including residence halls, administrative facilities, classrooms, hospitals and dining halls) and at all university-sponsored events – both indoor and outdoor, and to prohibit the sale and advertisement of tobacco products on campus. Smoking is allowed only at designated remote outdoor areas. Moreover, a tobacco prevention education curriculum was established and the smoke cessation hotline was opened to improve knowledge, attitudes and clinical competencies of students and faculty as well as to arouse public awareness to the dangers of tobacco addiction and exposure to second-hand smoke. Also supported by a specific CMB fund, WCCMS conducted a baseline survey to evaluate the changes in awareness, attitudes, and behaviors of medical students, teachers, and doctors as well as the changes of school policies and campus environment in 13 "smoke-free campus project" grantee universities.

The output of this project is the creation of a healthier and safer learning environment for all students, staff and visitors who are entitled to a totally smoke-free environment, and a healthier hospitals for the patients. What's more important is that it prevents the medical students who are the future health professionals from smoke addiction (Vázquez et al. 2014). The role and image of the health professional are essential in promoting tobacco-free lifestyles and cultures. In community and clinical settings, health professionals are the most knowledgeable in health matters and they are expected to act on the basis of this knowledge. Through their professional activities health professionals can help people by giving advice, guidance and answers to questions related to tobacco use and its health effects.

They can serve as a reference for the media, educating the public and policy-makers. They can also have an impact at national and international levels through their associations in influencing policy change for better tobacco control.

References

Alzyoud, S. A., & Bani-Hani, K. (2015). Social responsibility in higher education institutions: Application case from the Middle East. *European Scientific Journal, 11*(8), 122–129.

Brubacher, J. S. (1977). *On the philosophy of higher education.* San Francisco: Jossey-Bass Publishers.

Dima, A. M., Vasilache, S., Ghinea, V., & Agoston, S. (2013). A model of academic social responsability. *Transylvanian Review of Administrative Sciences, 9*(38), 23–43.

Fang, G. (2008). Views on social responsibility of modern university. *Peking University Education Review, 6*(2), 118–127.

Gibbon, M., Labonte, R., & Laverack, G. (2002). Evaluating community capacity. *Health and Social Care in the Community, 10*(6), 485–491.

Hill, R. P. (2004). The socially-responsible university: Talking the talk while walking the walk in the College of Business. *Journal of Academic Ethics, 2*(1), 89–100.

Li, T. Y., & Wang, H. Y. (2009). Improving the education system in rural communities to alleviate educational crisis of left-behind children. *Journal of Northeast Normal University (Philosophy and Social Sciences), 4*, 90–94.

Reed, D. (2004). Universities and the promotion of corporate responsibility: Reinterpreting the liberal arts tradition. *Journal of Academic Ethics, 2*(1), 3–41.

Vasilescu, R., Barna, C., Epure, M., & Baicu, C. (2010). Developing university social responsibility: A model for the challenges of the new civil society. *Procedia-Social and Behavioral Sciences, 2*(2), 4177–4182.

Vázquez, J. L., Aza, C. L., & Lanero, A. (2014). Are students aware of university social responsibility? Some insights from a survey in a Spanish university. *International Review on Public and Nonprofit Marketing, 11*(3), 195–208.

Wright, T. S. A. (2002). Definitions and frameworks for environmental sustainability in higher education. *International Journal of Sustainability in Higher Education, 3*(3), 203–220.

Chapter 16
University Social Responsibility: The PolyU Way

Timothy W. Tong, Angelina W.K. Yuen-Tsang and Daniel T.L. Shek

Abstract In view of the many complex global issues, there is a call to re-think higher education institutions' relationship with society and their role in improving global quality of life. Universities are now challenged to focus not only on individual institution's interest, prestige and graduate employment prospects, but also to be socially relevant and responsible by addressing societal needs, both locally and globally. This chapter aims to present and showcase how The Hong Kong Polytechnic University (PolyU) has been moving with the times and fulfilling its social responsibilities while coping with the social and economic changes in Hong Kong and the region.

Keywords The Hong Kong Polytechnic University · University social responsibility · Teaching, research, service

16.1 Introduction

Higher education in the 21st century has been facing various shifts in political, economic, social and environmental landscape. These have been precipitated by complex global issues including, for example, globalization, poverty, and climate change. As such, there has been a call to re-think higher education institutions' relationship with society. Universities are now challenged to focus not only on an individual institution's interest, prestige and the employment prospects of its

T.W. Tong · A.W.K. Yuen-Tsang · D.T.L. Shek (✉)
Office of the President, The Hong Kong Polytechnic University, Hunghom, Hong Kong
e-mail: daniel.shek@polyu.edu.hk

T.W. Tong
e-mail: president.office@polyu.edu.hk

A.W.K. Yuen-Tsang
e-mail: angie.yuen@polyu.edu.hk

© Springer Nature Singapore Pte Ltd. 2017
D.T.L. Shek and R.M. Hollister (eds.), *University Social Responsibility and Quality of Life*, Quality of Life in Asia 8,
DOI 10.1007/978-981-10-3877-8_16

255

graduates, but also to be socially relevant and responsible by addressing the needs of the society, both locally and globally. Historically, as university students and teachers possess more knowledge, they are expected to play the role of a "social conscience" when dealing with societal problems.

Influenced by the notion of corporate social responsibility (CSR), many universities are very sensitive to the importance of fulfilling their social responsibilities and have developed various initiatives to engage their stakeholders in dealing with a range of social issues. Some universities have even set up dedicated offices and devoted substantial resources to promoting university social responsibility (USR) programmes to meet societal needs. For example, an Office for Social Responsibility has been established in the University of Manchester and the University of Edinburgh has a Department for Social Responsibility and Sustainability. With different backgrounds and different cultural settings, there is not a "one-size fits all" USR model for universities to follow. However, some common objectives and principles regarding USR can be observed across universities. These include:

(a) creation of a socially responsible and sustainable community within the university and beyond;
(b) creation and nurturing of an inclusive environment in which all stakeholders can develop and excel;
(c) integration of the competitive interests of the institution and the interests of the wider society;
(d) promotion of a green world for future generations;
(e) promotion of society welfare;
(f) sensitive and responsible management of the operation of the institution, giving due consideration to its impact on the environment and society;
(g) balancing growth with sustainability;
(h) giving due attention to the common good, the betterment of our world and to the sacred dignity of all people, especially the poor and marginalized; and
(i) subscribing to the belief that all our activities should be pursued ethically, sustainably and for the public benefit.

With reference to the above common objectives, several strategies and approaches are commonly used to promote USR. These include to:

(a) support a culture of change;
(b) pursue excellence and innovation;
(c) embed social responsibilities in all activities;
(d) work collaboratively with the local and global community;
(e) pursue change across the following strategic areas—research with impact, socially responsible graduates, community engagement responsible processes and environmental sustainability;
(f) encourage an inclusive environment, based on mutual respect and without barriers to achievement, where students and staff are highly valued;

(g) embrace the principles of environmental responsibility and sustainable development;

(h) incorporate the values of Social Responsibility (SR) into the daily management of the university;

(i) promote the maintenance of principled standards, respect, and accountability across all institutional activities;

(j) commit to equality and diversity;

(k) treat employees with fairness and respect, including broad support for personnel and staff development activities;

(l) support fair trade and volunteering;

(m) ensure that the principles of CSR are embedded in the university strategy and are taken into account in the making of key decisions; and

(n) uphold high standards in relations with staff, students and communities.

16.2 PolyU—A Socially Responsible University for 80 Years

The Hong Kong Polytechnic University (PolyU) has a rich and proud heritage dating back to 1937 when its predecessor, the Government Trade School, was founded. Over the past eight decades, the institution, guided by the motto "To learn and to apply, for the benefit of mankind", has been moving with the times and fulfilling its social responsibilities while coping with the social and economic changes in Hong Kong and the region.

In its early years, when Hong Kong industries were expanding, the institution educated tens of thousands of professionals in the fields of construction, engineering, navigation, commerce and textiles. As society has progressed, PolyU has also nurtured a great number of health care, social services and management professionals. To support Hong Kong in its development into a major global centre of commerce, PolyU has expanded its programmes to include language and translation, logistics, design and tourism. More recently, taking into consideration the fast-changing and complex globalized economy, the University has moved beyond the provision of professional and academic education of students, striving to provide a variety of learning opportunities for them to also develop their all-round abilities, thus enabling them to be more competitive and more effective global citizens. Today, PolyU is highly commended for its commitment to nurturing professionals and leaders for the society, engaging in research that has an impact, practical value and social relevance, and for fostering partnerships with academia, government, business and industry.

In 2011, when PolyU re-drafted its vision and mission statement, the SR dimension of the university's core functions was explicitly highlighted. The new vision that was introduced stated that PolyU "be a leading university that excels in professional education, applied research and partnership for the betterment of Hong

Kong, the nation and the world". Coupled with this new vision, the mission statements included three key elements:

(a) to nurture graduates who are critical thinkers, effective communicators, innovative problem solvers, lifelong learners and ethical leaders;
(b) to advance knowledge and the frontiers of technology to meet the changing needs of society; and
(c) to support a University community in which all members can excel through education and scholarship.

16.3   USR in Practice

It is thus clear that PolyU has the conviction and determination to play a crucial role in societal development and SR. Various offices and departments in PolyU drive a wide variety of SR initiatives in different ways—in policies and processes, in learning and teaching, research and knowledge transfer, in advocating sustainable development within the campus and championing SR in the wider world, as well as in inspiring the students, supporting faculty members and engaging the university community. PolyU is also committed to developing its culture of social responsibilities further, making it a distinguishing feature of the University.

16.3.1   Policies and Processes

The policies and processes in PolyU intend to promote efficiency and good governance while creating social and environmental benefit for students and staff as well as for local and global communities. PolyU's commitment to its stakeholders is enhanced by the ways the University is undertaking its operational activities in governance, research, human resources as well as by its commitment to campus sustainability.

Aiming to ensure good governance and adherence to principles that include academic freedom and autonomy, quality performance, ethics and professionalism, transparency and public accountability, and social responsibility, the PolyU has developed a "University Governance Statement". To further ensure an effective framework for governance and management in directing and monitoring the University's operation and financial performance, the "University Governance Statement" has also stipulated a governance structure involving the Council, the Council Committees, the Senate, an executive-led management system, as well as an internal control and external reporting system.

In order to provide appropriate guidance for staff, the University has included in the Staff Handbook the following ethics guidelines:

- Code of Ethics in the Workplace
- Code of Ethics for Teaching
- Code of Ethics for Research
- Code of Ethics for the Use of Animal in Teaching and Research
- Code of Ethics for Research Involving Human Subjects
- Ethical Clearance for Teaching / Research Projects Involving the Use of Animals
- Ethical Clearance for Teaching / Research Projects or Investigation Involving Human Subjects

PolyU's human resources policies embrace equality and diversity in recruitment and promotion. Staff are encouraged to undertake outside activities such as serving the public through voluntary work; serving the business and industrial sectors through training and consultancy work; engaging in scholarly activities such as contributing to academic publications; and supporting the development of continued education by teaching courses offered by the PolyU or in collaboration with other institutions.

Health and safety policies also are introduced to ensure, as far as reasonably practicable, the health and safety of all staff at work, of students in the course of study and the general public using University premises. The University adopts standards over and above compliance with relevant statutory requirements. Additionally, to take a holistic approach to campus sustainability, several policies have been developed to govern related activities, including Sustainability Policy, Energy and Greenhouse Gas Policy, Green Procurement Policy, Sustainable Infrastructure Policy, Waste Management Policy, Water Conservation Policy and Environmental Policy.

16.3.2   Learning and Teaching

PolyU's overarching aim for learning and teaching, as specified in its strategic plan for the academic years 2012/13 to 2017/18, is "to provide students with a high quality, effective and rewarding learning experience that equips them with the wisdom, skills and attributes necessary to demonstrate knowledge and integrity, to progress in their career, to adapt to change, and to become responsible global citizens who make meaningful contributions to their profession and the community"[1]. This aim is seen best to be achieved through various academic programmes and specifically targeted Service-Learning (SL) programmes.

---

[1]http://www.polyu.edu.hk/cpa/splan/StrategicPlan2012.pdf (P. 14)

SR and key sustainable issues are incorporated into PolyU academic pro-grammes at PolyU. The undergraduate curriculum was reformed in 2012 with a view to nurturing the next generation of students into all-round global citizens with a strong sense of SR. Key SR elements and sustainable development issues are incorporated into teaching and learning. For example, the Faculty of Business has introduced into the undergraduate and postgraduate curricula elements such as business ethics, corporate social responsibility, responsible management and leadership. All research postgraduate students are also required to attend a com-pulsory course on "Ethics: Research, Professional and Personal Perspectives".

PolyU has been running community service learning programmes since 2004. Over the past decade, more than 8000 PolyU students and staff members have provided services to approximately 570,000 underprivileged people in Hong Kong as well as in the Chinese mainland and overseas. In the academic year 2012/13, in alignment with PolyU's goal of developing graduates into "responsible global citizens", the University introduced the SL requirement into the new undergraduate degree curriculum, with the aim of instilling a sense of SR among its students. Students are now required to complete a three-credit course designated to meet the SL requirement before graduation. PolyU was the first university in Hong Kong to make SL courses credit-bearing and mandatory for all undergraduate degree students.

To promote and support the institutionalization of SL at PolyU, the Office of Service-Learning was established in 2012, supporting growth in the scope of SL activity. Apart from local SL experience, students are offered opportunities to participate in SL projects in locations that include the Chinese mainland, Taiwan, Cambodia, Kyrgyzstan, Myanmar, Rwanda, and Vietnam. Six SL courses were offered to 189 undergraduate students in the academic year 2012/13 and the number of courses offered increased to 59 with the participation of 3121 students in the academic year 2014/15. In 2015/16, a total of 63 courses for around 3700 students were offered.

All students are required to undertake a three-credit subject related to "Leadership and Intra-personal Relationship" which provides students with theo-retical knowledge as well as experiential opportunities to enhance their leadership potential and to prepare them to become ethical leaders in our increasingly complex society. Moreover, an institutional level Global Youth Leadership Institute has been established since January 2016 to nurture our students to become socially responsible leaders of tomorrow through numerous formal and informal learning opportunities provided both locally and overseas.

To help students excel in their fields of study, PolyU's programmes place emphasis on professional knowledge, practical training, and meeting the needs of various industries, professions and the community. Starting from 2005/2006, all undergraduate students are required to complete a mandatory Work-Integrated Education (WIE) component as part of the curriculum. WIE comprises work-based learning experiences which take place in an organizational context relevant to a student's future profession, or the development of generic skills that will be valuable in that profession. This programme allows students to learn in the real-world while, at the same time, making a tangible contribution to industry and the community. As at today, PolyU is still the only university in Hong Kong that has implemented a WIE requirement. Currently, internship opportunities are available in about 25 countries and regions around the world and nine cities in the Chinese mainland, benefitting close to 1500 students in 2015/16.

PolyU also offers programmes which focus on issues of sustainability. With its emphasis on both environment and sustainable development, the BEng (Hons) programme in Environmental Engineering and Sustainable Development is the first of its kind offered by a Hong Kong higher education institution. A related master's programme, MSc in Environmental Management and Engineering, is also offered. A list of other academic programmes related to green buildings, environment and sustainability is given in Appendix 1. General Education Programme courses with a sustainability focus are also offered and include Chemistry and Sustainable Development, Green House Gases and Life, The Environmental Impact of the Dietary Culture in China, Climate Change, and Society, Ecological Perspectives: The Challenge of Our Times, and Business and Society: Corporate Social Responsibility.

16.3.3   Research

In research, PolyU aims to "foster a culture and environment in which research can thrive and excel."[2] Since setting the key research goals and strategies for the academic years 2012/13 to 2017/18, PolyU has made a significant contribution to many areas in society and created many research programmes to improve sustainable development and social well-being.

The Strategic Plan 2012/13 to 2017/18 specified one of the key goals of PolyU's research as "to identify, develop, and support emerging areas of research excellence that have a significant impact on the professions, the community, and the nation, and to build teams of excellent researchers."[3] PolyU researchers, with expertise in a wide range of disciplines, from cancer to food safety, from energy to climate change, strive to tackle the world's greatest challenges through research. For example, in recent years, PolyU research has achieved significant results and notable impact in areas that enhance sustainability (for example, eco blocks, myCar, green building technology, solar-powered air-conditioning system, air quality, buildings and their performance, transport, waste management, energy saving and renewable energy), facilitate economic and social development (for example, ultra-precision machinery technology, mega-structure diagnostic and prognostic system, and safety monitoring of high-speed railways), and improve quality of life

---

[2]http://www.polyu.edu.hk/cpa/splan/StrategicPlan2012.pdf (P. 20)
[3]http://www.polyu.edu.hk/cpa/splan/StrategicPlan2012.pdf (P. 22)

(for example, multi-potent drug against cancer, myopia control, food safety and robotic hand of hope).

Several research institutes at PolyU are committed to the promotion of sustainability. In 2012, PolyU established the Research Institute for Sustainable Urban Development to develop innovative solutions for the creation of sustainable high-density cities by capitalizing on the living laboratory of Hong Kong. Comprising 26 research groups each with an internationally recognized scholar as a leader, the Institue is committed to multi-disciplinary collaborations to address major urban planning and environmental issues.

Initiated by PolyU and The Hong Kong Jockey Club Charities Trust in 2012, the Jockey Club Design Institute for Social Innovation brings together university expertise, curates cross-disciplinary projects, and constructs partnerships for social well-being and positive systemic change. Being the first design institute dedicated to social innovation in Asia, it focuses on articulating creative and alternative solutions to some of today's complex challenges—including urban sustainability, ageing populations, family and youth, social entrepreneurship—as well as empowering technologies for the disadvantaged.

The Faculty of Business has established the Sustainability Management Research Centre to promote business sustainability through research and transfer of knowledge to the business community. It is multi-disciplinary in nature, aiming at promoting CSR as a model for achieving economic, social and environmental sustainability through management innovation. The centre's major research areas are Sustainability Strategy, Management and Performance, Green Transformation of Manufacturers in the Pearl River Delta Region, Social Enterprises, and Business Sustainability and Financial Performance. It also offers a Master of Science programme in business sustainability, with the objective of equipping management talents with professional knowledge of corporate social responsibility and thereby developing the sustainability of individual business corporations.

16.3.4   Knowledge Transfer

As one of the strategic areas of PolyU, the University encourages responsible knowledge transfer that helps the advancement of the community, promotes entrepreneurial thinking and contributes to the sustainable development of the University and the community. Through various schemes and projects, PolyU leverages its knowledge and technologies to facilitate and foster student-driven start-ups, to develop closer cooperation with local and global businesses—especially in the Institution's key knowledge areas, to create an environment of where innovation, entrepreneurship and community service are valued and to advocate social and ethical values within the university community and in the society at large.

PolyU transfers technological and other top-level expertise with application value in various ways through the Institute for Entrepreneurship (IfE), which was established by PolyU in 1999 to serve as an important platform to forge closer links between academics and business for their mutual benefit and the betterment of the wider community. I/E facilitates closer collaboration between industry and PolyU through:

(a) technology transfer and commercialization;
(b) entrepreneurship development;
(c) technology marketing;
(d) industrial networking; and
(e) corporate development and training.

To nurture socially responsible young entrepreneurs, PolyU established the "PolyU Micro Fund" Scheme in 2011 to provide seed funding for students and alumni in support of their pursuit of entrepreneurial venturing. Since its launch, the Scheme has gained community-wide recognition within PolyU and across local entrepreneurial communities. As of June 2016, the Scheme had supported 99 startup ventures and nurtured over 250 young entrepreneurs, from over 800 applications received. The various business ventures supported include those in the areas of information and communication technology, fashion and multimedia design, online learning, green education, upcycling and environmentally friendly products.

In addition to the Micro Fund, PolyU has established four further entrepreneurial funding schemes, namely the China Entrepreneurship Fund, HKSTP[4]-PolyU Technology Incubation Fund, PolyU Technology Launchpad Fund and Good Seed Programme, supporting startups in the Chinese mainland, technology ventures, social innovations and social enterprises. By June 2016, PolyU had supported over 150 startup ventures under various schemes and offered over 33,000 student-learning hours to nurture young entrepreneurs. Together with the Micro Fund, PolyU provides close to HK$ 10 million funding annually to support around 50 to 60 new startups.

PolyU has been actively involved in disaster reconstruction in Sichuan following its earthquake in 2008. PolyU secured a donation from The Hong Kong Jockey Club to set up China's first Institute for Disaster Management and Reconstruction with Sichuan University. The Institute is the first of its kind in disaster prepared-ness, disaster risk reduction and disaster reconstruction on the Chinese mainland and was officially opened in May 2013. It aims at enhancing disaster management capabilities through the provision of educational programmes, professional training in reconstruction and disaster management, undertaking interdisciplinary high-impact research, and offering disaster management facilities and services.

More than 12,000 people have been trained in disaster-related areas such as disaster nursing, physiotherapy, occupational therapy, prosthetics and orthopaedics, social work and psychology. The trainees included frontline healthcare profes-sionals, rehabilitation professionals, social workers, students from universities, school teachers, non-government organization workers and government officials. The two universities also run life education programmes to enhance participants'

---

[4]HKSTP—Hong Kong Science and Technology Park

disaster resilience. Over the years, around 4000 teachers and students from universities, secondary schools and primary schools have joined such programmes.

16.3.5 Campus Sustainability

In 2011, PolyU set up the Campus Sustainability Committee (CSC) to promote sustainability in planning, development, and operation of the University's campus environment and facilities as well as to develop sustainability initiatives in education, research and community service activities. Different units are involved in this initiative. The Health, Safety and Environmental Office, serves as the Secretary of CSC. The Campus Sustainability Office (CSO) is the executive arm which coordinates and monitors the University's environmental programmes, offers advice to the planning and implementation of sustainability policies and strategies, and drives a behavioral change among students and staff to embrace a sustainable lifestyle. CSO also manages a Green Concepts website (www.polyu.edu.hk/greencampus) to provide updated information about PolyU's sustainability initiatives. The Campus Development Office and Facilities Management Office are working hard in building new green campus buildings and retrofitting existing building utilities with energy efficient systems to improve the overall environmental performance of the campus.

PolyU's iconic building Jockey Club Innovation Tower showcases environment-friendly features including green decks, evaporative cooling towers, heat recovery system and many other energy efficient facilities.

To promote the concept of sustainability on campus, PolyU has launched PolyU Campus Sustainability Weeks since 2013, organized workshops, seminars, and exhibitions relating to sustainability, and participated in and promoted community campaigns such as World Wildlife Fund Earth Hour and Hong Kong No Air Con Night. The University also invests efforts to drive a sustainable culture, motivates students and staff to lead a green lifestyle, and promotes green campus through activities and campaigns such as recycling and upcycling, farming, Bring Your Own and food waste collection.

16.3.6 Community Engagement

Over the years, the University has carried out many initiatives to champion SR in the wider community. These have included:

(a) In November 2012, PolyU organized the first University Social Responsibility (USR) Summit to promote the concept of USR and to provide a platform for participants to share their views on the challenges and opportunities brought by USR, analyze related issues and discuss the way forward. The second

(USR) Summit was held in November 2014 and aimed at further promoting the scholarly development of the relevant theories, models, and tools of SL. Co-hosted by PolyU and Peking University, the third USR Summit took place in Beijing in November 2016, as a sub-forum of the Beijing Forum.

(b) In a bid to promote the understanding and adoption of CSR as a business model for achieving business sustainability in Hong Kong, PolyU's Department of Management and Marketing and the Hong Kong Productivity Council jointly launched the Hong Kong SME Business Sustainability Index in 2012 for small and medium-sized enterprises (SMEs). The Index is compiled with information about the best 40 of those SMEs with proven records of excellent performance in undertaking CSR initiatives by assessing their performance and achievement in the three areas: the value of CSR and sustainable development, their management and CSR projects, and their positive contribution to economic, social and environmental sustainability. The Index is a major initiative to promote CSR and business sustainability, encouraging SMEs to take up and perform CSR for the achievement of sustainable development and growth.

(c) Various departments organized conferences on sustainability. These have included an International Conference on Sustainable Energy Technologies in 2012, Motor Vehicle Emissions Control Workshop in 2014, "50 + 20 Agenda—Renewing Business Education in Asia" in 2014 and the Second International Conference on Sustainable Urbanization in 2015.

(d) PolyU operates the following units to provide services to the public with a view to enhancing the quality of life: Optometry Clinic, Integrative Community Health Centre, Integrative Health Clinic, Mobile Integrative Health Centre, Rehabilitation Clinic, Rehabilitation Engineering Clinic, Industrial Centre, Centre for Translation Studies and Speech Therapy Unit.

(e) The University has organized 58 Blood Donation Weeks since 1973. In 2014 The School of Nursing established an on-campus blood donor centre in collaboration with the Hong Kong Red Cross Blood Transfusion Service.

(f) Our teaching and research hotel, Hotel ICON, has been a food donor of the charitable "Food Angel" programme targeted to fight hunger and food waste since 2013.

(g) PolyU organized fundraising campaigns for the relief of victims in natural disasters such as for the victims in the floods in southern and southeastern parts of Chinese mainland in 1996, the earthquake in Hebei Province in 1998, the earthquake and tsunami in Southeast Asia in 2004, the earthquake in Sichuan in 2008, Taiwan typhoon in 2009, Qinghai earthquake in 2010, and Japan earthquake and tsunami in 2011.

(h) The official University-wide volunteer team, "The PolyU Volunteers", mainly comprising students, staff, alumni, and former staff, was established under the management of the Communications and Public Affairs Office (CPA) in September 2015 with a view to nurturing a stronger commitment to SR within the University community. Various community service initiatives that involved different faculties and departments and/or in collaboration with other NGOs and community partners have been organized by CPA to serve children, elderly and minorities.

16.3.7 University Social Responsibility Network

Further to the Second USR Summit held in 2014, roundtable discussion was held among collaborating institutions and other higher education establishments, where it was agreed that a network for advancing USR should be formed.

The University Social Responsibility Network (USR Network) held its first Executive Committee meeting in Hong Kong on 8 October 2015 while an inauguration ceremony was organized on the following day (9 October 2015) to officially commemorate the set up of the Network. The participating universities were invited to sign a "Declaration on University Social Responsibility" (Appendix 2) with a view to encouraging universities to include SR references in their mission, vision, and strategy, and to actively promoting collaborations among them.

Following the inauguration ceremony, PolyU also hosted the International Seminar on USR on the same day. The Founding Member Institutions' representatives made presentations on their respective university's USR initiatives. More than 150 local and overseas guests attended.

Serving as a global platform to connect and foster partnership among members, the USR Network shares ideas and resources to develop collaborative USR projects with varied scope and scale, advancing higher education as a catalyst for social change through education, research, and community service. Founding members of the Network agreed to further plan collaboration in research, SL programmes, student scholarships, staff visits and social responsibility related activities, as well as share insights and identify best practices for the ongoing development of USR.

16.3.8 University Social Responsibility Steering Committee

PolyU established the University Social Responsibility Steering Committee (USRSC) in 2015 with four major objectives:

(a) to foster a culture of social responsibility within the university community and encourage a commitment to social responsibility in the planning and development of education, research, knowledge transfer, and other activities;

(b) to set strategic directions for and approve plans of university-wide social responsibility initiatives;

(c) to enhance the co-ordination of social responsibility endeavours of various departments and offices for better synergies and results; and

(d) to review the progress and achievements of the university's social responsibility endeavours on an annual basis, identify issues of concern and advise the
way forward.

16.4 People Matter

PolyU inspires and supports its staff members, students, and alumni to become
socially responsible citizens. Most of our faculty members are actively engaged in
community service through serving as volunteers, sitting on various advisory
committees set up by the government or NGOs, or providing professional consultancy service to the needy sectors. They are keen to ensure that their knowledge
and their world-class work will benefit the wider community, not just in Hong
Kong, but also in the Chinese mainland and the rest of the world.

For PolyU students, apart from the compulsory SL programme and the WIE
requirement, many take the initiative to promote green culture and serve the
community. For example, students from The Green Society of The Hong Kong
Polytechnic University Students' Union, Green Hall of the two Student Halls of
Residence have contributed continuously and significantly in energy saving and
waste reduction in their communities. The Hong Kong Polytechnic University
Student-run Wellness Clinic is the first Hong Kong student-run social enterprise
that provides preventive care for the aged. The Clinic is jointly operated by students
from the Faculty of Business and Department of Rehabilitation Science. Students of
the Faculty of Business apply their business knowledge as well as management,
negotiation, and other skills to serve the community through FB CARES, a community service project initiated by the Faculty of Business.

Regarding their contribution, PolyU alumni have also devoted tremendous
efforts to serving the community. For example, the Federation of PolyU Alumni
Associations has for years co-organized with the University an annual tree planting
activity, which brings alumni and their friends and family members together, to
promote a greener living environment in Hong Kong and to educate the younger
generation in environmental care and sustainable development. Apart from planting
activities, various educational programmes on environmental protection such as
seminars, workshops and exhibitions have been organized.

16.5 The Way Forward

In order to consolidate the SR efforts on various fronts and to take its SR efforts to
the next level of excellence, in 2014 PolyU established a dedicated team to facilitate, co-ordinate and monitor the implementation of SR programmes by various
offices for better synergy and higher impact, as well as to identify new and worthy

initiative. In 2015, the USRSC was set up to help set the strategic direction for the development of SR in the University, as well as to foster a SR culture and nurture a commitment to SR within the university community.

The University is about to formulate the strategic plan for 2018/19-2022/23. It is expected that SR will command more attention as it sets its strategic objectives for teaching/ learning, research and knowledge transfer.

Further to the set up of the USR Network which is dedicated to be a platform for Network members to pursue and fulfill USR collectively and more effectively; and to spearhead the USR strategic development, PolyU as the secretariat for the Network will no doubt be actively involved to facilitate the achievement of the Network's vision and mission. PolyU is committed to advancing USR, not only within its own campus but also in the global higher education sector, collaborating with the Network members to address the economic, social, cultural and environmental challenges so as to make our world more just, inclusive, peaceful and sustainable.

Appendix 1: Academic Programmes Related to Green Buildings, Environment and Sustainability at PolyU in 2014

Faculty/school/department	Programme
Department of Applied Biology and Chemical Technology	BSc (Hons) in Chemical Technology
Department of Applied Biology and Chemical Technology	Higher Diploma in Chemical Technology
Department of Building and Real Estate	BSc (Hons) in Building Engineering and Management
Department of Building and Real Estate	BSc (Hons) in Surveying
Department of Building and Real Estate	Higher Diploma in Building Technology and Management (Engineering)
Department of Building Services Engineering	BEng (Hons) in Building Services Engineering
Department of Building Services Engineering	Higher Diploma in Building Services Engineering
Department of Civil and Environmental Engineering	BEng (Hons) Civil Engineering
Department of Civil and Environmental Engineering	BEng (Hons) in Environmental Engineering and Sustainable Development
Department of Civil and Environmental Engineering	BSc (Hons) in Environmental and Occupational Safety and Health
Department of Civil and Environmental Engineering	Higher Diploma in Civil Engineering
Faculty of Construction and Environment	MEng in Building Services Engineering

(continued)

(continued)

Faculty/school/department	Programme
Faculty of Construction and Environment	MSc in Building Services Engineering
Faculty of Construction and Environment	MSc in Environmental Management and Engineering
Faculty of Construction and Environment	MSc in Facility Management
Faculty of Construction and Environment	MSc in High Performance Buildings
Faculty of Construction and Environment	MSc in Sustainable Urban Development
Faculty of Construction and Environment	MSc/PgD in Fire and Safety Engineering
School of Design	BA (Hons) in Design (Environment and Interior)
School of Design	MDes in Urban Environments Design

Appendix 2: Declaration on University Social Responsibility

大學社會責任宣言

Together, we make our declaration on University Social Responsibility (USR) as follows:

我們謹此共同發表大學社會責任宣言如下:

We:

我們

1. Reaffirm that universities should include social responsibility references in their mission, vision and strategy, in a way that will have genuine impact on all their decisions and activities—management, learning and teaching, research, knowledge transfer and services, thereby driving the sustainable development of our society and our world.

   謹此重申,大學的使命、願景及策略均須涵蓋社會責任這一環,以期對大學的所有決定及活動 (包括管理、學與教、研究、知識轉移及服務)發揮實質影響,從而推動社會以至世界的持續發展。

2. Reaffirm that universities have a responsibility to promote and encourage, among students, faculty, staff and stakeholders, behaviors consistent with the values of justice, equality, social responsibility and sustainability.

   謹此重申,大學有責任向學生、教職員及持份者宣導與正義、平等、社會責任及持續發展這些價值取向一致的行為。

3. Reaffirm the role of universities in advancing the society's understanding of global issues of social, economic, scientific and cultural nature; as well as leading society to address the challenges through education and the generation of knowledge and technologies.

謹此重申,大學有責任促進社會了解與社會、經濟、科學及文化相關的全球問題,並透過教育、知識創造和科技創新,帶領社會應對挑戰。

4. Advocate cooperation amongst universities, and partnership between communities and universities, to identify and evaluate best practices for the continued development and promotion of USR policies and programmes.

謹此倡議,大學與大學之間,以及大學與社會各個界別應加強合作,就大學社會責任的政策及活動的發展和宣傳探究最佳模式。

Part IV
Conclusion

Chapter 17
Conclusion: Global Experience to Date and Future Directions

Robert M. Hollister

Abstract The theoretical chapters and institutional accounts document that USR is a robust and growing global movement, characterized by considerable common vision and strategy, as well as diversity of context and approach. University-community partnerships are an essential ingredient of successful USR, and are most successful when universities forge truly reciprocal and mutually beneficial collaborations with community partners. Significant organizational change is a key dimension in virtually all of the institutional case studies. USR often has received increased priority in the institutions' most recent strategic planning, and as a result several institutions have created higher level positions and coordinating councils in charge of USR. National policies have been influential drivers of USR in a few of the cases. Expansion of student programs is a major component of all of the institutional experience, often including a major increase in service learning, and some institutions have started to systematically evaluate student learning outcomes. Major opportunities are identified for cross-national research and other collective action. The University Social Responsibility Network can be an important vehicle for future research and joint projects, building on its current collaborative activities, and working in partnership with other global and regional alliances.

Keywords University social responsibility · Institutional accounts · Common themes · Future directions

The opening theoretical chapters and the preceding institutional accounts document that university social responsibility (USR) is indeed a robust and growing global

Robert M. Hollister, Professor Emeritus, Tufts University; Founding Dean Emeritus, Tisch College of Civic Life, Tufts University; Founding Executive Director Emeritus, Talloires Network.

R.M. Hollister (✉)
Department of Urban and Environmental Policy and Planning,
Tufts University, Medford, USA
e-mail: robert.hollister@tufts.edu

© Springer Nature Singapore Pte Ltd. 2017
D.T.L. Shek and R.M. Hollister (eds.), *University Social Responsibility and Quality of Life*, Quality of Life in Asia 8,
DOI 10.1007/978-981-10-3877-8_17

movement. They illustrate a great deal of common visions and strategies, and considerable diversity of contexts and approaches as well. What will the future hold? This mosaic of the work of 12 universities demonstrates a shared deep commitment to USR, suggesting that the next stage can be a period of continuing innovation and of additional cross-national comparison and collaboration. The vital energy and momentum for continuing improvement expressed in each of the institutional cases indicates that the prospects are very good for further development of the social responsibility approaches and programs of these universities. In addition, the individual accounts also suggest some very promising opportunities for more extensive inter-university collaboration.

The institutional account about the University of Pretoria concludes with a compelling reflection about the national situation in South Africa, summing up well the current reality and future opportunity in a global context:

> While there is still no national consensus on what form it should take, social responsibility is receiving serious attention at all public institutions. The lack of a uniform definition should not be seen as an obstacle or problem but rather as indicative of a dynamic higher education sector where diversity and freedom to experiment with different approaches allows for the emergence of robust programs. Continued debate and research are required to analyze what has been learned, to give voice to new ideas and new interventions. In the process, the role of higher education in addressing social and economic development will be strengthened. In the current context, the university is a central institutional actor of scientific and technological changes, but also of other dimensions – of capacity to educate and train skills responsive to the changing economic and social conditions and a significant contributor to equalization of chances and democratization of society.

This quote outlines eloquently the possibilities for all universities in the period ahead—a rich diversity of approaches that gives rise to vigorous debate and research, continuing elevation in the role of universities in advancing social and economic development *and also* promoting equal opportunity and democracy.

A first common theme that emerges from the institutional descriptions is *university-community partnerships*, confirming that, and illustrating how they are an essential component and ingredient of successful USR. They are vital infrastructure for effective community-engaged teaching and engaged research. The experiences reported herein show the impressive positive results that well-organized and supported university-community partnerships can yield, and the significant complexities and challenges as well. Community partnerships are a defining element in virtually all of the cases and received particular emphasis on the chapters about University of Haifa, The University of Manchester, University of São Paulo, Kyoto University, and Washington University in St. Louis. Effective university-community partnerships require that university representatives operate with a strong commitment to forging truly reciprocal and mutually beneficial collaborations. Building and sustaining strong partnerships also requires significant investments of time and resources in planning, organizing and running these efforts. Challenges include resource needs, power sharing, cultural differences, and managing diverging interests and priorities.

This dimension of USR in the future would be enhanced by additional documentation of especially successful models and more research on the impacts of alternative approaches. What strategies are proving to be most effective in addressing the common challenges noted immediately above and in maximizing impacts on community conditions and on the SR learning of student participants?

All of the institutional accounts are stories of significant recent and ongoing *organizational changes*, changes that aim to strengthen USR. These changes have been driven and shaped by several factors, including facilitating influences such as national policies, the visions and skills of individual leaders, new demands from other sectors, and collaboration with external partners (including other universities). The processes of an organizational change have taken time and they rarely have been fully linear. Navigating through and overcoming counter-pressures and priorities (such as competing financial needs, rating systems that advantage basic rather than applied research, traditional academic culture, and faculty rewards and incentives) is a shared feature of all of the narratives. Although the cases describe a variety of organizational structures to promote USR, a number of common features are noteworthy. In several instances, USR emerged as a high priority in the institution's most recent strategic planning. These same institutions often have assigned special responsibility for leading and coordinating USR activities to a new position, always at a higher level in the overall structure of the university, and to new coordinating councils or committees.

In the years ahead, universities that are seriously committed to USR can be expected to continue to develop new organizational arrangements to support this work. A new wave of structural innovations will be needed in order to fully address the next-stage challenges and opportunities. High on the list: mechanisms to organize and support interdisciplinary applied research; to build and sustain university-community partnerships; to build the capabilities of professors, students and other actors in USR; and to regularly assess the impacts of USR programs.

National policies that promote USR have been significant in several of the institutions (University of Haifa, University of Pretoria, and all of the Chinese universities—Beijing Normal University, Peking University, Sichuan University, and The Hong Kong Polytechnic University) and much less so in others. The fact that national policies have played an important role in some countries suggests that this arena has high potential for future action and research. Future opportunities include the development of pro-USR policies where at present these do not exist, or are limited. This also is a promising area for cross-national comparative research and for fostering exchange among both university personnel and government officials internationally. In what specific ways have the national policies had positive impacts and how have these results been achieved? To what extent and how are the national policies actually implemented and supported (and not)? What are alternative mechanisms of accountability? What are the consequences of universities' performance with respect to the national expectations?

This collection of institutional profiles underscores that *student programming* is an especially robust and exciting aspect of USR work. Participating universities are engaged in substantial and growing efforts to expand and strengthen their efforts to develop socially responsible graduates. They operate a diverse mix of student volunteer programs and many are rapidly increasing their service learning programs. A number of institutions discuss the importance of preparing students to be effective in community service activities and the approaches taken by their institutions to increase students' capabilities before and during their SR activities (including Kyoto University, The University of New South Wales, Washington University in St. Louis, Beijing Normal University, Peking University, Sichuan University and The Hong Kong Polytechnic University). It is encouraging that increasing numbers of universities are systematically evaluating student learning outcomes, addressing: what and how do students learn SR values and skills through different kinds of programs? This area of activity is still relatively new. One hopes that those institutions that have undertaken significant assessment efforts will continue and deepen these efforts and share broadly what they are learning.

Looking ahead, the assessment of student learning outcomes is an especially fertile area for international comparative research—to learn from one another, and also to aggregate the research findings of individual institutions. The field will make the greatest progress on this topic to the extent that institutions adopt common definitions of learning goals, common measures, and common assessment methodologies.

Applied research is a universal component of USR; it is discussed in all of the cases, but more through brief examples than in-depth analysis. The role of applied research to address societal challenges is described mostly in relation to selected topics—for example, health care for the elderly and economic development. The overall extent of applied research that rates highly in terms of SR goals is impressive. What is not clear is how to support and to evaluate the overall accomplishments of a university on this aspect of USR. One avenue for filling this gap would be for universities to test out the assessment framework presented in Carlos Wing-Hung Lo et al.'s "University Social Responsibility: Conceptualization and an Assessment Framework" (Chap. 4).

Universities' corporate social responsibility is noted in some of the institutional accounts (The Hong Kong Polytechnic University, Sichuan University, Tufts University, and University of Pretoria), but overall this dimension of USR received comparatively modest attention in the institutional cases. In settings of increased societal expectations and scarcity of resources, it is likely that there will be greater pressures—both external and internal—on universities to elevate their corporate social responsibility. At present, we know far too little about how university corporate social responsibility does, or does not, reinforce other aspects of USR— SR-oriented teaching and learning, and research. This question calls out for systematic exploration and inquiry. This issue could be addressed as part of a broader inquiry into: how does the full range of USR functions interact within individual institutions? To what extent do they actually reinforce one another or are they mostly parallel activities that do not strengthen one another?

The University Social Responsibility Network (USRN) can be an important vehicle for seizing some of the opportunities for global collaboration noted above. As noted in the first chapter, USRN already has started a number of collaborative activities—joint research and publications, international student programs and scholarships, and periodic conferences. The Network also plans to establish a faculty exchange and visiting fellowship program. USRN can bring distinctive strengths to future international collaborative endeavors. Because a number of Chinese universities are founding members of USRN, there may be a unique opportunity associated with the continuing expansion of the Chinese higher education system and the strong role of the national government in setting priorities for the higher education sector. Might USR become a significant element in this national higher education system that is unique in its rate of expansion and opportunities to innovate?

Future action and research can and should be informed by, and also involve, other higher education alliances that are providing creative leadership on these topics. Potential partners include The Talloires Network, other international coalitions, such as the Global Alliance on Community-Engaged Research, The Global University Network for Innovation, and the International Consortium for Higher Education, Civic Responsibility, and Democracy, and national and regional networks such as the South African Higher Education Community Engagement Forum, Engagement Australia, the Latin American Center for Service-Learning, and Campus Engage (Ireland).

Index

© Springer Nature Singapore Pte Ltd. 2017
D.T.L. Shek and R.M. Hollister (eds.), *University Social Responsibility and Quality of Life*, Quality of Life in Asia 8,
DOI 10.1007/978-981-10-3877-8